DayBook
~OF~
PROMISE

Copyright © 2014 Worthy Inspired,
a division of Worthy Media, Inc.

ISBN 978-1-61795-383-5

Published by Worthy Inspired, a division of Worthy Media, Inc.,
134 Franklin Road, Suite 200,
Brentwood, Tennessee 37027.

Cover Design by ThinkPen Designs
Page Layout by Bart Dawson

Printed in China

1 2 3 4 5—RRD—18 17 16 15 14

DayBook
~OF~
PROMISE

Classic Selections

FROM EVERY CENTURY AND
TRADITION OF THE CHURCH

WORTHY
Inspired

Day 1

STANDING ON
THE PROMISES OF GOD

I am now going the way of all the earth, and you know with all your heart and all your soul that none of the good promises the LORD your God made to you has failed. Everything was fulfilled for you; not one promise has failed.

Joshua 23:14

Today, there are few certainties that we can count on daily in our life. When we try and predict our outcomes, we often feel frustrated and/or defeated by the results which can become burdens for us to carry. That is why there is a peace and comfort in knowing that the only results we can fully rely on come from the Lord. He is the true sustainer in our life. God is always faithful and He will never leave us or disappoint us But are we always willing to be patient?

God's timing is His timing. He answers the "why" and the "how." All we have to do is seek His direction and be faithful to what He promises. However, being patient is not easy. We tell ourselves "I can't..." or "I don't have time to..." or "I can't afford to..." It's easy to allow the "voice within" to breakdown your outlook of encouragement and hope and trade it in for a variety of problems that can turn into a dark, heavy cloud overhead. But when we turn to God and stand firmly on His promises, then that is when we encounter "true peace" that passes all understanding.

May this collection of classic written devotions serves as a firm foundation to strengthen your faith throughout the year.

YOU CAN MAKE A DIFFERENCE

So they removed the stone. Then Jesus raised His eyes and said, "Father, I thank You that You heard Me. I know that You always hear Me, but because of the crowd standing here I said this, so they may believe You sent Me."

John 11:41–42

Those who have left the deepest impression on this sin-cursed earth have been men and women of prayer. You will find that prayer has been the mighty power that has moved not only God, but man also.

We read that Elijah brought fire down on Mount Carmel (see 1 Kings 18:17–39). The prophets of Baal cried long and loud, but no answer came. The God of Elijah heard and answered his prayer. Let us remember that the God of Elijah still lives. As we go to the throne of grace, let us always remember that God answers prayer.

All through the Scriptures you will find that when believing prayer went up to God, the answer came down.

~ D. L. Moody (1837–1899)

DAILY PROMISES TO STRENGTHEN YOUR FAITH

Put on the full armor of God so that you can stand against the tactics of the Devil. For our battle is not against flesh and blood, but against the rulers, against the authorities, against the world powers of this darkness, against the spiritual forces of evil in the heavens.

This is why you must take up the full armor of God, so that you may be able to resist in the evil day, and having prepared everything, to take your stand. Stand, therefore, with truth like a belt around your waist, righteousness like armor on your chest, and your feet sandaled with readiness for the gospel of peace.

In every situation take the shield of faith, and with it you will be able to extinguish all the flaming arrows of the evil one. Take the helmet of salvation, and the sword of the Spirit, which is God's word.

Pray at all times in the Spirit with every prayer and request, and stay alert in this with all perseverance and intercession for all the saints.

Peace to the brothers, and love with faith, from God the Father and the Lord Jesus Christ. Grace be with all who have undying love for our Lord Jesus Christ.

~ Ephesians 6:11–18, 23, 24

PEACE WITH GOD

LORD, You will establish peace for us, for You have also done all our work for us.

Isaiah 26:12

There is Peace that comes from submission; tranquility of spirit, which is the crown and reward of obedience; repose, which is the very smile upon the face of faith, and all these things are given unto us along with the Grace and Mercy of our God. And the man that possesses this is at Peace with God, and at Peace with himself, so he may bear in his heart that singular blessing of a perfect tranquility and quiet amidst the distractions of duty, of sorrows, of losses, and of cares.

"In everything by prayer and supplication with thanksgiving let your requests be known unto God; and the Peace of God which passeth all understanding shall keep your hearts and minds in Christ Jesus." And he who is thus at friendship with God, and in harmony with himself, and at rest from sorrows and cares, will surely find no enemies amongst men with whom he must needs be at war, but will be a son of Peace, and walk the world, meeting in them all a friend and a brother. So all discords may be quieted; even thought still we have to fight the good fight of faith, we may do, like Gideon of old, build an altar to "Jehovah Shalom," the God of Peace.

~ Alexander Maclaren (1826–1910)

SACRILEGE

Therefore, brothers, by the mercies of God, I urge you to present your bodies as a living sacrifice, holy and pleasing to God; this is your spiritual worship.

Romans 12:1

Sacrilege we have always thought was the breaking into a church and stealing there from. That is not so; it is going into Church and putting something on the plate. Do not forget that.

Sacrilege is centered in offering God something which costs nothing, because you think God is worth nothing. God looks for the giving at His alter of a gift that costs something. Men are perpetually bringing into the Christian church the things they do not need themselves. I know there is much sacrificial giving, thank God, but there is also an enormous amount of sacrilegious giving abroad in the world today, giving devoid of sacrifice. We offer to God in the Church, things which we would never offer to our governors. This is sacrilege. If the giving in the Church of God today was of the type and the pattern of the gift of the widow to the treasury in the days long since passed away, the work of God would never have to go begging to men and women outside the Church.

～ G. Campbell Morgan (1898–1945)

THE HEART OF JESUS

And He took bread, gave thanks, broke it, gave it to them, and said, "This is My body, which is given for you. Do this in remembrance of Me."

Luke 22:19

The Best Preparation is—to look into the heart of Jesus. When you understand what He that sits on the throne desires for you, how He longs after you, what He has prepared for you, this will more than aught else set your desires and longings in motion, and impart to you the right preparation. That word of Jesus at the Paschal table enables me to look into His heart. He knew that He must go from that feast to the cross. He knew that His body must be broken, and His blood shed, in order that He might be really your Passover. He knew how in that night they should grieve and betray Him, and yet He says: "With desire have I desired to eat this Passover with you." What a love this is!

And Jesus is still the same. Even with you, poor sinner, He earnestly desires to eat the Passover. Yea, on the throne of heaven, He looks forward with longing to the day of the Supper, to eat with you, and to quicken you. O man, let your sluggishness put you to shame: Jesus earnestly desires—Jesus greatly longs—to observe the Supper with you; He would not enjoy the food of heavenly life alone; He would fain eat of it along with you.

— Andrew Murray (1828–1917)

A READY VESSEL

*Seek the L*ORD *while He may be found; call to Him while He is near.*

Isaiah 55:6

Pick at random a score of great saints whose lives and testimonies are widely known. Let them be Bible characters or well-known Christians of post-biblical times. You will be struck instantly with the fact that the saints were not alike. Sometimes the dissimilarities were so great as to be positively glaring. The differences are as wide as human life itself—differences of race, nationality, education, temperament, habit, and personal qualities. Yet they all walked, each in his day, upon a high road of spiritual living far above the common way.

I venture to suggest that the one vital quality which they had in common was *spiritual receptivity*. Something in them was open to heaven, something which urged them Godward. I shall say simply that they had spiritual awareness and that they went on to cultivate it until it became the biggest thing in their lives.

~ A. W. Tozer (1897–1963)

PARADISE

I wait for Yahweh; I wait and put my hope in His word.

Psalm 130:5

What is Paradise? All things that are. For all things are good and pleasant, and may therefore fitly be called Paradise. It is also said, that Paradise is an outer court of heaven. In the same way, this world is truly an outer court of the eternal, or of eternity; and this is specially true of any temporal things or creatures which manifest the Eternal or remind us of eternity; for the creatures are a guide and path to God and eternity.

Thus the world is an outer court of eternity, and therefore it may well be called a Paradise, for so indeed it is. And in this Paradise all things are lawful except one tree and its fruit. That is to say, of all things that exist, nothing is forbidden or contrary to God, except one thing only. That one thing is self-will, or to will otherwise than as the eternal Will would have it. Not that everything which is so done is in itself contrary to the eternal Will, but in so far as it is done from a different will, or otherwise than from the Eternal and Divine Will.

~ Johannes Eckhart (1260–1327)

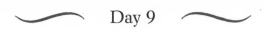

Day 9

ASSURANCE

Now faith is the reality of what is hoped for, the proof of what is not seen.

Hebrews 11:1

Assurance will make us active and lively in God's service; it will excite prayer, and quicken obedience. As diligence begets assurance, so assurance begets diligence. Assurance will not (as the papists say) breed self-security in the soul, but industry.

Doubting discourages us in God's service, but the assurance of His favour breeds joy. "The joy of the Lord is our strength." Assurance makes us mount up to heaven, as eagles, in holy duties; it is like the Spirit in Ezekiel's wheels, that moved them, and lifted them up. Faith will make us walk, but assurance will make us run: we shall never think we can do enough for God. Assurance will be as wings to the birds, as weights to the clock, to set all the wheels of obedience running.

~ Thomas Watson (1620–1686)

A CALL TO CHRIST

*In Christ there is not Greek and Jew, circumcision and uncircumcision,
barbarian, Scythian, slave and free; but Christ is all and in all.*

Colossians 3:11

Abraham Lincoln, the great emancipator, is reported to have said:
"Those who deny freedom to others deserve it not for themselves,
and, under a just God, cannot long retain it." On more than one
occasion Jesus laid down this principle concerning the use and
abuse of gospel gifts and privileges: "For whosoever hath (made
gain), to him shall be given (still more to invest), and he shall have
more abundance; but whosoever hath not (made gain), from him
shall be taken away even that he hath." It is as though He had said,
Make gain with your spiritual gifts, your earthly riches, your gospel
freedoms—pass then on to others. Use them, or lose them—it is
divine law.

~ Abraham Lincoln (1809–1865)

HIS EXAMPLE

The one who says he remains in Him should walk just as He walked.

1 John 2:6

Our Lord Christ with His Doctrine and Example, is the Mirror, the Guide of the Soul, the Way and the only door by which we enter into those Pastures of Life Eternal…Hence it follows, that the Remembrance of the Passion and Death of our Saviour ought not wholly to be blotted out: nay, it is also certain, that whatsoever high elevation of Mind the Soul may be raised to, it ought not in all things to separate from the most holy Humanity. But then it follows, not from hence neither, that the Soul accustomed to internal recollection, that can no longer ratiocinate, should always be meditating on, and considering…the most holy Misteries of our Saviour.

It is holy and good to Meditate; and would to God that all men of this World practiced it. And the Soul, besides that meditates, reasons and considers with facilitie; ought to be let alone in that state, and not pushed on to another higher, so long as in that of Meditation it finds nourishment and profit. It belongs to God alone, and not to the spiritual Guide, to promote the Soul from Meditation to Contemplation; because, if God through His special Grace, call it not to this state of Prayer, the Guide can do nothing with all his Wisdom and Instructions.

~ Miguel de Molinos (1628–1696)

CHRIST THE COMFORTER

But the Counselor, the Holy Spirit—the Father will send Him in My name—will teach you all things and remind you of everything I have told you.

John 14:26

Job had comforters, and I think he spoke the truth when he said, "Miserable comforters are ye all." But I dare say they esteemed themselves wise; and when the young man Elihu rose to speak, they thought he had a world of impudence. Were they not "grave and reverend seigniors"? Did not they comprehend his grief and sorrow?…But they did not find out the cause…It is a bad case when the doctor mistakes a disease and gives a wrong prescription, and so perhaps kills the patient.

Sometimes, when we go and visit people, we mistake their disease; we want to comfort them on this point, whereas they do not require any such comfort at all, and they would be better left alone, than spoiled by such unwise comforters as we are. But oh, how wise the Holy Spirit is! He takes the soul, lays it on the table, and dissects it in a moment; He finds out the root of the matter, He sees where the complaint is, and then He applies the knife where something is required to be taken away, or puts a plaster where the sore is; and He never mistakes. O how wise is the blessed Holy Ghost; from ever comforter I turn, and leave them all, for thou art He who alone givest the wisest consolation.

∼ Charles Haddon Spurgeon (1834–1892)

GOD, OUR PROVISION

And my God will supply all your needs according to His riches in glory in Christ Jesus.

Philippians 4:19

What can we possibly need that we do not find provided in Him? Do we hopelessly groan under the curse of the broken law, hanging menacingly over us? Christ has "redeemed us from the curse of the law, having been made a curse for us" (Gal. 3:13). Do we know that only he that worketh righteousness is acceptable to God, and despair of attaining life on so unachievable a condition? Christ Jesus "hath of God been made unto us righteousness" (1 Cor. 1:30). Do we loathe ourselves in the pollution of our sins, and know that God is greater than we, and that we must be an offence in His holy sight? The blood of Christ cleanseth us from all sin (1 John 1:7). But do we not need faith, that we may be made one with Him and so secure these benefits? Faith, too, is the gift of God: and that we believe on Him is granted by God in the behalf of Christ (Phil. 1:29).

Nothing has been forgotten, nothing neglected, nothing left unprovided. In the person of Jesus Christ, the great God, in His perfect wisdom and unfailing power, has taken our place before the outraged justice of God and under His perfect law, and has wrought out a complete salvation.

~ B. B. Warfield (1851–1921)

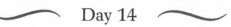

BELIEVERS EXPERIENCES

I thank God through Jesus Christ our Lord! So then, with my mind I myself am a slave to the law of God, but with my flesh, to the law of sin.

Romans 7:25

A *believer* is to be known not only by his peace and joy, but by his warfare and distress. His peace is peculiar: it flows from Christ; it is heavenly, it is holy peace. His warfare is as peculiar: it is deep-seated, agonising, and ceases not till death. If the Lord will, many of us have the prospect of sitting down next Sabbath at the Lord's table.

Coming to Christ takes away your fear of the law; but it is the Holy Spirit coming into your heart that makes you love the law. The Holy Spirit is no more frightened away from that heart; He comes and softens it; He takes out the stony heart and puts in a heart of flesh; and there He writes the holy, holy, holy law of God…The law of God is sweet to that soul…Oh that all the world but knew that holiness and happiness are one! Oh that all the world were one holy family, joyfully coming under the pure rules of the gospel!

Try yourselves by this. Can you say, "I delight," etc.? Do you remember when you hated the law of God? Do you love it now? Do you long for the time when you shall live fully under it—holy as God is holy, pure as Christ is pure?

～ Robert Murray McCheyne (1813–1843)

WHAT IS GOD'S WILL?

Then he said, "The God of our fathers has appointed you to know His will, to see the Righteous One, and to hear the sound of His voice."

Acts 22:14

When God puts down His great will beside me telling me to do it, He puts down just beside it as great a thing, His Love. And as my soul trembles at the fearfulness of will, Love comes with its calm omnipotence, and draws it to Himself; then takes my timid will and twines it around His, till mine is fierce with passion to serve, and strong to do His will. Just as if some mighty task were laid to an infant's hand, and the engine-grasp of a giant strengthened it with his own. Where God's law is, is God's love. Look at Law—it withers your very soul with its stern inexorable face. But look at Love, or look at God's will, which means look at Love's will, and you are re-assured, and your heart grows strong. No martyr dies for abstract truth. For a person, for God, he will die a triple death.

So no man will die for God's law. But for God he will do it. Where God's will, then, seems strong to command, God's love is strong to obey. Hence the profound texts, "Love is the fulfilling of the law." "And this is the love of God that we keep His commandments, and His commandments are not grievous."

〜 Henry Drummond (1851–1897)

THE LAMB ON THE THRONE

On Calvary we're adoring stood, And gazed on that wondrous cross; Where holy, spotless Lamb of God Was slain in His love for us; How our hearts have stirred at that solemn cry, While the sun was en-wrapt in night, "E-li, E-li lama sabachthani!" Most blessed, most awful sight. Our sins were laid on His sacred head, The curse by our Lord was borne; For us a victim our Savior bled, And endured that death of scorn; Himself He gave our poor hearts to win—(Was ever love, Lord, like Thine!) From paths of folly and shame and sin, And fill them with joys divine. We've watched by the tomb where our Savior lay When He entered the gloomy grave; And by death the pow'r of death might slay And His lambs from the lion save. O, glorious time when the Victor rose! He liveth, no more to die; He hath bruised the head of our mighty foes, For us was His victory!

The gates of heav'n are open wide, At His name all the angels bow; The Son of Man who was crucified Is the King of glory now. We love to look up and behold him there, The Lamb for His chosen slain; And soon shall His saints all His glories share, With their Head and their Lord shall reign. And now we draw near to the throne of grace, For His blood and the Priest are there; And we joyfully seek God's holy face, With our censer of praise and prayer. The burning mount and the mystic vail, With our terrors and guilt, are gone; Our conscience has peace that can never fail, 'Tis the Lamb on high on the throne.

⁓ James G. Deck (1807–1884)

CHRIST THE DELIVERER

And the world with its lust is passing away, but the one who does God's will remains forever.

1 John 2:17

Christ is God's Deliverer for the world: This is God's method of deliverance. He gives us in Christ a new center, and the wheel of life runs truly and smoothly because it is truly centered. But because Christ is the center of the whole kingdom of God, in heaven and on earth, the life that is centered in Him is thereby in harmony with God and all His kingdom, the world of order, harmony, peace, and joy, the world where one will alone prevails, the will of God—and being such, is therefore eternal But for the same reason which a life is eccentric, out of center, with that portion of the universe, heavenly and earthly, which is not centered in Christ.

If two sets of powerful machinery were at work in the same space, there would arise friction, clash, damage. In this age, this situation induces conflict of spirit and practical trouble for the Christ-centered man. But he can endure with patience and confidence, seeing that he knows that Christ has conquered this world, and that His world, the heavenly, will prevail finally. Christ is God's Savior for the individual and for the world: association with Him, by faith and obedience, if God's method of salvation. There is no other, nor can there be (John 3:35–36).

～ G.H. Lang (1874–1958)

THE WORKING CHRIST

"Isn't this the carpenter, the son of Mary, and the brother of James, Joses, Judas, and Simon? And aren't His sisters here with us?" So they were offended by Him.

Mark 6:3

There are few places where human nature can be better studied than in a country village; for there one sees the whole of each individual life and knows all one's neighbors thoroughly. In a city far more people are seen, but far fewer known; it is only the outside of life that is visible. In a village it is the view outwards of life that is visible. In a village the view outwards if circumscribed; but the view downwards is deep, and the view upwards unimpeded. Nazareth was a notoriously wicked town, as we learn from the proverbial question, Can any good thing come out of Nazareth?

Jesus had no acquaintance with sin in His own soul, but in the town He had a full exhibition of the awful problem with which it was to be His life-work to deal. He was still further brought into contact with human nature by His trade. That He worked as a carpenter in Joseph's shop there can be no doubt. Who could know better than His own townsmen, who asked, in their astonishment at His preaching, Is not this the carpenter? It would be difficult to exhaust the significance of the fact that God chose for His Son, when He dwelt among men, out of all the possible positions in which He might have place Him, the lot of a working man. It stamped men's common toils with everlasting honor. It acquainted Jesus with the feelings of the multitude, and helped Him to know what was in man. It was afterwards said that He knew this so well that He needed not that any man should teach Him.

~ James Stalker (1848–1927)

CALVARY'S CROSS

Keeping our eyes on Jesus, the source and perfecter of our faith, who for the joy that lay before Him endured a cross and despised the shame and has sat down at the right hand of God's throne.

Hebrews 12:2

We take a Red Cross, and with it symbolize the ministry of healing. Our poets and hymn-writers sing to us of "the wondrous cross," "the blessed cross." But all this ought not to hide from us the fact that originally the cross was a thing unspeakable shameful and degrading. "Cursed is everyone that hangeth on a tree," said Paul, quoting Deuteronomy. That was how Jewish feeling expressed it; and Roman sentiment was the same. "This cruelest, most hideous of punishments," said Cicero, using words in which you can almost hear the shudder—"*crudelissimum taeterrimumque supplicium.*" "Never may it," he said elsewhere, "come near the bodies of Roman citizens, never near their thoughts or eyes or ears!"

Devised in the first instance in semi-barbaric Oriental lands, death by crucifixion was reserved by the Romans for slaves and for criminals of the most abandoned kind. It was a fate of utter ignominy…That the Messiah should die such a death was utterly beyond belief. Yet so it was. Everything which Christ ever touched— the cross included—He adorned and transfigured and haloed with splendour and beauty; but let us never forget out of what appalling depths He has set the cross on high.

⁓ James S. Stewart (1783–1858)

REDEEMED

"This is why the Father loves Me, because I am laying down My life so I may take it up again. No one takes it from Me, but I lay it down on My own. I have the right to lay it down, and I have the right to take it up again. I have received this command from My Father."

John 10:17, 18

The death of Christ is, my friends, the most wonderful event past, present, or future in the whole universe. It is so in the eye of God. "Therefore doth My Father love Me, because I lay down My life." There is nothing in the whole world so lovely as His Son. It is not only for His Godhead, but on account of His manhood, through which He laid down His life. "Therefore doth My Father love Me, because I laid down My life." These words of Christ, "I lay down My life," are dearer to God than a thousand worlds. It is the same in the eyes of the redeemed.

All the redeemed love Christ, because He laid down His life. John says, "I beheld, and lo, in the midst of the throne, and of the four beasts, and in the midst of the elders, stood a lamb as it had been slain. And when he had taken the book, the four beasts, and four and twenty elders fell down before the Lamb, having every one of them harps, and golden vials full of odours, which are the prayers of saints. And they sang a new song, saying, Thou art worthy to take the book, and to open the seals thereof; for thou was slain, and hast redeemed us to God by thy blood.

～ Robert Murray McCheyne (1813–1843)

IN HUMILITY

Make your own attitude that of Christ Jesus.... Instead He emptied Himself by assuming the form of a slave, taking on the likeness of men. And when He had come as a man in His external form, He humbled Himself by becoming obedient to the point of death—even to death on a cross.

Philippians 2:5, 7–8

Although Jesus made His entry on the stage of life so humbly and silently; although the citizens of Bethlehem dreamed not what had happened in their midst; although the emperor of Rome knew not that his decree had influenced the nativity of a king who was yet to bear rule, not only over the Roman world, but over many a land where Rome's eagles never flew; although the history of mankind went thundering forward next morning in the channels of its ordinary interests, quite unconscious of the event which had happened, yet it did not altogether escape notice.

As the babe leaped in the womb of the aged Elizabeth when the mother of her Lord approached her, so when He who brought the new world with Him appeared, there sprang up anticipation and forebodings of the truth in various representatives of the old world that was passing was. There went through sensitive and waiting soul, here and there, a dim and half-conscious thrill, which drew them round the Infant's cradle. Look at the group which gathered to gaze on Him! It represented in miniature the whole of His future history.

~ James Stalker (1848–1927)

HE IS A GOD OF POWER

Far above every ruler and authority, power and dominion, and every title given not only in this age but also in the one to come.

Ephesians 1:21

There is no want of power in God to cast wicked men into hell at any moment. Men's hands cannot be strong when God rises up. The strongest have no power to resist Him, nor can any deliver out of His hands. He is not only able to cast wicked men into hell, but He can most easily do it.

Sometimes an earthly prince meets with a great deal of difficulty to subdue a rebel, who has found means to fortify himself, and has made himself strong by the numbers of his followers. But it is not so with God…Though hand join in hand, and vast multitudes of God's enemies combine and associate themselves, they are easily broken in pieces. They are as great heaps of light chaff before the whirlwind; or large quantities of dry stubble before devouring flames. We find it easy to tread on and crush a worm that we see crawling on the earth; so it is easy for us to cut or singe a slender thread that any thing hangs by: thus easy is it for God, when He pleases, to cast His enemies down to hell. What are we, that we should think to stand before Him, at whose rebuke the earth trembles, and before whom the rocks are thrown down?

～ Jonathan Edwards (1703–1758)

A JOYOUS HEART

Then he said to them, "Go and eat what is rich, drink what is sweet, and send portions to those who have nothing prepared, since today is holy to our Lord. Do not grieve, because the joy of the LORD is your stronghold."

Nehemiah 8:10

"The sad heart tires in a mile," is a frequent proverb. What a difference there is between the energy of the healthy, joyous heart and the forced activity of the morbid and depressed one! The one leaps to its task, the other creeps to it. The one discovers its meat and drink in self-sacrifice, the other limps, and stoops, and crawls. If you want to be strong for life's work, be sure to keep a glad heart. But, be equally sure to be glad with the joy of Lord. There is a counterfeit of it in the world, of which we must beware—an outward merry-making, jesting, and mad laughter, which hides an aching and miserable heart…Ours must be the joy of the Lord.

It begins with the assurance of forgiveness and acceptance in the Beloved. It is nourished in trial and tribulation, which veil outward sources of consolation, and lead us to rejoice in God through our Lord Jesus…It lives not in the gifts of God, but in God Himself. It is the fruit of the Spirit, who begets in us love, joy, peace, long-suffering. Get the Lord Himself to fill your soul, and joy will be as natural as the murmur of a brook to its flow.

～ F. B. Meyer (1847–1929)

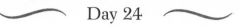
CHRIST, THE TEACHER

This man came to Him at night and said, "Rabbi, we know that You have come from God as a teacher, for no one could perform these signs You do unless God were with him."

John 3:2

John calls Jesus "Word of God." What is a word? It is the invisible thought taking form: Wordsworth says, "Language is the incarnation of thought." Spoken words are sounds, articulate and significant: sounds in which there is soul. Written words are visible signs of intelligence and intellect; thought has determined their exact form, order, relation.

God is represented as pure Spirit, and cannot be known by sense. He would communicate with man, and so puts His thought and love in a visible form in Christ, who is therefore beautifully called the living "Word of God." As God does everything perfectly, we are justified in looking for such an expression of His mind and heart in His incarnate Son as shall excel all other revelations of Himself. In Christ, as the Word of God, we may properly expect to find the clear and unmistakable stamp of the divine mind. In His teaching there must be a divine authority, majesty, originality, spirituality, vitality, essential worth and practical power, such as no merely human teaching could display.

— Jonathan Edwards (1703–1758)

PSALM 8

O Lord, our Lord, how wondrous great Is Thine exalted name! The glories of Thy heav'nly state Let men and babes proclaim. When I behold Thy works on high The moon that rules the night, And stars that well adorn the sky, Those moving worlds of light. Lord, what is man, or all his race, Who dwells so far below, That Thou should visit him with grace, And love his nature so? That Thine eternal Son should bear To take a mortal form; Made lower than His angels are, To save a dying worm? Yet while He lived on earth unknown, And men would not adore, The obedient seas and fishes own His Godhead and His power. The waves lay spread beneath His feat; And fish, at His command, Bring their large shoals to Peter's net, Bring tribute to His hand.

Those lesser glories of the son Shone through the fleshly cloud; Now, we behold Him on His throne, And men confess Him God. Let Him be crowned with majesty, Who bowed His head to death; And be His honors sounded high, By all things that have breath. Jesus, our Lord, how wondrous great Is Thine exalted name! The glories of Thy heavenly state Let the whole earth proclaim.

～ King David(10th Century B.C.) and Isaac Watts (1674–1748)

GOD'S PEACE

Let no man dare to say, if he would speak the truth, that the question of preparation for national defense is a question of war or of peace. If there is one passion more deep seated in the hearts of our fellow countrymen than another, it is the passion for peace. No nation in the world ever more instinctively turned away from the thought of war than this Nation to which we belong. Partly because in the plentitude of its power, in the unrestricted area of its opportunities, it has found nothing to covet in the possession and power of other nations. There is no spirit of aggrandizement in America.

There is no desire on the part of any thoughtful and conscientious American man to take one foot of territory from any other nation in the world...It is not permissible for any man to say that anxiety for the defense of the Nation has in it the least tinge of desire for a power that can be used to bring on war. But gentlemen, there is something that the American people love better than they love peace. They love the principles upon which their political life is founded. They are ready at any time to fight for the vindication of their character and of their honor. They will not at any time seek the contest, but they will at no time cravenly avoid it; because if there is one thing that the individual ought to fight for, and that the Nation ought to fight for, it is the integrity of its own convictions. We cannot surrender our convictions. I would rather surrender territory than surrender those ideals which are the staff of the soul itself...

⁓ Woodrow Wilson (1856–1924)

GROW IN KNOWLEDGE

But grow in the grace and knowledge of our Lord and Savior Jesus Christ. To Him be the glory both now and to the day of eternity. Amen.

2 Peter 3:18

The knowledge of a person is not the same as the knowledge of a creed or of a thought or of a book. We are to grow in the knowledge of Christ, which includes but is more than the intellectual apprehension of the truths concerning Him. He might turn the injunction into "Increase your acquaintance with your Savior." Many Christians never get to be any more intimate with Him than they were when they were first introduced to Him.

They are on a kind of bowing acquaintance with their Master, and have little more than that. We sometimes begin an acquaintance which we think promises to ripen into a friendship, but are disappointed. Circumstances or some want of congeniality which is discovered prevents its growth. So with not a few professing Christians. They have got no nearer to Jesus Christ than when they first knew Him. Their friendship has not grown. It has never reached the stage where all restraints are laid aside and there is perfect confidence. "Grow in the knowledge of your Lord and Savior Jesus Christ." Get more and more intimate with Him, nearer to Him, and franker and more cordial with Him day by day.

~ Alexander Maclaren (1826–1910)

THE SPHERE OF
THE BELIEVER'S LIFE

For the wages of sin is death, but the gift of God is eternal life in Christ Jesus our Lord.

Romans 6:23

Those three short words, in Christ Jesus, are, without doubt, the most important ever written...to express the mutual relation of the believer and Christ...Sometimes we meet the expression, in Christ or in Christ Jesus, and again in Him, or in whom, etc. And sometimes this sacred name, or its equivalent pronoun, is found associated with other prepositions—through, with, by; but the thought is essentially the same. Such repetition and variety must have some intense meaning. When, in the Word of God, a phrase like this occurs so often, and with such manifold applications, it cannot be a matter of accident; there is a deep design.

God's Spirit is bringing a truth of the highest importance before us, repeating for the sake of emphasis, compelling even the careless reader to give heed as to some vital teaching...a further evidence of the vital importance of the phrase, in Christ, in the fact that these two words unlock and interpret every separate book in the New Testament. Here is God's own key, whereby we may open all the various doors and enter all the glorious rooms in this Palace Beautiful...where the door is opened into heaven...some new benefit or blessing enjoyed by him who is thus in Christ Jesus...

~ A. T. Pierson (1867–1911)

PERSONAL REVELATION OF GOD

In the beginning was the Word, and the Word was with God, and the Word was God.

John 1:1

No one can too fully understand, or too deeply feel, the necessity of taking home the Bible with all it contains, as a message sent from Heaven to him; nor can too earnestly desire or seek the promised Spirit to teach him the true spiritual import of all its contents. He must have the Bible made a personal revelation of God to his own soul. It must become his own book. He must know Christ for himself. He must know him in his different relations. He must know him in his blessed and infinite fullness, or he cannot abide in him, and unless he abide in Christ, he can bring forth none of the fruits of holiness. "Except a man abide in me, he is cast forth as a branch, and is withered" (John 15:6). ["Sanctify them through Thy Truth: Thy Word is Truth" (John 17:17)]…

The foregoing are some of the relations which Christ sustains to us as to our salvation. I could have enlarged greatly, as you perceive, upon each of these, and easily have swelled this part of our course of study to a large volume…["And there are also many other things which Jesus did, the which, if they should be written every one, I suppose that even the world itself could not contain the books that should be written. Amen" (John 21:25).]

~ Charles G. Finney (1792–1875)

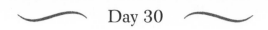

THE PREPARATION

In My Father's house are many dwelling places; if not, I would have told you. I am going away to prepare a place for you.

John 14:2

There are some people who depend so much upon their reason that they reason away God. They say God is not a person we can ever see. They say God is a Spirit. So He is, but He is a person too; and became a man and walked the earth once. Scripture tells us very plainly that God has a dwelling-place. There is no doubt whatever about that. A place indicates personality. God's dwelling-place is in heaven. He has a dwelling-place, and we are going to be inmates of it.

Therefore we shall see Him…We believe this is just as much a place and just as much a city as is New York, London, or Paris. We believe in it a good deal more, because earthly cities will pass away, but this city will remain forever. It has foundations whose builder and maker is God. Some of the grandest cities the world has ever known have not had foundations strong enough to last.

～ Dwight L. Moody (1837–1899)

I WANT TO BE LIKE YOU, LORD!

And walk in love, as the Messiah also loved us and gave Himself for us,
a sacrificial and fragrant offering to God.

Ephesians 5:2

O Thou who hast redeemed me to be a Son of God, and called me from vanity to inherit all things, I praise Thee, that having loved me and given Thyself for me, Thou commandest us saying, As I have loved you, so do ye also love one another. Wherein Thou hast commanded all men, so to love me, as to lay down their lives for my peace and welfare. Since Love is the end for which heaven and earth was made, enable me to see and discern the sweetness of so great a treasure.

And since Thou hast advanced me into the Throne of God, in the bosom of all Angels and men; commanding them by this precept, to give me an union and communion with Thee in their dearest affection; in their highest esteem; and in the most near and inward room and seat in their hearts; give me the grace which Saint Paul prayed for, that I may be acceptable to the Saints, fill me with Thy Holy Spirit, and make my soul and life beautiful, make me all wisdom goodness and love, that I may be worthy to be esteemed and accepted of them. That being delighted also with their felicity, I may be crowned with Thine, and with their glory.

∼ Thomas Traherne (1636–1674)

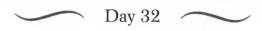
THE SHEPHERD,
THE LIBERATOR

As God's slaves, live as free people, but don't use your freedom as a way to conceal evil.

1 Peter 2:16

The world has never had a good definition of the word *liberty*, and the American people, just now, are much in want of one. We all declare for liberty; but in using the same word we do not all mean the same thing.

With some the word *liberty* may mean for each man to do as he pleases with himself, and the product of his labor; while with some others the same word many mean for some men to do as they please with other men, and the product of the other men's labor… The shepherd drives the wolf from the sheep's throat, for which the sheep thanks the shepherd as a liberator, while the wolf denounces him for the same act as the destroyer of liberty…Plainly the sheep and the wolf are not agreed upon a definition of the word liberty; and precisely the same difference prevails today among us human creatures…

~ Abraham Lincoln (1809–1865)

GOD'S COMPENSATION PLAN

Dishonest scales are detestable to the LORD, but an accurate weight is His delight.

Proverbs 11:1

Years ago, in the astronomical world, it was found that certain changes are taking place which threaten the very existence of the order of the universe. For example: the orbits of the planets are inclined to each other by an angle which does not remain uniform. From the earliest ages the inclination of the earth's equator to the ecliptic has been decreasing, say about half a second a year.

Should this decrease continue, in about 85,000 years the equator and ecliptic would coincide—the order of nature would be entirely changed, and the succession of seasons would give place to one unchanging spring. But in fact, by and by this decrease will reach its limit, and the angle of inclination will then increase, and so the seasons will keep revolving, and seed time and harvest time shall not fail.

God has provided a compensation for what at first seemed a disturbing cause, and as by the chronometer of balance in a model time-piece, regularity of movement is insured, in the end. The action of this compensating law may consume two hundred millenniums, but this shows nothing more than the vast scale on which this machine is constructed.

~ Arthur T. Pierson (1867–1911)

JESUS' SURRENDER OF HIMSELF

Christ also loved the Church, and gave Himself for it; that He might sanctify and cleanse it…just as Christ loved the church and gave Himself for her to make her holy, cleansing her with the washing of water by the word. He did this to present the church to Himself in splendor, without spot or wrinkle or anything like that, but holy and blameless.

Ephesians 5:25–27

Hear still a word of God: "Who gave Himself for us, that He might redeem us from all iniquity, and purify unto Himself a people for His own possession, zealous of good works." Yes: it is to prepare for Himself a pure people, a people of His own, a zealous people, that Jesus gives Himself. When I receive Him, when I believe that He gave Himself to do this for me, I shall certainly experience it. I shall be purified through Him, shall be held fast as His possession, and be filled with zeal and joy to work for Him.

And mark, further, how the operation of this surrender of Himself will especially be that He shall then have us entirely for Himself: "'that He might present us to Himself.' `that He might purify us to Himself, a people of His own'…" The surrender is a mutual one: the love comes from both sides. His giving of Himself makes such an impression on my heart, that my heart with the self-same love and joy becomes entirely His. Through giving Himself to me, He of Himself takes possession of me; He becomes mine and I His. I know that I have Jesus wholly for me, and that He has me wholly for Him.

— Andrew Murray (1827–1917)

WALKING WITH GOD
(PART 1)

Enoch walked with God; then he was not there because God took him.

Genesis 5:24

Various are the pleas and arguments which men of corrupt minds frequently urge against yielding obedience to the just and holy commands of God. But, perhaps, one of the most common objections that they make is this, that our Lord's commands are not practicable, because contrary to flesh and blood; and consequently, that He is "an hard master, reaping where he has not sown, and gathering where he has not strewed." These we find were the sentiments entertained by that wicked and slothful servant mentioned in the 25th of St. Matthew; and are undoubtedly the same with many which are maintained in the present wicked and adulterous generation.

The Holy Ghost foreseeing this, hath taken care to inspire holy men of old, to record the examples of many holy men and women; who, even under the Old Testament dispensation, were enabled cheerfully to take Christ's yoke upon them, and counted His service perfect freedom. The large catalogue of saints, confessors, and martyrs, drawn up in the 11th chapter to the Hebrews, abundantly evidences the truth of this observation. What a great cloud of witnesses have we there presented to our view? All eminent for their faith, but some shining with a greater degree of luster than do others.

～ George Whitefield (1714–1777)

WALKING WITH GOD
(PART 2)

The proto-martyr Abel leads the van. And next to him we find Enoch mentioned, not only because he was next in order of time, but also on account of his exalted piety…have here a short but very full and glorious account, both of his behavior in this world, and the triumphant manner of his entry into the next. The former is contained in these words, "And Enoch walked with God'. The latter in these, 'and he was not: for God took him."

He was not; that is, he was not found, he was not taken away in the common manner, he did not see death; for God had translated him. Who this Enoch was, does not appear so plainly…he seems to have been a person of public character…like Noah, a preacher of righteousness. And, if we may credit the apostle Jude, he was a flaming preacher. For he quotes one of his prophecies, wherein he saith, "Behold, the Lord cometh with ten thousands of his saints, to execute judgment upon all, and to convince all that are ungodly among them, of all their ungodly deeds which they have ungodly committed, and of all their hard speeches, which ungodly sinners have spoken against him." But whether a public or private person, he has a noble testimony given him in the lively oracles.

～ George Whitefield (1714–1777)

WALKING WITH GOD
(PART 3)

The author of the epistle to the Hebrews saith, that before his translation he had this testimony, "that he pleased God"; and his being translated, was a proof of it beyond all doubt. And I would observe, that it was wonderful wisdom in God to translate Enoch and Elijah under the Old Testament dispensation, that hereafter, when it should be asserted that the Lord Jesus was carried into heaven, it might not seem a thing altogether incredible to the Jews; since they themselves confessed that two of their own prophets had been translated several hundred hears before.

But it is not my design to detain you any longer, by enlarging, or making observations, on Enoch's short but comprehensive character: the thing I have in view being to give a discourse, as the Lord shall enable, upon a weighty and a very important subject; I mean, walking with God. "And Enoch walked with God." If so much as this can be truly said of you and me after our decease, we shall not have any reason to complain that we have lived in vain.

~ George Whitefield (1714–1777)

LET GOD LEAD

"Why do you call Me 'Lord, Lord,' and don't do the things I say?"

Luke 6:46

Struggle not to over do, for when it is time convenient, and thou canst be any way useful to thy Neighbour; God will call thee forth, and put thee in the employment that will best suit with thee: That thought belongs only to Him, and to thee, to continue in thy rest, disengaged, and wholly resigned up to the Divine will and pleasure. Don't think that in that condition thou art idle: He is busied enough, who is always ready waiting to perform the Will of God.

Who takes heed to himself for God's sake, does every thing; because, one pure Act of internal Resignation, is more worth than a hundred thousand Exercises for ones own Will. Though the Cistern be capable to contain much Water, yet it must still be without it, till Heaven favour it with Rain. Be at rest…humble and resigned, to every thing that God shall be pleased to do with thee, leave the care to God, for He as a Loving Father, knows best…conform thy self totally to His Will, perfection being founded in that, inasmuch as he who doeth the will of the Lord…Think not that God esteemeth him most, that doeth most. He is most beloved who is most humble…and most correspondent to his own Internal Inspiration, and to the Divine will and pleasure.

~ Miguel de Molinos (1628–1696)

THE CHRISTIAN LIFE

What will it benefit a man if he gains the whole world yet loses his life?
Or what will a man give in exchange for his life?

Matthew 16:26

There is not one command in all the Gospel for public worship...
religion or devotion which is to govern the ordinary actions of our
life is to be found in almost every verse of Scripture. Our blessed
Saviour and His Apostles are wholly taken up in doctrines that
relate to common life.

They call us to renounce the world...to renounce all its goods,
to fear none of its evils, to reject its joys, and have no value for its
happiness: to be as new-born babes, that are born into a new state
of things: to live as pilgrims in spiritual watching, in holy fear, and
heavenly aspiring after another life: to take up our daily cross, to
deny ourselves, to profess the blessedness of mourning, to seek the
blessedness of poverty of spirit: to forsake the pride and vanity of
riches, to take no thought for the morrow, to live in the profoundest state of humility, to rejoice in worldly sufferings: to reject the
lust of the flesh, the lust of the eyes, and the pride of life: to bear
injuries, to forgive and bless our enemies, and to love mankind as
God loveth them: to give up our whole hearts and affections to
God, and strive to enter through the strait gate into a life of eternal
glory.

— William Law (1686–1761)

GO YE…

Go, therefore, and make disciples of all nations, baptizing them in the name of the Father and of the Son and of the Holy Spirit.

Matthew 28:19

It very often happens that the converts that are born in excitement die when the excitement is over. They are like certain insects which are the product of an exceedingly warm day, and die when the sun goes down. Certain converts live like salamanders, in the fire; but they expire at a reasonable temperature. I delight not in the religion which needs or creates a hot head. Give me the godliness which flourishes upon Calvary rather than upon Vesuvius.

The utmost zeal for Christ is consistent with common sense and reason: raving, ranting, and fanaticism are products of another zeal which is not according to knowledge. We would prepare men for the chamber of communion, and not for the padded room at Bedlam. No one is more sorry than I that such a caution as this should be needful; but remembering the vagaries of certain wild revivalists, I cannot say less, and I might say a great deal more. What is the real winning of a soul for God? So far as this is done by instrumentality, what are the processes by which a soul is led to God and to salvation? I take it that one of its main operations consists in instructing a man that he may know the truth of God. Instruction by the gospel is the commencement of all real work upon men's minds.

～ Charles H. Spurgeon (1834–1892)

KEEP COMPANY WITH GOD, AND WITH THE PEOPLE OF GOD

I am the good shepherd. I know My own sheep, and they know Me.

John 10:14

Intimacy with God is the very essence of religion, and the foundation of discipleship. It is in intercourse with Father, Son, and Spirit that the most real parts of our lives are lived; and all parts that are not lived in fellowship with Him, "in whom we live, and move, and have our being," are unreal, untrue, unsuccessful, and unsatisfying. The understanding of doctrine is one thing, and intimacy with God is another. They ought always to go together; but they are often seen asunder; and, when there is the former without the latter, there is a hard, proud, hollow religion. Get your teaching from God (Job 36:22; Jer. 23:30); take your doctrine from His lips; learn truth upon your knees. Beware of opinions and speculations: they become idols, and nourish pride of intellect; they furnish no food to the soul; they make you sapless and heartless; they are like winter frost-work on your windowpane, shutting out the warm sun. Let God be your companion, your bosom-friend, your instructor, your counselor.

~ F. Horatius Bonar (1808–1889)

THE CHARACTER OF
THE RESURRECTION

*And I have a hope in God, which these men themselves also accept,
that there is going to be a resurrection, both of the righteous and the
unrighteous.*

Acts 24:15

Scripture teaches us to look forward to a BODILY resurrection,
similar to the resurrection of Christ. The redemption in Christ will
include the body, Rom. 8:23; 1 Cor. 6:13–20. Such a resurrection
is clearly taught in 1 Cor. 15, and in Rom. 8:11. It will include
both the righteous and the wicked, but will be an act of deliverance
and glorification only for the former. For the latter the re-union of
body and soul will issue in the extreme penalty of eternal death.
According to Scripture the general resurrection will coincide with
the return of Christ and the end of the world, and will immediately
precede the final judgment.

Pre-millennarians teach a double resurrection: one of the just
at the return of Christ, and another of the unjust a thousand years
later, at the end of the world. But the Bible speaks of the resurrection of both in a single breath. It connects the judgment of the
wicked with the coming of Christ, and places the resurrection of
the just at the last day.

⁓ Louis Berkoff (1809–1833)

DEVOTED TO GOD

"Still other seed fell on good ground; when it sprang up, it produced a crop: 100 times what was sown." As He said this, He called out, "Anyone who has ears to hear should listen!"

Luke 8:8

That same state and temper of mind which makes our alms and devotions acceptable, must also make our labour, or employment, a proper offering unto God. If a man labours to be rich, and pursues his business, that he may raise himself to a state of figure and glory in the world, he is no longer serving God in his employment; he is acting under other masters, and has no more title to a reward from God, than he that gives alms, that he may be seen, or prays, that he may be heard of men. For vain and earthly desires are no more allowable in our employments, than in our alms and devotions.

For these tempers of worldly pride, and vain-glory, are not only evil, when they mix with our good works, but they have the same evil nature, and make us odious to God, when they enter into the common business of our employment…But as our alms and devotions are not an acceptable service, but when they proceed from a heart truly devoted to God, so our common employment cannot be reckoned a service to Him, but when it is performed with the same temper and piety of heart.

⌒ William Law (1686–1761)

A FAITH PINNACLE

You will keep the mind that is dependent on You in perfect peace, for it is trusting in You.

Isaiah 26:3

The belief of the resurrection of our Lord from the dead, and of His ascension into heaven, has strengthened our faith by adding a great buttress of hope…shows how freely He laid down His life for us when He had it in His power thus to take it up again. With what assurance, then, is the hope of believers animated, when they reflect how great He was who suffered so great things for them while they were still in unbelief!

And when men look for Him to come from heaven as the judge of quick and dead, it strikes great terror into the careless, so that they retake themselves to diligent preparation, and learn by holy living to long for His approach, instead of quaking at it on account of their evil deeds…what imagination can conceive, the reward He will bestow at the last, when we consider that for our comfort in this earthly journey He has given us so freely of His Spirit, that in the adversities of this life we may retain our confidence in, and love for, Him whom as yet we see not; and that He has also given to each gifts suitable for the building up of His Church, that we may do what He points out as right to be done, not only without a murmur, but even with delight?

〜 St. Augustine (354–430)

Day 45

DIVINE INSPIRATION

For I am Yahweh your God, so you must consecrate yourselves and be holy because I am holy. You must not defile yourselves by any swarming creature that crawls on the ground.

Leviticus 11:44

The Spirit of the triune God, breathed into...was that alone which made him a holy creature in the image and likeness of God. Had he not been...God in him and he in God ...brought into the world as a true offspring and real birth of the Holy Spirit, no dispensation of God to fallen man would have directed him to the Holy Spirit, or ever have made mention of his inspiration in man...And had not the Holy Spirit been his first life, in and by which he lived, no inspired prophets among the sons of fallen Adam had ever been heard of, or any holy men speaking as they were moved by the Holy Ghost.

For the thing would have been impossible, no fallen man could have been inspired by the Holy Spirit, but because the first life of man was a true and real birth of it; and also because every fallen man had, by the mercy and free grace of God, a secret remains of his first life preserved in him, though hidden, or rather swallowed up by flesh and blood; which secret remains, signified and assured to Adam by the name of a "bruiser of the serpent," or "seed of the woman," was his only capacity to be called and quickened again into his first life, by new breathings of the Holy Spirit in him.

⁓ William Law (1686–1761)

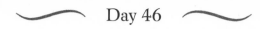
LOVE ONE ANOTHER

"This is My command: Love one another as I have loved you."

John 15:12

The disciples loved one another. This was the blessed fruit of Christ's dying precept to His disciples, and His dying prayer for them… They were dead to this world…evidence of the grace of God in them. They did not take away others' property, but they were indifferent to it…they had, in affection, forsaken all for Christ…they were of one heart and soul, when they sat so loose to the wealth of this world. In effect, they had all things common; for there was not any among them who lacked, care was taken for their supply. The money was laid at the apostles' feet.

Great care ought to be taken in the distribution of public charity, that it be given to such as have need…those who are reduced to want for well-doing, and for the testimony of a good conscience, ought to be provided for. Here is one in particular mentioned, remarkable for this generous charity; it was Barnabas. As one designed to be a preacher of the gospel, he disentangled himself from the affairs of this life. When such dispositions prevail, and are exercised according to the circumstances of the times, the testimony will have very great power upon others.

— Matthew Henry (1662–1714)

A CHRISTIAN MUST

So faith comes from what is heard, and what is heard comes through the message about Christ.

Romans 10:17

The soul can do without everything except the word of God…it is rich and wants for nothing, since that is the word of life, of truth, of light, of peace, of justification, of salvation, of joy, of liberty, of wisdom, of virtue, of grace, of glory, and of every good thing. It is on this account that the prophet in a whole Psalm 119…sighs for and calls upon the word of God with so many groanings and words…there is no more cruel stroke of the wrath of God than when He sends a famine of hearing His words just as there is no greater favour from Him than the sending forth of His word… Christ was sent for no other office than that of the word…

The Apostle Paul explains what it is, namely the Gospel of God, concerning His Son, incarnate, suffering, risen, and glorified, through the Spirit, the Sanctifier. For the word of God cannot be received and honoured by any works, but by faith alone…the soul needs the word alone for life and justification, so it is justified by faith alone, and not by any works. For if it could be justified by any other means, it would have no need of the word, nor consequently of faith.

～ Martin Luther (1483–1546)

THY KINGDOM COME

For we conclude that a man is justified by faith apart from the works of the law.

Romans 3:28

Works…cannot glorify God, although they may be done to the glory of God, if faith be present. But at present we are inquiring, not into the quality of the works done, but into him who does them, who glorifies God, and brings forth good works. This is faith of heart, the head and the substance of all our righteousness. Hence that is a blind and perilous doctrine which teaches that the commandments are fulfilled by works. The commandments must have been fulfilled previous to any good works, and good works follow their fulfillment, as we shall see…we must know that in the Old Testament God sanctified to Himself every first-born male.

The birthright was of great value, giving a superiority over the rest by the double honour of priesthood and kingship. For the first-born brother was priest and lord of all the rest. Under this figure was foreshown Christ, the true and only First-born of God the Father and of the Virgin Mary, and a true King and Priest, not in a fleshly and earthly sense. For His kingdom is not of this world; it is in heavenly and spiritual things that He reigns and acts as Priest; and these are righteousness, truth, wisdom, peace, salvation, etc.

~ Martin Luther (1483–1546)

THE PURPOSE OF GOD

We know that all things work together for the good of those who love God: those who are called according to His purpose.

Romans 8:28

The purpose of God is one, and only one. It is always referred to in the singular; "Called according to His purpose." "According to the purpose…." (Eph. 1:11). "According to the eternal purpose" (Eph. 3:11). "According to His purpose and grace" (2 Tim. 1:9). It is not a variety or number of things; it is just one. And what is the one, single, comprehensive purpose? The answer is Christ! "His Son, Jesus Christ." And when we ask further, What about His Son?

The answer is, to have Him fill all things and to have all things in Him. That this is so is made clear in the definite statements of Scripture; "In Him were all things created, in the heavens and upon the earth, things visible and things invisible… all things have been created through Him, and unto Him." "For it was the good pleasure of the Father that in Him should all the fullness dwell" (Col. 1:16, 19). "Whom He appointed heir of all things, through Whom also He made the worlds (ages)" (Heb. 1:2)…So, then, in the counsels of God, all things must head up in Christ. God's occupation is with bringing Christ in, and bringing into Christ. If we would be "God's fellow-workers," this must be our single-eyed aim and business. This defines precisely the purpose of the Church.

~ T. Austin-Sparks (1888–1971)

HIS VOICE

*So he answered me, "This is the word of the L*ord *to Zerubbabel: 'Not by strength or by might, but by My Spirit,' says the L*ord *of Hosts."*

Zechariah 4:6

The Holy Spirit has His own grammar. Grammar is useful everywhere, but when the subject is greater than can be comprehended by the rules of grammar and philosophy, it must be left behind. In grammar, analogy works very well: Christ is created. Therefore Christ is a creature. But in theology, nothing is more useless. Wherefore our eloquence must be restrained, and we must remain content with the patterns prescribed by the Holy Spirit. We do not depart [from grammar] without necessity, for the subject is ineffable and incomprehensible.

A creature, in the old use of language, is that which the creator has created and distinguished from himself, but this meaning has no place in Christ the creature. There the creator and the creature are one and the same...as once Augustine spoke, moved by the greatest joy: "Is this not a marvelous mystery? He who is the Creator, wished to be a creature." This is to be forgiven the holy Father, who was moved by surpassing joy to speak thus...And the Fathers are to be forgiven, because they spoke thus because of surpassing joy, wondering that the Creator was a creature...it does not matter how you speak, and I am not harmed if you say: Christ is thirst, humanity, captivity, creature.

~ Martin Luther (1483–1546)

GRACE AND PEACE

…Grace to you and peace.

1 Thessalonians 1:1

Grace to you and peace, etc. Nothing is more desirable than to have God propitious to us, and this is signified by grace; and then to have prosperity and success in all things flowing from Him, and this is intimated by peace; for however things may seem to smile on us, if God be angry, even blessing itself is turned to a curse.

The very foundation then of our felicity is the favor of God, by which we enjoy true and solid prosperity, and by which also our salvation is promoted even when we are in adversities. And then as he prays to God for peace, we must understand, that whatever good comes to us, it is the fruit of divine benevolence. Nor must we omit to notice, that he prays at the same time to the Lord Jesus Christ for these blessings. Worthily indeed is this honor rendered to him, who is not only the administrator and dispenser of his Father's bounty to us, but also works all things in connection with him. It was, however, the special object of the Apostle to show, that through him all God's blessings come to us.

～ John Calvin (1509–1564)

JUSTIFICATION

Who can bring an accusation against God's elect? God is the One who justifies.

Romans 8:33

Justification may fitly be extended to the unremitted continuance of God's favor, from the time of our calling to the hour of death; but as Paul uses this word throughout the Epistle, for gratuitous imputation of righteousness…What Paul indeed had in view was to show that a more precious compensation is offered to us, than what ought to allow us to shun afflictions; for what is more desirable than to be reconciled to God, so that our miseries may no longer be tokens of a curse, nor lead us to ruin?…those who are now pressed down by the cross shall be glorified; so that their sorrows and reproaches shall bring them no loss.

Though glorification is not yet exhibited except in our Head, yet as we in a manner behold in Him our inheritance of eternal life, His glory brings to us such assurance respecting our own glory, that our hope may be justly compared to a present possession.…"Those whom God now, consistently with His purpose, exercises under the cross, are called and justified, that they may have a hope of salvation, so that nothing of their glory decays during their humiliation; for though their present miseries deform it before the world, yet before God and angels it always shines forth as perfect."

～ John Calvin (1509–1564)

GODLY WISDOM

"Therefore take care how you listen. For whoever has, more will be given to him; and whoever does not have, even what he thinks he has will be taken away from him."

Luke 8:18

If we had a religion that consisted in absurd superstitions…people might well be glad to have some part of their life excused from it. But as the religion of the Gospel is only the refinement and exaltation of our best faculties, as it only requires a life of the highest reason…to live in such tempers as are the glory of intelligent beings, to walk in such wisdom as exalts our nature, and to practise such piety as will raise us to God; who can think it grievous to live always in the spirit of such a religion, to have every part of his life full of it, but he that would think it much more grievous to be as the Angels of God in Heaven?…

Our Saviour has assured us, it be more blessed to give than to receive, we ought to look upon those that ask our alms, as so many friends and benefactors, that come to do us a greater good than they can receive, that come to exalt our virtue, to be witnesses of our charity, to be monuments of our love, to be our advocates with God, to be to us in Christ's stead, to appear for us in the day of judgment, and to help us to a blessedness greater than our alms can bestow on them.

～ William Law (1686–1761)

THE GREAT PHYSICIAN

Therefore, confess your sins to one another and pray for one another, so that you may be healed. The urgent request of a righteous person is very powerful in its effect.

James 5:16

IF we were well accustomed to the exercise of the presence of God, all bodily diseases would be much alleviated thereby. God often permits that we should suffer a little, to purify our souls, and oblige us to continue with Him. Take courage, offer Him your pains incessantly, pray to Him for strength to endure them. Above all, get a habit of entertaining yourself often with God, and forget Him the least you can. Adore Him in your infirmities, offer yourself to Him from time to time; and, in the height of your sufferings, beseech Him humbly and affectionately (as a child his father) to make you conformable to His holy will…God has many ways of drawing us to Himself.

He sometimes hides Himself from us: but faith alone, which will not fail us in time of need, ought to be our support, and the foundation of our confidence, which must be all in God. I know not how God will dispose of me: I am always happy: all the world suffer; and I, who deserve the severest discipline, feel joys so continual, and so great, that I can scarce contain them…Let us be always with Him. Let us live and die in His presence.

⁓ Brother Lawrence (1749–1832)

HIS DELIGHT

How happy is the man who does not follow the advice of the wicked or take the path of sinners or join a group of mockers! Instead, his delight is in the LORD's instruction, and he meditates on it day and night.

Psalm 1:1–2

A proverb saith, "He that has begun well, has half done": so he that has begun to live by rule, has gone a great way towards the perfection of his life. By rule, must here be constantly understood, a religious rule observed upon a principle of duty to God. For if a man should oblige himself to be moderate in his meals, only in regard to his stomach; or abstain from drinking, only to avoid the headache; or be moderate in his sleep, through fear of a lethargy; he might be exact in these rules, without being at all the better man for them. But when he is moderate and regular in any of these things, out of a sense of Christian sobriety and self-denial, that he may offer unto God a more reasonable and holy life, then it is, that the smallest rule of this kind is naturally the beginning of great piety.

For the smallest rule in these matters is of great benefit, as it teaches us some part of the government of ourselves, as it keeps up a tenderness of mind, as it presents God often to our thoughts, and brings a sense of religion into the ordinary actions of our common life.

～ William Law (1686–1771)

GOD'S LOVE COMMENDED TO US

But God proves His own love for us in that while we were still sinners, Christ died for us!

Romans 5:8

So long as we think of God only as One to be feared, not to be loved, there will be a prejudice against Him as more an enemy than a friend. Yet, God would lead us to serve Him in love and not in bondage. He would draw us forth into the liberty of the sons of God. He loves to see the obedience of the heart. He would inspire love enough to make all our service free and cheerful and full of joy. If you wish to make others love you, you must give them your love. Show your servants the love of your heart, so will you break their bondage, and make their service one of love. In this way God commends His love towards us in order to win our hearts to Himself, and thus get us ready and fit to dwell forever in His eternal home. His ultimate aim is to save us from our sins that He may fill us forever with His own joy and peace.

～ Charles Grandison Finney (1792–1875)

WIFE'S PASSING

The death of His faithful ones is valuable in the LORD's sight.

Psalm 116:15

Almighty and most merciful Father, who lovest those whom thou Punishest, and turnest away thine anger from the penitent, look down with pity upon my sorrows, and grant that the affliction which it has pleased thee to bring upon me, may awaken my conscience, enforce my resolutions of a better life, and impress upon me such conviction of thy power and goodness, that I may place in thee my only felicity, and endeavor to please thee in all my thoughts, words, and actions.

Grant, O Lord, that I may not languish in fruitless and unavailing sorrow, but that I may consider from whose hand all good and evil is received, and may remember that I am punished for my sins, and hope for comfort only by repentance. Grant, O merciful God, that by the assistance of thy Holy Spirit I may repent, and be comforted, obtain that peace which the world cannot give, pass the residue of my life in humble resignation and cheerful obedience; and when it shall please thee to call me from this mortal state, resign myself into thy hands with faith and confidence, and finally obtain mercy and everlasting happiness, for the sake of Jesus Christ our Lord. Amen.

~ Samuel Johnson (1709–1784)

INTEGRITY

The integrity of the upright guides them, but the perversity of the treacherous destroys them.

Proverbs 11:3

It is a great mercy to young people…to have those about them who will instruct them to do what is right in the sight of the Lord; and they do wisely and well for themselves, when willing to be counselled and ruled. The temple was out of repair; Jehoash orders the repair of the temple. The king was zealous. God requires those who have power, to use it for the support of religion, the redress of grievances, and repairing of decays. The king employed the priests to manage…the work. But nothing was done effectually till the twenty-third year of his reign. Another method was therefore taken.

When public distributions are made faithfully, public contributions will be made cheerfully. While they were getting all they could for the repair of the temple, they did not break in upon the stated maintenance of the priests. Let not the servants of the temple be starved, under colour of repairing the breaches of it. Those that were intrusted did the business carefully and faithfully. They did not lay it out in ornaments for the temple, till the other work was completed; hence we may learn, in all our expenses, to prefer that which is most needful, and, in dealing for the public, to deal as we would for ourselves.

— Matthew Henry (1662–1714)

THE PRESENCE OF CHRIST

Immediately Jesus spoke to them. "Have courage! It is I. Don't be afraid."

Matthew 14:27

Think, first, of the presence of Christ lost. You know the disciples loved Christ, clung to Him, and with all their failings, they delighted in Him. But what happened? The Master went up into the mountain to pray, and sent them across the sea all alone without Him; there came a storm, and they toiled, rowed, and laboured, but the wind was against them, they made no progress, they were in danger of perishing, and how their hearts said, "Oh, if the Master only were here!" But His presence was gone. They missed Him.

Once before, they had been in a storm, and Christ had said, "Peace, be still," and all was well; but here they are in darkness, danger, and terrible trouble, and no Christ to help them. Ah, isn't that the life of many a believer at times? I get into darkness, I have committed sin, the cloud is on me, I miss the face of Jesus; and for days and days I work, worry, and labour; but it is all in vain, for I miss the presence of Christ. Oh, beloved, let us write that down —the presence of Jesus lost is the cause of all our wretchedness and failure.

⁓ Andrew Murray (1828–1917)

THE STILL, SMALL VOICE

Instead, I have calmed and quieted myself like a little weaned child with its mother; I am like a little child.

Psalm 131:2

God said, "Be still, and know that I am God." Then came the conflict of thoughts for tomorrow, and its duties and cares; but God said, "Be still." As I listened, it became to me the voice of prayer, the voice of wisdom, the voice of duty, and I did not need to think so hard, or pray so hard, or trust so hard; but that "still small voice" of the Holy Spirit in my heart was God's prayer in my secret soul, was God's answer to all my questions, was God's life and strength for soul and body, and became the substance of all knowledge, and all prayer and all blessing: for it was the living God Himself as my life, my all.

It is thus that our spirit drinks in the life of our risen Lord, and we go forth to life's conflicts and duties like a flower that has drunk in, through the shades of night, the cool and crystal drops of dew. But as dew never falls on a stormy night, so the dews of His grace never come to the restless soul.

∼ A. B. Simpson (1843–1919)

BIBLICAL WORSHIP

God is spirit, and those who worship Him must worship in spirit and truth.

John 4:24

I believe that the greatest challenge facing the Christian community today is to correct out misunderstanding and mis-representation of biblical worship. We have made people believe that worship consists only of what we do for an hour or so on Sunday mornings at the place we call the church. We have made it something we "go to" and "leave from" at the appropriate times. In doing so, we have reduced to an hour what God said must be our entire loves. "Therefore, I urge you, brothers, in view of God's mercy, to offer your bodies as living sacrifices, holy and pleasing to God-this is your spiritual act of worship" (Rom. 12:1).

True worship is the offering to God of one's body, one's entire life. Worship is a life given in obedience to God. When we meet together to encourage, teach, and equip for service, we are being obedient and therefore worshiping, but no more than when we obey Him anywhere else at any other time. A man may say he is going to the assembly to worship God, but he should also say he is going to the factory, the office, the school, the ball field, or the restaurant to worship God. Real worship is offering every moment and every action of every day to God.

~ Randy Cordell (1954–)

A DIRECTORY FOR PRAYER

Pray at all times in the Spirit with every prayer and request, and stay alert in this with all perseverance and intercession for all the saints.

Ephesians 6:18

To pray always may import as much as to pray in all conditions; that is, in prosperity as well as in adversity...it holds at all times equally, and as much in prosperity as in adversity. Indeed, when God doth afflict, he puts an especial season for prayer into our hands; but when he enlargeth our state, he doth not discharge us of the duty, as if we might then lay it aside, as the traveller doth his cloak when the weather is warm. Prayer is not a winter garment.

It is then to be warn indeed; but not to be left off in the summer of prosperity. If you would find some at prayer you must stay till it thunders and lightens; not go to them except it be in a storm or tempest...This is not to pray always; not to serve God, but to serve ourselves of God; to visit God, not as a friend for love of his company, but as a mere beggar for relief of our present necessity... for a net to compass in some mercy we want, and when the fish is got then to throw away the duty.

~ William Gurnall (1617–1679)

ALL SPIRITUAL BLESSINGS

Praise the God and Father of our Lord Jesus Christ, who has blessed us in Christ with every spiritual blessing in the heavens.

Ephesians 1:3

Jesus Christ, by His atoning death and by His resurrection and ascension to the right hand of the Father, has obtained for every believer in Him every possible spiritual blessing. There is no spiritual blessing that any believer enjoys that may not be yours. It belongs to you now; Christ purchased it by His atoning death, and God has provided it in Him. It is there for you; but it is your part to claim it, to put out your hand and take it. God's appointed way of claiming blessings, or putting out your hand and taking hold of the blessings that are procured for you by the atoning death of Jesus Christ, is by prayer. Prayer is the hand that takes to ourselves the blessings that God has already provided in His Son.

~ R. A. Torrey (1856–1928)

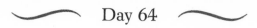

THERE IS A GOOD DARKNESS

He made darkness His hiding place, dark storm clouds His canopy around Him.

Psalm 18:11

There are two sorts of darkness...the first are such as arise from sin, and are unhappy, because they lead the Christian to an eternal precipice. The second are those which the Lord suffers to be in the Soul, to ground and settle it in vertue; and these are happy, because they enlighten it, fortifie it, and cause greater light therein, so that thou oughtest not to grieve and disturb thy self, nor be disconsolate in seeing thy self obscure and darksom, judging that God hath failed thee, and the light also that thou formerly had the experience of; thou oughtest rather at that time persevere constantly in Prayer, it being a manifest sign, that God of his infinite mercy intends to bring thee into the inward path, and happy way of Paradise... embrace it with peace and resignation, as the instrument of perfect quiet, true light, and of all thy spiritual good... See now if darkness be not to be esteemed and embraced.

What thou oughtest to do amidst them, is to believe, that thou art before the Lord, and in his Presence; but thou oughtest to do so, with a sweet and quiet attention; not desire to know any thing, nor search after delicacies, tenderness or sensible devotions, nor do any thing but what is the good will and pleasure of God...

～ Miguel de Molinos (1628–1696)

CAREFUL TREATMENT
REQUIRED

Therefore, the person who rejects this does not reject man, but God, who also gives you His Holy Spirit.

1 Thessalonians 4:8

The need of divine guidance is never more deeply felt than when one undertakes to give instruction in the work of the Holy Spirit—unspeakably tender is the subject, touching the inmost secrets of God and the soul's deepest mysteries. We shield instinctively the intimacies of kindred and friends from intrusive observation, and nothing hurts the sensitive heart more than the rude exposure of that which should not be unveiled, being beautiful only in the retirement of the home circle.

Greater delicacy befits our approach far below the social life where language is formed and usage determines the meaning of words. Glimpses of this life have been revealed, but the greater part has been withheld. It is like the life of Him who did not cry, nor lift up nor cause His voice to be heard in the street. And that which was heard was whispered rather than spoken—a soul-breath, soft but voiceless, or rather a radiating of the soul's own blessed warmth. Sometimes the stillness has been broken by a cry or a raptured shout; but there has been mainly a silent working, a ministering of stern rebuke or of sweet comfort by that wonderful Being in the Holy Trinity whom with stammering tongue we adore as the Holy Spirit.

~ Abraham Kuyper (1837–1920)

OBEYING AND PRAYING

Dear friends, if our conscience doesn't condemn us, we have confidence before God and can receive whatever we ask from Him because we keep His commands and do what is pleasing in His sight.

1 John 3:21–22

The one who expects God to do as he asks Him must on his part *do whatever God bids him.* If we give a listening ear to all God's commands to us, He will give a listening ear to all our petitions to Him. If, on the other hand, we turn a deaf ear to His precepts, He will be likely to turn a deaf ear to our prayers. Here we find the secret of much unanswered prayer. We are not listening to God's Word, and therefore He is not listening to our petitions. If we would have power in prayer, we must be earnest students of His Word to find out what His will regarding us is, and then having found it, do it. One un-confessed act of disobedience on our part will shut the ear of God against many petitions.

~ R. A. Torrey (1856–1928)

A PSALM

Sing to Yahweh, you His faithful ones, and praise His holy name.

Psalm 30:4

A psalm is souls' calm, herald of peace, hushing the swell and agitation of thoughts. It soothes the passions of the soul; it brings her license under law. A psalm is welder of friendship, atonement of adversaries, reconciliation of haters. Who can regard a man as his enemy, when they have lifted up one voice to God together? So Psalmody gives us the best of all boons, love. Psalmody has bethought her of concerted singing as a mighty bond of union, and links the people together in a symphony of one song.

A psalm puts fiends to flight, and brings the aid of angels to our side; it is armour in the terrors of the night; in the toils of the day it is refreshment; to infants it is a protection, to men in life's prime a pride, to elders a consolation, to women an adornment. It turns wastes into homes. It brings wisdom into marts and meetings. To beginners it is an alphabet, to all who are advancing an improvement, to the perfect a confirmation. It is the voice of the church. It gladdens feasts. It produces godly sorrow. It brings a tear even from a heart of stone. A psalm is angels' work, the heavenly conversation, the spiritual sacrifice…those whose souls are musical and harmonious find their road to the things that are above most easy.

~ Henry Wace (1836–1924)

TREASURE IN EARTHEN VESSELS

Now we have this treasure in clay jars, so that this extraordinary power may be from God and not from us.

2 Corinthians 4:7

The principle of the world is "self-glorification," and the principle of the Christian is "self-crucifixion." The principle of the world is "exalt yourself," and the principle of the Christian is "crucify yourself." The principle of men is greatness, bigness, pomp, and show; the principle of the cross is death. Therefore, whenever a man has seen the glory of God in the face of Jesus Christ…at once he comes right into a head-on collision within his own personal living, with all of his principles and motives upon which he has lived until this moment…. if there is to be a continual manifestation of Holy Spirit life, there must be a constant submission to the crucifixion of the flesh, not simply sometimes, but always…

Why is it that so many Christians behave like kindergarten children? Because they have not seen His face!… And the cost in the Christian life… Deep down in the Christian's life, always and all the time, there is to be a "no" to every demand that the flesh may make for recognition, and every demand that the flesh may make for approval, and every demand that the flesh may make for vindication. Always the Christian must bear about in his body the marks of the Lord Jesus.

~ Alan Redpath (1907–1989)

PRAYER CHANGES THINGS

For nothing will be impossible with God.

Luke 1:37

We grouse before God, we are apologetic or apathetic, but we ask very few things. Yet what a splendid audacity a childlike child has! Our Lord says—"Except ye become as little children." Ask, and God will do. Give Jesus Christ a chance, give Him elbow room, and no man will ever do this unless he is at his wits' end.

When a man is at his wits' end it is not a cowardly thing to pray, it is the only way he can get into touch with Reality. Be yourself before God and present your problems, the things you know you have come to your wits' end over. It is not so true that "prayer changes things" as that prayer changes me and I change things. God has so constituted things that prayer on the basis of Redemption alters the way in which a man looks at things. Prayer is not a question of altering things externally, but of working wonders in a man's disposition.

~ Oswald Chambers (1874–1917)

THE WORD OF ENCOURAGEMENT TO BATTLE

Finally, be strengthened by the Lord and by His vast strength.

Ephesians 6:10

A soul deeply possessed with fear, and dispirited with strong apprehensions of danger, is in no posture for counsel. As we see in any army when put to flight by some sudden alarm, or apprehension of danger, it is hard rallying them into order until the fright occasioned thereby is over; therefore the apostle first raiseth up their spirits, "be strong in the Lord." As if he should say, Perhaps some drooping souls find their hearts fail them, while they see their enemies so strong, and they so weak; so numerous, and they so few; so well appointed, and they so naked and unarmed; so skilful and expert at arms, but they green and raw soldiers…with undaunted courage march on, and be strong in the Lord, on whose performance lies the stress of battle, and not on your skill or strength.

It is not the least of a minister's care and skill in dividing the word, so to press the Christian's duty, as not to oppress his spirit with the weight of it, by laying it on the creature's own shoulders, and not on the Lord's strength, as here our apostle teacheth us. In this verse…We have, A familiar appellation, "my brethren," An exhortation, "be strong," A cautionary direction annexed to the exhortation, "in the Lord," An encouraging amplification of the direction, "and in the power of his might," or in his mighty power.

~ William Gurnall (1617–1679)

OUR WILL

The will always follows the last dictate of the understanding. But then the understanding must be taken in a large sense, as including the whole faculty of perception or apprehension, and not merely what is called reason or judgment. If by the dictate of the understanding is meant what reason declares to be best, or most for the person's happiness, taking in the whole of its duration, it is not true, that the Will always follows the last dictate of the understanding.

Such a dictate of reason is quite a different matter from things appearing now most agreeable, all things being put together which pertain to the mind's present perceptions in any respect: although that dictate of reason, when it takes place, has concern in the compound influence which moves Will; and should be considered in estimating the degree of that appearance of good which the Will always follows; either as having its influence added to other things, or subducted from them. When such dictate of reason concurs with other things, then its weight is added to them, as put into the same scale; but when it is against them, it is as a weight in the opposite scale, resisting the influence of other things: yet its resistance is often overcome by their greater weight, and so the act of the Will is determined in opposition to it.

～ Jonathan Edwards (1703–1758)

STAND UP!—STAND UP FOR JESUS

Stand up!—stand up for Jesus, Ye soldiers of the Cross!
Lift high His royal banner, It must not suffer loss.
From vict'ry unto vict'ry His army shall He lead
Till ev'ry foe is vanquished And Christ is Lord indeed.

Stand up!—stand up for Jesus! The trumpet-call obey;
Forth to the mighty conflict In this His glorious day!
Ye that are men, now serve Him Against unnumbered foes;
Let courage rise with danger And strength to strength oppose.

Stand up!—stand up for Jesus! Stand in His strength alone;
The arm of flesh will fail you, Ye dare not trust your own.
Put on the Gospel armor, Each piece put on with prayer;
Where duty calls or danger, Be never wanting there.

Stand up!—stand up for Jesus! The strife will not be long;
This day the noise of battle, The next, the victor's song.
To him that overcometh A crown of life shall be;
He with the King of Glory Shall reign eternally.

~ George Duffield (1818–1888)

KEEP GOING

"The LORD our God spoke to us at Horeb: 'You have stayed at this mountain long enough. Resume your journey and go to the hill country of the Amorites and their neighbors in the Arabah, the hill country, the Judean foothills, the Negev and the sea coast—to the land of the Canaanites and to Lebanon as far as the Euphrates River."

Deuteronomy 1:6–7

When our Lord said, "One of you will betray Me," thank God those disciples had enough spirituality that nobody said, "Lord, is it he?" Every one of those disciples said, "Lord, is it I?" If they would not have so responded there could not have been a Pentecost. But because they were humble enough to point the finger in their own direction the Holy Spirit fell upon them.

Self-righteousness is terrible among God's people. If we feel that we are what we ought to be, then we will remain what we are. We will not look for any change or improvement in our lives. This will quite naturally lead us to judge everyone by what we are. This is the judgment of which we must be careful. To judge others by ourselves is to create havoc in the local assembly. I hear the voice of Jesus saying to us, "You have stayed long enough where you are. Break camp and advance into the hill country." This would be a new spiritual experience that God has for us.

~ A. W. Tozer (1897–1963)

HAVE NOT I, THE LORD?

Yahweh said to him, "Who made the human mouth? Who makes him mute or deaf, seeing or blind? Is it not I, Yahweh?"

Exodus 4:11

Mental pain is less dramatic than physical pain, but it is more common and also more hard to bear. The frequent attempt to conceal mental pain increases the burden: it is easier to say, "My tooth is aching" than to say, "My heart is broken." Yet if the cause is accepted and faced, the conflict will strengthen and purify the character and in time the pain will usually pass. Sometimes, however, it persists and the effect is devastating; if the cause is not faced or not recognized, it produces the dreary state of the chronic mental pain.

They often produce brilliant work and strengthen, harden, and sharpen their characters till they become like tempered steel. In actual insanity the picture is darker. In the whole realm of medicine there is nothing so terrible to contemplate as a man with chronic melancholia. But most of the insane are not unhappy, or, indeed, conscious of their condition. In either case, if they recover, they are surprisingly little changed. Often they remember nothing of their illness. Pain provides an opportunity for heroism; the opportunity is seized with surprising frequency.

～ C. S. Lewis (1898–1963)

CALL FOR CHASTITY

For it is written, Be holy, because I am holy.

1 Peter 1:16

Could I influence the thought of contemporary youth and set the intent of their hearts, minds, and souls upon one subject in particular, that subject would be chastity. For I believe that of all the cardinal virtues that youth might aspire after, it is the one most under attack in our society. Chastity means sexual purity. It means abstinence from sex, except for sex in the marriage bond between male and female. Chastity has found favor with noble persons both inside and outside of Christianity.

Degradation unchecked knows no shame, no limits. So it is not surprising that in recent decades, pornography and the sexual abuse of children have become major problems. Practicing homosexuals demand special treatment. Sexologists seek to have incest legitimized. Did men and women and youth desire purity and fidelity as much as they cuddle up to temptation and lust, we would be freed as individuals, and as a nation, from the sordid costs of unbridled sexual passion and perversion. Oh that our churches, our literature, our schools, and our politics might resound with the call to chastity. Sex is as fire: purposeful in its proper bounds, the bounds of committed marriage, but destructive outside of those boundaries.

~ Raymond V. Banner (1937–)

ARIDITIES TO BE BORNE IN LOVE

I said about laughter, "It is madness," and about pleasure, "What does this accomplish?" I explored with my mind how to let my body enjoy life with wine and how to grasp folly—my mind still guiding me with wisdom—until I could see what is good for people to do under heaven during the few days of their lives.

Ecclesiastes 2:2–3

Though God has no other desire than to impart Himself to the loving soul that seeks Him, yet He frequently conceals Himself from it, that it may be roused from sloth, and impelled to seek Him with fidelity and love. But with what abundant goodness does He recompense the faithfulness of His beloved! And how often are these apparent withdrawings of Himself succeeded by the caresses of love! At these seasons we are apt to believe that it proves our fidelity, and evinces a greater ardor of affection to seek Him by an exertion of our own strength and activity; or that such a course will induce Him the more speedily to revisit us.

No, dear souls, believe me, this is not the best way in this degree of prayer; with patient love, with self-abasement and humiliation, with the reiterated breathings of an ardent but peaceful affection, and with silence full of veneration, you must await the return of the Beloved. Thus only can you demonstrate that it is HIMSELF alone, and his good pleasure, that you seek; and not the selfish delights of your own sensations in loving Him.

~ Jeanne Marie Vouvier de la Mothe Guyon (1647–1711)

PROOF:
GOD IS THE MASTER

Now I know that Yahweh is greater than all gods, because He did wonders when the Egyptians acted arrogantly against Israel.

Exodus 18:11

The famous clock in Strasburg Cathedral has a mechanism so complicated, that it seems to the ignorant and superstitious almost a work of superhuman skill. The abused and offended maker, yet unpaid for his work, came one day and touched its secret springs, and it stopped. All the patience and ingenuity of a nation's mechanics and artisans failed to restore its disordered mechanism and set it in motion. Afterward, when his grievances were redressed, that maker came again, touched the inner springs and set it again in motion, and all its multiplied parts revolved again obedient to his will.

When thus, by a touch, he suspended and restored those marvelous movements, he gave to any doubting mind proof that he was the maker—certainly the master, of that clock. And when Jesus of Nazareth brings to a stop the mechanism of nature, makes its mighty wheels turn back or in any way arrests its grand movement—more than all, when He cannot only stop, but start again, the mysterious clock of human life, He gives to an honest mind overwhelming proof that God is with him. For a malignant power might arrest or destroy, but only He could reconstruct and restore!

⌒ Arthur T. Pierson (1867–1911)

JESUS' PREACHING

Your kingdom come. Your will be done on earth as it is in heaven.

Matthew 6:10

When we come to inquire what the matter of Jesus' preaching consisted of, we perhaps naturally expect to find Him expounding the system of doctrine which we are ourselves acquainted with, in the forms, say, of the Catechism or the Confession of Faith. But what we find is very different. He did not make use of any system of doctrine.

We can scarcely doubt, indeed, that all the numerous and varied ideas of His preaching, as well as those which He never expressed, co-existed in His mind as one world of rounded truth. But they did not so co-exist in His teaching. He did not use theological phraseology, speaking of the Trinity, of predestination, of effectual calling, although the ideas which these terms cover underlay His words, and is it the undoubted task of science to bring them forth. But He spoke in the language of life, and concentrated His preaching on a few burning points, that touched the heart, the conscience, and the time. The central idea and the commonest phrase of His preaching was "the kingdom of God." Jesus announced that it had come, and that He had brought it. The time of waiting was fulfilled.

— James Stalker (1848–1927)

TRUE HAPPINESS

"The LORD your God is with you, isn't He? And hasn't He given you rest on every side? For He has handed the land's inhabitants over to me, and the land has been subdued before the LORD and His people. Now determine in your mind and heart to seek the LORD your God. Get started building the LORD God's sanctuary so that you may bring the ark of the LORD's covenant and the holy articles of God to the temple that is to be built for the name of Yahweh."

1 Chronicles 22:18–19

It may be you are struggling hard for the rewards of this world. Perhaps you are straining every nerve to obtain money, or place, or power, or pleasure. If that be your case, take care. You are sowing a crop of bitter disappointment. Thousands have trodden the path you are pursuing, and have awoke too late to find it end in misery and eternal ruin. They have fought hard for wealth, and honour, and office, and promotion, and turned their backs on God, and Christ, and heaven, and the world to come. And what has their end been? Often, far too often, they have found out that their whole life has been a grand mistake.

For your own happiness' sake resolve this day to join the Lord's side. Shake off your past carelessness and unbelief. Come out from the ways of a thoughtless, unreasoning world. Take up the cross, and become a good soldier of Christ. Fight the good fight of faith, that you may be happy as well as safe.

~ J. C. Ryle (1816–1900)

SHELTER OF THE MOST HIGH

God, hear my cry; pay attention to my prayer. I call to You from the ends of the earth when my heart is without strength. Lead me to a rock that is high above me, for You have been a refuge for me, a strong tower in the face of the enemy. I will live in Your tent forever and take refuge under the shelter of Your wings. Selah

Psalm 61:1–4

During the time when Indonesia was almost taken over by the Communist, our Baptist Hospital was to be demonstrated against with the ultimate goal of destroying it and the missionaries who worked there. We were given three days to prepare. Needless to say, prayer was THE preparation. The day of the demonstration came. Thousands had gathered at the soccer field with their knives and kerosene cans ready to march to the excitement. My husband, Jim, had already gone over to the hospital and was seeing the few patients who dared to venture out. My Christian helpers and I gathered around the dining table.

As a child of missionaries growing up in China, I was quite used to trusting God during dangerous times. Reading Psalm 91 we all were encouraged and reminded that we serve a Faithful, All Powerful God who would protect us, our three little girls, other missionaries and our Christian Indonesians. God did answer all of our prayers in Kediri because when the word came from the Communist leaders, "Destroy" there was only silence and one by one the three thousand people dropped their rocks, turned around and went home. God proved once again, we "live in the shelter of the Most High."

~ Joyce S. Carpenter (1931–)

NOT SO DIFFERENT?

*To reveal His Son in me, so that I could preach Him among the
Gentiles, I did not immediately consult with anyone.*

Galatians 1:16

A strong young man dressed in a loincloth steps off the mountain
path and disappears into the dense jungle. His hand grasps a sharp
machete. Over his shoulder hang two beautifully carved hardwood
cups. Up the same steep trail comes another tribesman—There's a
flash of steel, and without a cry he drops to the ground, headless.
The young warrior fills the cups with the warm blood and quickly
makes his way back to the village where his bride awaits him.

The headman calls the villagers together. Bride and groom
kneel on a red cloth placed on the dirt floor of the small hut. As
the tribes people begin their strange chant of joy, bride and groom
drink the human blood. The marriage ceremony is over. No one
will argue with me over whether or not this is a heathen custom. I
pick up my morning newspaper in Suburbia, U.S.A., and find on
the front page, "Brilliant college senior kills coed who refuses his
lustful advances." Or the headlines scream, "Well-respected doctor
shoots wife in order to live with paramour." The papers today are
filled with items of murder, rape, adultery, robbery, and all other
forms of moral decay. Is not all this just as heathen? There is only
one answer—yes!

∼ Dick Hillis (1913–2005)

NEW CREATURES BECAUSE OF GOD'S LOVE

Look at how great a love the Father has given us that we should be called God's children. And we are! The reason the world does not know us is that it didn't know Him.

1 John 3:1

There is no condemnation to them that are in Christ Jesus; but if you cannot fall finally, you may fall foully, and may go with broken bones all your days. Take care of backslidings; for Jesus Christ's sake, do not grieve the Holy Ghost you may never recover your comfort while you live.

I have paid dear for backsliding. Our hearts are so cursedly wicked, that if you take not care, if you do not keep up a constant watch, your wicked hearts will deceive you, and draw you aside. It will be sad to be under the scourge of a correcting Father...

Let me, therefore, exhort you that have got peace to keep a close walk with Christ. I am grieved with the loose walk of those that are Christians, that have had discoveries of Jesus Christ; there is so little difference betwixt them and other people, that I scarce know which is the true Christian. Christians are afraid to speak of God, they run down with the stream; if they come into worldly company, they will talk of the world as if they were in their element; this you would not do when you had the first discoveries of Christ's love; you could talk then of Christ's love for ever, when the candle of the Lord shined upon your soul.

~ George Whitefield (1714–1770)

HIS PEACE

Abundant peace belongs to those who love Your instruction; nothing makes them stumble.

Psalm 119:165

As God can send a nation or people no greater blessing than to give them faithful, sincere, and upright ministers, so the greatest curse that God can possibly send upon a people in this world, is to give them over to blind, unregenerate, carnal, lukewarm, and unskilled guides. And yet, in all ages, we find that there have been many wolves in sheep's clothing, many that daubed with untempered mortar, that prophesied smoother things than God did allow.

As it was formerly, so it is now; there are many that corrupt the Word of God and deal deceitfully with it. It was so in a special manner in the prophet Jeremiah's time; and he, faithful to his Lord, faithful to that God who employed him, did not fail from time to time to open his mouth against them, and to bear a noble testimony to the honor of that God in whose name he from time to time spake… This is what I design at present, that I may deliver my soul, that I may be free from the blood of those to whom I preach that I may not fail to declare the whole counsel of God. I shall, from the words of the text, endeavor to show you what you must undergo, and what must be wrought in you before you can speak peace to your hearts.

~ George Whitefield (1714–1770)

MARVEL NOT

"Do not be amazed that I told you that you must be born again."

John 3:7

A man cannot enter the intellectual world except he have brains, or the artistic world except he have taste. And he cannot make or find brains or taste. They must be born in him. A man cannot make a poetical mind for himself. It must be created in him. Hence "the poet is born—not made," we say. So the Christian is born, not made… If human nature makes it necessary, much more does the Divine nature.

When Christ shall present His Church to God, it must be as a spotless Bride. In that eternal kingdom saints are more than subjects: they are the companions of the King. They must be a select number. They must be a highborn company. Marvel not if you and I are to be there—as if it were unnecessary that we must be born again. "Lord, who shall abide in Thy tabernacle—who shall dwell in Thy holy hill? He that hath clean hands and a pure heart." "There shall in no wise enter into it anything that defileth." Marvel not as if it were unnecessary that our robes should be washed white. But marvel if you are. Marvel if you are not. Marvel that you may be today.

~ Henry Drummond (1851–1897)

GOD REMAINS UNCHANGED AND UNCHANGEABLE

Now where there is forgiveness of these, there is no longer an offering for sin.

Hebrews 10:18

Our faith becomes a fixed attitude, once it begins to rest in this wonderful fact. Then it can be, if necessary, "rejected indeed of men, but chosen of God, and precious" (1 Peter 2:4 ASV). This is the steadying influence most believers are in need of today. A century ago, J. B. Stoney wrote:

> The blessed God never alters nor diverges from the acceptance in which He has received us because of the death and resurrection of Jesus Christ. Alas! We diverge from the state in which God can ever be toward us as recorded in Romans 5:1–11. Many suppose that because they are conscious of sins, that hence they must renew Their acceptance with God.
>
> The truth is that God has not altered. His eye rests on the work accomplished by Christ for the believer. When you are not walking in the Spirit you are in the flesh: you have turned to the old man which was crucified on the cross Rom. 6:6). You have to be restored to fellowship, and when you are, you find your Acceptance with God unchanged and unchangeable… He certainly will judge the flesh if we do not, but He never departs from the love which He has expressed to the prodigal, and we find… His love, blessed be His Name, had never changed.

~ Miles Stanford (1914 –1999)

WITH HELP FROM THE HOLY SPIRIT

In the same way the Spirit also joins to help in our weakness, because we do not know what to pray for as we should, but the Spirit Himself intercedes for us with unspoken groanings.

Romans 8:26

We realize that we are energized by the Holy Spirit for prayer; we know what it is to pray in the Spirit; but we do not so often realize that the Holy Spirit Himself prays in us prayers which we cannot utter. When we are born again of God and are indwelt by the Spirit of God, He expresses for us the unutterable. "He [the Spirit in you] maketh intercession for the saints according to the will of God," and God searches your heart not to know what your conscious prayers are, but to find out what is the prayer of the Holy Spirit.

Have we recognized that our body is the temple of the Holy Ghost? If so, we must be careful to keep it undefiled for Him. We have to remember that our conscious life, though it is only a tiny bit of our personality, is to be regarded by us as a shrine of the Holy Ghost. He will look after the unconscious part that we know nothing of; but we must see that we guard the conscious part for which we are responsible.

~ Oswald Chambers (1874–1917)

GRACE COVENANT

He has made us competent to be ministers of a new covenant, not of the letter, but of the Spirit. For the letter kills, but the Spirit produces life.

2 Corinthians 3:6

When one person assigns a stipulated work to another person with the promise of a reward upon the condition of the performance of that work, there is a covenant. Nothing can be plainer than that all this is true in relation to the Father and the Son. The Father gave the Son a work to do; He sent Him into the world to perform it, and promised Him a great reward when the work was accomplished. Such is the constant representation of the Scriptures.

We have, therefore, the contracting parties, the promise, and the condition. These are the essential elements of a covenant. Such being the representation of Scripture, such must be the truth to which we are bound to adhere. It is not a mere figure, but a real transaction, and should be regarded and treated as such if we would understand aright the plan of salvation. In Psalm 40, expounded by the Apostle as referring to the Messiah, it is said, "Lo, I come: in the volume of the book it is written of me, I delight to do Thy will," i.e., to execute Thy purpose, to carry out Thy plan. Christ came, therefore, in execution of a purpose of God, to fulfill a work which had been assigned Him.

⁓ Charles Hodge (1797–1887)

THE CONSEQUENCES OF SIN

For all have sinned and fall short of the glory of God.

Romans 3:23

Some sense of sin, and some serious and humbling apprehension of our danger and misery in consequence of it, must indeed be necessary to dispose us to receive the grace of the Gospel, and the Saviour who is there exhibited to our faith. But God is pleased sometimes to begin the work of His grace in the heart almost from the first dawning of reason, and to carry it on by such gentle and insensible degrees, that very excellent persons, who have made the most eminent attainments in the Divine life, have been unable to recount any remarkable history of their conversion...this is most frequently the case with those of them who have enjoyed the benefit of a pious education... God forbid, therefore, that any should be so insensible of their own happiness as to fall into perplexity with relation to their spiritual state...

I have spoken my sentiments on this head so fully in the eighth of my Sermons on Regeneration, that I think none who has read and remembers the general contents of it can be ill danger of mistaking my meaning here...and I am much obliged to that worthy and excellent person who kindly reminded me of the expediency of doing it.

~ Philip Doddridge (1702–1751)

HOLY SPIRIT CONVICTED

When He comes, He will convict the world about sin, righteousness, and judgment.

John 16:8

These words contain part of a gracious promise, which the blessed Jesus was pleased to make to His weeping and sorrowful disciples. The time was now drawing near, in which the Son of man was first to be lifted up on the cross, and afterwards to heaven. Kind, wondrous kind! Had this merciful High-priest been to His disciples, during the time of His tabernacling amongst them. He had compassion on their infirmities, answered for them when assaulted by their enemies, and set them right when out of the way, either in principle or practice.

He neither called nor used them as servants, but as friends; and He revealed His secrets to them from time to time. He opened their understandings, that they might understand the scriptures; explained to them the hidden mysteries of the kingdom of God, when He spoke to others in parables: nay, He became the servant of them all, and even condescended to wash their feet. The thoughts of parting with so dear and loving a Master as this, especially for a long season, must needs affect them much. When on a certain occasion He intended to be absent from them only for a night, we are told, He was obliged to constrain them to leave Him…

～ George Whitefield (1714 –1770)

THE POWER OF OBEDIENCE

He then took the covenant scroll and read it aloud to the people. They responded, "We will do and obey everything that the LORD has commanded."

Exodus 24:7

All God's revelations are sealed to us until they are opened to us by obedience. You will never get them open by philosophy or thinking. Immediately you obey, a flash of light comes. Let God's truth work in you by soaking in it, not by worrying into it. Obey God in the thing He is at present showing you, and instantly the next thing is opened up.

 We read tomes on the work of the Holy Spirit when five minutes of drastic obedience would make things clear as a sunbeam. We say, "I suppose I shall understand these things some day." You can understand them now: it is not study that does it, but obedience. The tiniest fragment of obedience and heaven opens up and the profoundest truths of God are yours straight away. God will never reveal more truth about Himself till you obey what you know already. Beware of being wise and prudent.

⌒ Oswald Chambers (1874–1917)

THE NEW COVENANT

In the same way He also took the cup after supper and said, "This cup is the new covenant established by My blood; it is shed for you."

Luke 22:20

The Lord's Supper is a covenant meal…It is of great importance to understand the New Covenant thoroughly. It is something quite different from the Old Covenant—infinitely better and more glorious. The Old Covenant which God made with Israel was indeed glorious, but yet not adapted for sinful man, because he could not fulfill it. God gave to His people His perfect law, with the glorious promises of His help, His guidance, His blessing, if they should continue in the observance of it. But man in his inner life was still under the power of sin: he was lacking in the strength requisite for abiding in the covenant of His God.

God promised to make a New Covenant… God promised to bestow the most complete forgiveness of sins and to take man altogether into His favor…to communicate to him His law, not externally as written on tables, but inwardly and in his heart, so that he should have strength to fulfill its precepts. He was to give him a new heart and a new spirit—in truth, His own Holy Spirit. Man was not called on in the first instance to promise that he would walk in God's law. God rather took the initiative in promising that He would enable him to do so.

⁓ Andrew Murray (1828–1917)

FRUIT GROWN IN THE HEART OF A CHRISTIAN

"My Father is glorified by this: that you produce much fruit and prove to be My disciples."

John 15:8

God judgeth the fruit by the heart from whence it comes? "A good man, out of the good treasure of his heart, bringeth forth that which is good; and an evil man, out of the evil treasure of his heart, bringeth forth that which is evil" (Luke 4:45). Nor can it be otherwise concluded, but that thou art an evil man, and so that all thy supposed good is nought but badness; for that thou hast made it to stand in the room of Jesus, and hast dared to commend thyself to the living God thereby: for thou hast trusted in thy shadow of righteousness, and committed iniquity. Thy sin hath melted away thy righteousness, and turned it to nothing but dross; or, if you will, to the early dew, like to which it goeth away, and so can by no means do thee good, when thou shalt stand in need of salvation and eternal life of God.

∼ John Bunyan (1628–1688)

PRAYER AND FAITH

"And if you believe, you will receive whatever you ask for in prayer."
Matthew 21:22

Faith does the impossible because it brings God to undertake for us, and nothing is impossible with God. How great—without qualification or limitation—is the power of faith! If doubt be banished from the heart, and unbelief made stranger there, what we ask of God shall surely come to pass, and a believer hath vouchsafed to him "whatsoever he saith." Prayer projects faith on God, and God on the world. Only God can move mountains, but faith and prayer move God. In His cursing of the fig-tree our Lord demonstrated His power.

Following that, He proceeded to declare, that large powers were committed to faith and prayer, not in order to kill but to make alive, not to blast but to bless... We turn to a saying of our Lord, which there is need to emphasize, since it is the very keystone of the arch of faith and prayer. "Therefore I say unto you, What things soever ye desire when ye pray, believe that ye receive them, and ye shall have them." We should ponder well that statement— "Believe that ye receive them, and ye shall have them." Here is described a faith which realizes, which appropriates, which takes. Such faith is a consciousness of the Divine, an experienced communion, a realized certainty.

~ E. M. Bounds (1835–1913)

GOD'S PEACEMAKERS

The peacemakers are blessed, for they will be called sons of God.

Matthew 5:9

It does not belong to all of us Christians, and I doubt whether it belongs to the Christian Church as such at all, to fling itself into the movements to which I have referred. But if a man go and carry to men the great message of a reconciled and a reconciling God manifest in Jesus Christ, and bringing Peace between men and God, he will have done more to sweeten society and put an end to hostility than I think he will be likely to do by any other method.

Christian men and women, whatever else you and I are here for, we are here mainly that we may preach, by lip and life, the great message that in Christ is our Peace, and that God—there is no nobler office for Christians than to seek to damp down all these devil's flames of envy and jealousy and mutual animosity. We have to do it, first, by making very sure that we do not answer scorn with scorn, gibes with gibes, hate with hate, but "seek to overcome evil with good." It takes two to make a quarrel, and your most hostile antagonist cannot break the Peace unless you help him. If you are resolved to keep it, kept it will be.

~ Alexander Maclaren (1826–1810)

SELF-EXAMINATION

I will instruct you and show you the way to go; with My eye on you, I will give counsel.

Psalm 32:8

True proving of ourselves consists of three parts: 1) In the first place, let everyone in his own heart reflect on his sin and condemnation, in order that he may loathe himself and humble himself before God: seeing that the wrath of God against sin is so great that, rather than suffer it to remain unpunished, He punished it in His dear Son Jesus Christ, in the bitter and ignominious death of the Cross.

2) In the second place, let everyone examine his heart as to whether he also believes this sure promise of God, that only on the ground of the suffering and death of Jesus Christ all his sins are forgiven him, and the perfect righteousness of Christ is bestowed upon him and imputed to him as his own: yea, as completely as if he himself in his own person had atoned for all his sins and performed all righteousness.

3) In the third place, let everyone examine his conscience as to whether he is prepared, henceforth and with his whole life, to manifest true thankfulness toward God the Lord, and to walk uprightly in God's sight. All who are so disposed, God will assuredly receive into His favor, and regard as worthy communicants at the table of His Son Jesus Christ. On the other hand, those that have no such testimony in their hearts, eat and drink judgment to themselves.

~ Andrew Murray (1828–1917)

MEDITATE ON THE LORD

Rest in God alone, my soul, for my hope comes from Him.

Psalm 62:5

The Contemplative life appertaineth only to such men and women as for the love of God have forsaken all notorious sins, both of the flesh and of the world, and have given over all intermeddling with the affairs and businesses of the world, or with worldly goods, as also all care and charge over others, and all superiority or offices that concern the government of others (if ever they had any such) and make themselves poor and, as it were, naked from all the things of this life save for what their corporal nature doth merely need and of necessity require.

Unto these men and women it appertaineth diligently and seriously to employ themselves in internal exercises for to get thereby (through the grace of our Lord) cleanness in heart and peace in conscience by destroying of sin and gaining of virtue, and so to come to Contemplation; since such cleanness (necessary for Contemplation) cannot be had without much exercise of body and continual travail or industry in spirit, by devout prayers, fervent desires and spiritual meditation.

～ Walter Hilton (1340–1396)

CARING FOR AGING PARENTS

Honor your father and your mother so that you may have a long life in the land that the LORD your God is giving you.

Exodus 20:12

"Honor thy father and thy mother" is one of the Ten Commandments. While Christ hung upon the cross He remembered His own mother Mary and charged the beloved Apostle John to care for her. Caring for and serving the weak and needy and old and sick has been a mark of Christianity from its inception and this application is most pertinent to the members of one's own family. The church father Gregory of Nazianzus was raised in a devout Christian family.

In his example of deeds and funeral orations of words, Gregory exemplified this tender aspect of Christianity when he returned to his hometown of Nazianzus to take charge of the affairs of his dead brother and then served as, in succession, his beloved sister, father and mother died. Some times the child must give many years of physical assistance and bear the emotional burdens and restrictions of such care. Some times there have been ruptures in family relations where forgiveness, humility, and submissive self-sacrifice are necessary for the sanctified carrying out of such service. Such service and ministering is often tedious and burdensome, seldom glamorous. But it can be made sweet and rewarding by the grace of God and the spirit of Him who "came, not to be ministered unto but to minister..."

⁓ Raymond V. Banner (1937–)

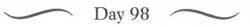
GRACE, MERCY, AND PEACE

Grace, mercy, and peace will be with us from God the Father and from Jesus Christ, the Son of the Father, in truth and love.

2 John 1: 3

"Grace, Mercy, and Peace," stand related to each other in a very interesting manner—as it were, from the fountain head, and slowly traces the course of the blessing down to its lodgment in the heart of man. There is the fountain, and the stream, and, if I may so say, the great still lake in the soul, into which its waters flow, and which the flowing waters make. There is the sun, and the beam, and the brightness grows deep in the heart of man.

Grace, referring solely to the Divine attitude and thought: Mercy, the manifestation of grace in act, referring to the workings of that great Godhead in its relation to humanity: and Peace, which is the issue in the soul of the fluttering down upon it of the Mercy which is the activity of the Grace. So these three come down…a great, solemn, marble staircase from the heights of the Divine Mind…down to the level of earth; and the blessings which are shed along the earth…All begins with Grace; and the end and purpose of Grace, when it flashes into deed, and becomes Mercy, is to fill my soul with quiet repose, and shed across all the turbulent sea of human love a great calm, a beam of sunshine that gilds, and miraculously stills while it gilds, the waves.

— Alexander Maclaren (1826–1910)

A CALL TO BE HOLY

For He chose us in Him, before the foundation of the world, to be holy and blameless in His sight. In love…

Ephesians 1:4

We must come out from the world and be separate, and must not be conformed to it in our characters…no longer share in its spirit or its ways. Our conversation must be in Heaven, and we must seek those things that are above…We must walk through the world as Christ walked…have the mind that was in Him. As pilgrims and strangers we must abstain from fleshly lusts that war against the soul. As good soldiers of Jesus Christ, we must disentangle ourselves from the affairs of this life as far as possible…

We must abstain from all appearance of evil. We must be kind one to another, tenderhearted, forgiving one another, even as God, for Christ's sake, hath forgiven us. We must not resent injuries or unkindness, but must return good for evil, and turn the other cheek to the hand that smites us. We must take always the lowest place among our fellowmen; and seek not our own honor, but the honor of others. We must be gentle, and meek, and yielding; not standing up for our own rights, but for the rights of others. All that we do must be done for the glory of God. And, to sum it all up, since He which hath called us is holy, so we must be holy…

～ Hannah Whitall Smith (1832–1911)

GROWTH

But grow in the grace and knowledge of our Lord and Savior Jesus Christ. To Him be the glory both now and to the day of eternity. Amen.

2 Peter 3:18

These are the last words of an old man, written down as his legacy to us. He was himself a striking example of his own precept. It would be interesting study to examine these two letters of the Apostle Peter in order to construct from them a picture of what he became, and to contrast it with his own earlier self when full of self confidence, rashness, and instability. It took a life time for Simon, the son of Jonas, to grow into Peter; but it was done. And the very faults of the character became strength.

What he had proved possible in his own case he commands and commends to us, and from the height to which he has reached, he looks upwards to the infinite ascent which he knows he will attain when he puts off this tabernacle; and then downwards to his brethren, bidding them, too, climb and aspire. His last word is like that of the great Roman Catholic Apostle to the East Indies: "Forward!" He is like some trumpeter on the battlefield who spends his last breath in sounding an advance. Immortal hope animates his dying injunction: "Grow! Grow in Grace, and in the knowledge of our Lord and Savior."

⁓ Alexander Maclaren (1826–1910)

PERSEVERANCE

How far you go in life depends on your being tender with the young, compassionate with the aged, sympathetic with the striving and tolerant of the weak and strong. Because someday in your life you will have been all of these.

I love to think of nature as an unlimited broadcasting station, through which God speaks to us every hour, if we will only tune in.

Ninety-nine percent of the failures come from people who have the habit of making excuses.

Nothing is more beautiful than the loveliness of the woods before sunrise.

Our creator is the same and never changes despite the names given Him by people here and in all parts of the world. Even if we gave Him no name at all, He would still be there, within us, waiting to give us good on this earth.

When I was young, I said to God, God, tell me the mystery of the universe. But God answered, that knowledge is for me alone. So I said, God, tell me the mystery of the peanut. Then God said, well, George, that's more nearly your size.

Reading about nature is fine, but if a person walks in the woods and listens carefully, he can learn more than what is in books, for they speak with the voice of God.

Where there is no vision, there is no hope.

~ George Washington Carver (1860–1943)

SURRENDER

And do not offer any parts of it to sin as weapons for unrighteousness. But as those who are alive from the dead, offer yourselves to God, and all the parts of yourselves to God as weapons for righteousness.

Romans 6:13

Have you confessed, renounced, and surrendered? If you have, then all you have to do is to believe. God will then give you a supernatural faith and you will be able to trust Him for the fullness of the Holy Spirit. Remember, the Holy Spirit is more anxious to fill you than you are to be filled. Nature abhors a vacuum. So it is with the Holy Ghost. As soon as your heart is ready He will come in and then He will complete the transformation until you are finally changed into Christlikeness.

There may not be any great emotional experience. God never promises it. No two are filled the same. When there is a lot of sin there may be a tremendous experience. When there is a big dam and it is suddenly taken away, there will be a mighty rush and roar as the water pours over. If there is no great dam, then, as you quietly yield, He will flow in in His fullness and fill you without any tremendous upheaval, but it will be real nevertheless. The result will be seen in your ministry. You will be used by God. Conviction will grip the hearts of those to whom you preach, or witness. God will work in you and through you for His glory.

～ J. Oswald Smith (1889–1986)

GAZE UPON CHRIST

But those who trust in the LORD will renew their strength; they will soar on wings like eagles; they will run and not grow weary; they will walk and not faint.

Isaiah 40:31

To those who set their gaze on Christ, no present from which He wishes them to remove can be so good for them as the new conditions into which He would have them pass. It is hard to leave the spot, though it be in the desert, where we have so long encamped that it has come to look like home. We may look with regret on the circle of black ashes on the sand where our little fire glinted cheerily, and our feet may ache and our hearts ache more as we begin our tramp once again, but we must set ourselves to meet the God appointed change cheerfully, in the confidence that nothing will be left behind which it is not good to lose, nor anything met, which does not bring a blessing, however its first aspect may be harsh or sad…

A heart that waits and watches for God's direction—that uses common sense as well as faith to unravel small and great perplexities, and is willing to sit loose to the present, however pleasant, in order that it may not miss the indications which say "Arise! this is not your rest"—fulfills the conditions on which, if we keep them, we may be sure that He will guide us by the right way, and bring us at last to the city of habitation.

～ Alexander Maclaren (1826–1910)

HE WILL DO

He that believeth on Me, the works that I do shall he do also; and greater works than these shall he do; because I go unto My Father. And whatsoever ye shall ask in My Name, that will I do, that the Father may be glorified in the Son. If ye shall ask anything in My Name, I will do it. How wonderful are these statements of what God will do in answer to prayer! Of how great importance these ringing words, prefaced, as they are, with the most solemn verity! Faith in Christ is the basis of all working, and of all praying. All wonderful works depend on wonderful praying, and all praying is done in the Name of Jesus Christ. Amazing lesson, of wondrous simplicity, is this praying in the name of the Lord Jesus! All other conditions are depreciated, everything else is renounced, save Jesus only.

The name of Christ—the Person of our Lord and Savior Jesus Christ—must be supremely sovereign, in the hour and article of prayer. If Jesus dwells at the fountain of my life; if the currents of His life have displaced and superseded all self-currents; if implicit obedience to Him be the inspiration and force of every movement of my life, then He can safely commit the praying to my will, and pledge Himself, by an obligation as profound as His own nature, that whatsoever is asked shall be granted. Nothing can be clearer, more distinct, more unlimited both in application and extent, than the exhortation and urgency of Christ, "Have faith in God."

〜 E. M. Bounds (1835–1913)

ZION'S JOY

Sing for joy, Daughter Zion; shout loudly, Israel! Be glad and rejoice with all your heart, Daughter Jerusalem!.

Zephaniah 3:14, 17

What a wonderful rush of exuberant gladness there is in these words! The swift, short clauses, the triple invocation in the former verse, the triple promise in the latter, the heaped together synonyms all help the impression. The very words seem to dance with joy. But more remarkable than this is the parallelism between the two verses. Zion is called to rejoice in God because God rejoices in her. She is to shout for joy and sing because God's joy too has a voice, and breaks out into singing.

For every throb of joy in man's heart, there is a wave of gladness in God's. The notes of our praise are at once the echoes and the occasions of His. We are to be glad because He is glad: He is glad because we are so. We sing for joy, and He joys over us with singing because we do. We are solemnly warned by "profound thinkers" of letting the shadow of our emotions fall upon God. No doubt there is a real danger there; but there is a worse danger, that of conceiving of a God who has no life and heart; and it is better to hold fast by this—that in Him is that which corresponds to what in us is gladness.

~ Alexander Maclaren (1826–1919)

ALL FOR HIM

For you were bought at a price. Therefore glorify God in your body.

1 Corinthians 6:20

God having made the heavens and the earth, which do not feel the happiness of their being, He has willed to make beings who should know it, and who should compose a body of thinking members. For our members do not feel the happiness of their union, of their wonderful intelligence, of the care which has been taken to infuse into them minds, and to make them grow and endure. How happy they would be if they saw and felt it!

But for this they would need to have intelligence to know it, and good-will to consent to that of the universal soul. But if, having received intelligence, they employed it to retain nourishment for themselves without allowing it to pass to the other members, they would be not only unjust, but also miserable, and would hate rather than love themselves; their blessedness, as well as their duty, consisting in their consent to the guidance of the whole soul to which they belong, which loves them better than they love themselves. To be a member is to have neither life, being, nor movement, except through the spirit of the body, and for the body.

～ Blaise Pascal (1623–1662)

REVIVAL

For I will pour water on the thirsty land and streams on the dry ground; I will pour out My Spirit on your descendants and My blessing on your offspring. They will sprout among the grass like poplars by flowing streams.

Isaiah 44:3–4

God has given much honor to His ministers, but not the privilege of pouring out the Spirit. He keeps that in His own hand: "I will pour." "It is not by might, nor by power, but by My Spirit, saith the Lord of hosts." Alas! we would have little hope, if it depended upon ministers, for where are our men of might now? God is as able to do it today as He was at the day of Pentecost; but men are taken up with ministers, and not with God. As long as you look to a minister, God cannot pour, for you would say it came from man—Prayer is more powerful than preaching.

It is prayer that gives preaching all its power. I observe that some Christians are very ready to censure ministers and to complain of their preaching, of their coldness, their unfaithfulness. God forbid that I should ever defend unfaithful preaching, or coldness, or deadness, in the ambassador of Christ! May my right hand sooner forget its cunning! But I do say, where lies the blame of unfaithfulness? Where, but in the lack of faithful praying? Why, the very hands of Moses would have fallen down, had they not been held up by his faithful people.

~ Robert Murray McCheyne (1813–1843)

INSPIRATION OF SCRIPTURE

And when he had said this, he breathed on them, and saith unto them, Receive ye the Holy Ghost.

John 20:22 KJV

"We believe that the Holy Bible was written by men divinely inspired, and is a perfect treasure of heavenly instruction; that it has God for its author, salvation for its end, and truth without any mixture of error for its matter; that it reveals the principles by which God will judge us; and therefore is, and shall remain to the end of the world, the true center of Christian union, and the supreme standard by which all human conduct, creeds, and opinions shall be tried." This is the first Article of Faith of a great many Baptist churches in our Southland.

This brings us at once to the subject of the inspiration of the Scriptures. The word inspiration is derived from the Latin word *inspiro*, which means to breathe on or to breathe into. That is the literal meaning of the word. The theological meaning is to breathe on or to breathe into for the purpose of conveying the Holy Spirit, in order that those inspired may speak or write what God would have spoken or written.

A Scriptural example of this is found in John 20:22: "And when he said this he breathed on them and saith unto them, Receive ye the Holy Spirit." Following that, verse 23 gives the result: "Whosoever sins ye forgive, they are forgiven unto them; whosoever sins ye retain, they are retained." That is, an inspired man can declare exactly the terms of remission of sins, and the terms upon which sins cannot be remitted, because he is speaking for God. The book that a man, so breathed on, writes is called *theopneustos*, a Greek word meaning "God-inspired." The Holy Bible!

⁓ B. H. Carroll (1843–1914)

KINGDOM BUILDING...
GOD'S WAY

"But seek first the kingdom of God and His righteousness, and all these things will be provided for you."

Matthew 6:33

Immediately we look at these words of Jesus, we find them the most revolutionary statement human ears ever listened to. "Seek ye first the kingdom of God." We argue in exactly the opposite way, even the most spiritually-minded of us—"But I must live; I must make so much money; I must be clothed; I must be fed." The great concern of our lives is not the kingdom of God, but how we are to fit ourselves to live. Jesus reverses the order: Get rightly related to God first, maintain that as the great care of your life, and never put the concern of your care on the other things.

Jesus is not saying that the man who takes thought for nothing is blessed—that man is a fool. Jesus taught that a disciple has to make his relationship to God the dominating concentration of his life, and to be carefully careless about every thing else in comparison to that. It is one of the severest disciplines of the Christian life to allow the Holy Spirit to bring us into harmony with the teaching of Jesus in these verses.

∼ Oswald Chambers (1874–1917)

THE ADVENT OF OUR KING

The advent of our King
Our prayers must now employ,
And we must hymns of welcome sing
In strains of holy joy.
The everlasting Son Incarnate deigns to be;
Himself a servant's form puts on
To set His servants free.
O Zion's Daughter, rise
To meet thy lowly King,
Nor let thy faithless heart despise
The peace He comes to bring.
As Judge, on clouds of light,
He soon will come again
And His true members all unite
With Him in heaven to reign.
Before the dawning day
Let sin's dark deeds be gone,
The old man all be put away,
The new man all put on.
All glory to the Son,
Who comes to set us free,
With Father, Spirit, ever One,
Through all eternity.

~ Charles Coffin (1676–1749)

THE FATHER'S LOVE

Look at how great a love the Father has given us that we should be called God's children. And we are! The reason the world does not know us is that it didn't know Him.

1 John 3:1

Learn this solemn truth that the Father loves you, the Father wants you to be saved, the Father wants you to believe on the Son; the very Father who commanded Christ to lay down His life for sinners. You will notice from this that the Father is clear from the blood of all men. He does not want you to perish. "Turn ye, turn ye. why will ye die?" He is not willing that any should perish. "He willeth all men to be saved, and to come to the knowledge of the truth." He does not want you to perish.

He commands Christ to go into the world, and lay down his life for sinners. Oh! it is true: the Father does not want you to perish. "God so loved the world, that he gave his only begotten Son." "God sent not his Son into the world to condemn the world; but that the world through him might be saved." God the Father is as earnest in your salvation as Christ is. It was God's part to send the Son, and the Son's part to come and die. And as God the Son has done His part, so God the Father has done His. So that, sinners, if you perish, it is because you will not come to Him, that you may have life.

～ Robert Murray McCheyne (1813–1843)

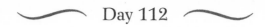
THE GREAT APOSTASY AND THE GREAT TRIBULATION

Now concerning that day and hour no one knows—neither the angels in heaven, nor the Son—except the Father only.

Matthew 24:36

The Bible teaches repeatedly that toward the end of time there will be a great falling away. Iniquity will increase, and the love of many will wax cold. Wickedness crying to high heaven will result in a terrible tribulation "such as hath not been from the beginning of the world until now, no, nor ever shall be" (Matt. 24:21 ASV). If those days were not shortened no flesh would be saved; but they will be shortened for the sake of the elect.

The Bible also refers to striking signs as marking the beginning of the end. There will be wars, famines, and earthquakes in diverse places, which are called the beginning of travail, to be followed by the rebirth of the universe; and also fearful portents in heaven, when the powers of the heavens will be shaken. After these signs the Son of Man will be seen coming on the clouds of heaven. Some believe that the coming of Christ is imminent, that is, may now occur at any time. But the Bible teaches us that the events and signs mentioned in the foregoing must precede the return. From God's point of view the coming is always near; but no one can determine the exact time, not even the angels nor the Son of Man.

◯ Louis Berkoff (1809–1833)

AFFLICTION

Suppose someone says to God, "I have endured my punishment; I will no longer act wickedly. Teach me what I cannot see; if I have done wrong, I won't do it again."

Job 34:31–32

This world is a world of trouble: "Man that is born of woman, is of few days, and full of trouble." "We dwell in cottages of clay, our foundation is in the dust, we are crushed before the moth" (Job 4:19). This world has sometimes been called "a vale of tears." Trials come into all your dwellings; the children of God are not excepted; there is a need be that you be in many temptations. "Count it not strange when you fall into diverse temptations, as though some strange thing happened unto you."

If this be so, of how great importance is it, that you and I be prepared to meet it. The darkest thunder cloud only covers the heavens for a time…Remember, it is right to learn contentment. What right have you to complain? What right have you to challenge God's dealings with you? If little children were to take upon them to decide upon the proceedings of both houses of Parliament, what would you think of it? And what right have you to challenge God's government? We should say, with Job, "The Lord gave, and the Lord hath taken away; blessed be the name of the Lord.

～ Robert Murray McCheyne (1813–1843)

PEACE WITHIN

Don't worry about anything, but in everything, through prayer and petition with thanksgiving, let your requests be made known to God.

Philippians 4:6

Paul would have us understand that Christ imparts a measure of His own peace to our worshipping hearts when we make everything pertaining to life a matter of prayer. We can readily comprehend the possibilities of prayer when we perceive that mortal man can obtain a measure of the peace which the God of Peace possesses in His divine nature.

It is not necessary for the children of God to enter heaven in order to enjoy the priceless possession of peace. Christ wills to give the heavenly heritage of His Peace to all the sons of God. He revealed this truth when He said in John 14:27, "Peace I leave with you; My peace I give to you; not as the world gives do I give to you. Do not let your heart be troubled, nor let it be fearful."

~ T. M. Anderson (1888–1979)

OF COMMUNION WITH GOD

Jesus answered, "If anyone loves Me, he will keep My word. My Father will love him, and We will come to him and make Our home with him."

John 14:23

Our communion with God consisteth in His communication of Himself unto us, with our returnal unto Him of that which He requireth and accepteth, flowing from that unions which in Jesus Christ we have with Him… Perfect and complete, in the full fruition of His glory and total giving up of ourselves to Him, resting in Him as our utmost end; which we shall enjoy when we see Him as He is… Initial and incomplete, in the first fruits and dawnings of that perfection which we have Here in grace…that mutual communication in giving and receiving, after a most holy and spiritual manner, which is between God and the saints while they walk together in a covenant of peace, ratified in the blood of Jesus, whereof we are to treat.

And this we shall do, if God permit; in the meantime praying the God and Father of our Lord and Saviour Jesus Christ, who has, of the riches of His grace, recovered us from a state of enmity into a condition of communion and fellowship with Himself… may have such a taste of His sweetness and excellencies therein, as to be stirred up to a farther longing after the fulness of His salvation, and the eternal fruition of Him in glory.

~ John Owen (1616 –1683)

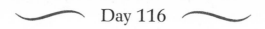

A PRAYER FOR PEACE

For the mind-set of the flesh is death, but the mind-set of the Spirit is life and peace.

Romans 8:6

God grant me the serenity
to accept the things I cannot change;
courage to change the things I can;
and wisdom to know the difference.
Living one day at a time;
enjoying one moment at a time;
accepting hardships as the pathway to peace;
taking, as He did, this sinful world
as it is, not as I would have it;
trusting that He will make all things right
if I surrender to His Will;
that I may be reasonably happy in this life
and supremely happy with Him
forever in the next.
Amen.

~ Reinhold Niebuhr (1892–1971)

AN EXHORTATION TO HUMILITY

The fear of the LORD is what wisdom teaches, and humility comes before honor.

Proverbs 15:33

Let us therefore, brethren, be of humble mind, laying aside all haughtiness, and pride, and foolishness, and angry feelings; and let us act according to that which is written (for the Holy Spirit saith, "Let not the wise man glory in his wisdom, neither let the mighty man glory in his might, neither let the rich man glory in his riches; but let him that glorieth glory in the Lord, in diligently seeking Him, and doing judgment and righteousness"), being especially mindful of the words of the Lord Jesus which He spake, teaching us meekness and long-suffering.

For thus He spoke: "Be ye merciful, that ye may obtain mercy; forgive, that it may be forgiven to you; as ye do, so shall it be done unto you; as ye judge, so shall ye be judged; as ye are kind, so shall kindness be shown to you; with what measure ye mete, with the same it shall be measured to you." By this precept and by these rules let us establish ourselves, that we walk with all humility in obedience to His holy words. For the holy word saith, "On whom shall I look, but on him that is meek and peaceable, and that trembleth at My words?"

~ Philip Schaff (1819–1893)

FROM GROANS TO PRAISE

Hallelujah! Sing to the LORD a new song, His praise in the assembly of the godly.

Psalm 149:1

Truly we are more than conquerors through Him that loved us; for we can give thanks before the fight is done. Yes, even in the thickest of the battle we can look up to Jesus, and cry, Thanks to God. The moment a soul groaning under corruption rests the eye on Jesus, that moment his groans are changed into songs of praise. In Jesus you discover a fountain to wash away the guilt of all your sin. In Jesus you discover grace sufficient for you—grace to hold you up to the end—and a sure promise that sin shall soon be rooted out all together. "Fear not, I have redeemed thee. I have called thee by My name; thou art Mine."

Ah, this turns our groans into songs of praise! How often a psalm begins with groans and ends with praises! This is the daily experience of all the Lord's people. Is it yours? Try yourselves by this. Oh, if you know not the believer's song of praise, you will never cast your crowns with them at the feet of Jesus! Dear believers, be content to glory in your infirmities, that the power of Christ may rest upon you. Glory, glory, glory to the Lamb!

~ Robert Murray McCheyne (1813–1843)

CONSECRATED WHOLLY TO GOD

I am weary from grief; strengthen me through Your word.

Psalm 119:28

But who am I, and what is my people, that we should be able to offer so willingly after this sort? For all things come of Thee, and of Thine own have we given Thee. To be and abide in continual dependence upon God. Become nothing, begin to understand that you are nothing but an earthen vessel into which God will shine down the treasure of His love. Blessed is the man who knows what it is to be nothing, to be just an empty vessel meet for God's use. Work, the Apostle says, for it is God who worketh in you to will and to do.

Brethren, come and take tonight the place of deep, deep dependence on God. And then take the place of child-like trust and expectancy. Count upon your God to do for you everything that you can desire of Him. Honour God as a God who gives liberally. Honour God and believe that He asks nothing from you but what he is going first to give. And then come praise and surrender and consecration. Praise Him for it! Let every sacrifice to Him be a thank-offering. What are we going to consecrate? First of all our lives.

⁓ Andrew Murray (1828–1917)

THE CHURCH DOOR

Then said Jesus unto them again, "Verily, verily, I say unto you, I am the door of the sheep. All that ever came before me are thieves and robbers: but the sheep did not hear them. I am the door: by me if any man enter in, he shall be saved, and shall go in and out, and find pasture. The thief cometh not, but for to steal, and to kill, and to destroy: I am come that they might have life, and that they might have it more abundantly." Christ is the kindest of all teachers. He was speaking to a crowd of ignorant and prejudiced Jews, and yet how kindly he deals with them.

He told them one parable, but they understood not. "This parable spake Jesus unto them; but they understood not what things they were he spake unto them." And yet, we are told, Christ spake unto them again. He hath given them a description of the true and false shepherd, and of the door into the sheepfold; but they seem to have been at a loss to know what the door meant; therefore He says, "Verily, verily, I say unto you, I am the door of the sheep." You see how kindly He tries to instruct them. My brethren, Christ is the same kind teacher still. Are there not many stupid and prejudiced persons here? And yet has He not given you "precept upon precept, precept upon precept; line upon line, line upon line; here a little, and there a little" (Isa. 13:28). He has broken down the bread for you.

～ Robert Murray McCheyne (1813–1843)

MAKING HIM KING!

I have done this so that we may not be taken advantage of by Satan. For we are not ignorant of his schemes.

2 Chronicles 2:11

God's loving appointment in making Jesus King will be apparent when we remember how beautiful He is in His personal character; how closely He is identified with our nature; the might of His arm with which He shields, the patience wherewith He bears, the redemption which He has wrought out and brought in for all who believe. What could God's love have done better to approve itself? Is He your King? Never till He is so, will you know the fulness of God's love.

Those who question or refuse His authority are always in doubt about the love of God to themselves and to the world. Those, on the other hand, who acknowledge His claims, and crown Him as King, suddenly find themselves admitted to a standpoint of vision in which doubts and disputations vanish, and the secret love of God is unfolded. Then they experience the wise and gentle tendency of the Divine love in its most entrancing characteristics. All is love where Jesus reigns. Nothing is more indicative of God's benevolence than His incessant appeal to men to make Jesus King. "Go, spread your trophies at His feet, And crown Him Lord of all!"

— F. B. Meyer (1847–1929)

HUMBLE RESIGNATION

But remember that the LORD your God gives you the power to gain wealth, in order to confirm His covenant He swore to your fathers, as it is today.

Deuteronomy 8:18

When God had a mind to instruct His own Captain Moses, and give Him the two Tablets of the Law (Exodus 24) written in Stone, he called him up to the Mountain, at what time God being there with him, the Mount was Darkened and environed with thick Clouds, Moses standing idle, not knowing what to think or say. Seven days after God commanded Moses to come up to the top of the Mountain where He show'd him His Glory, and filled him with great Consolation.

So in the Beginning, when God intends after an extraordinary manner, to guide the Soul into the School of the divine and loving Notices of the internal Law, He makes it go with Darkness, and Dryness, that He may bring it near to Himself, because the Divine Majesty knows very well, that it is not by the means of one's own Ratiocination, or Industry, that a Soul draws near to Him, and understands the Divine Documents; but rather by silent and humble Resignation.

～ Miguel de Molinos (1628–1696)

WALK WITH CHRIST

We used to have close fellowship; we walked with the crowd into the house of God.

Psalm 55:14

"There is a path which no fool knoweth, and which the vulture's eye hath not seen: the lion's whelps have not trodden it, nor the fierce lion passed by it." What an unspeakable mercy for one who really desires to walk with God, to know that there is a way for him to walk in! God has prepared a pathway for His redeemed in which they may walk with all possible certainty, calmness and fixedness. It is the privilege of every child of God, and every servant of Christ, to be as sure that he is in God's way as that his soul should be saved.

This may seem a strong statement; but the question is, Is it true? If is be true, it cannot be too strong. No doubt it may, in the judgment of some, savor a little of self confidence and dogmatism to assert, in such a day as that in which we live, and in the midst of such a scene as that through which we're passing, that we are sure of being in God's path…the selfsame voice that tells us of God's salvation for our souls, tells us also of God's pathway for our feet.

~ C. H. Mackintosh (1820–1896)

SUFFERING

Praise the God and Father of our Lord Jesus Christ, the Father of mercies and the God of all comfort. He comforts us in all our affliction, so that we may be able to comfort those who are in any kind of affliction, through the comfort we ourselves receive from God.

2 Corinthians 1:3–4

Men who love God are so far from complaining of their sufferings, that their complaint and their suffering is rather because the suffering which God's will has assigned them is so small. All their blessedness is to suffer by God's will, and not to have suffered something, for this is the loss of suffering. This is why I said, Blessed are they who are willing to suffer for righteousness, not, Blessed are they who have suffered. All that a man bears for God's sake, God makes light and sweet for him.

If all was right with you, your sufferings would no longer be suffering, but love and comfort. If God could have given to men anything more noble than suffering, He would have redeemed mankind with it: otherwise, you must say that my Father was my enemy, if he knew of anything nobler than suffering. True suffering is a mother of all the virtues.

～ Johannes Eckhart (1260–1327)

WALK OF FAITH

Jesus replied to them, "Have faith in God."

Mark 11:22

The blessed apostle declares himself not ashamed of the gospel: "for it is the power of God unto salvation to everyone that believeth; to the Jew first, and also to the Greek. For therein is the righteousness of God revealed, on the principle of faith, to faith: as it is written, the just shall live by faith." "…but that no man is justified by the law in the sight of God, it is evident: For, the just shall live by faith."

Finally, in the tenth of Hebrews, where the object is to exhort believers to hold fast their confidence, we read, "Cast not away therefore your confidence, which hath great recompense of reward. For ye have need of patience, that, after ye have done the will of God, ye might receive the promise. For yet a little while, he that shall come will come, and will not tarry. Now the just shall live by faith." Here we have faith presented not only as the ground of righteousness, but as the vital principle by which we are to live, day by day, from the starting-post to the goal of the Christian course. there is no other way of righteousness, no other way of living, but by faith. It is by faith we are justified, and by faith we live. By faith we stand, and By faith we walk.

~ C. H. Mackintosh (1820–1896)

SAVIOR OF THE NATIONS, COME

Savior of the nations, come,
Virgin's Son, make here Thy home!
Marvel now, O heaven and earth,
That the Lord chose such a birth.
Not by human flesh and blood,
By the Spirit of our God,
Was the Word of God made flesh—
Woman's Offspring, pure and fresh.
Wondrous birth! O wondrous
Child Of the Virgin undefiled!
Though by all the world disowned,
Still to be in heaven enthroned.
From the Father forth He came
And returneth to the same,
Captive leading death and hell—
High the song of triumph swell!
Thou, the Father's only Son,
Hast o'er sin the victory won.
Boundless shall Thy kingdom be
When shall we its glories see?
Brightly doth Thy manger shine,
Glorious is its light divine
Let not sin o'ercloud this light;
Ever be our faith thus bright.
Praise to God the Father sing,
Praise to God the Son, our King,
Praise to God the Spirit be Ever and eternally.

～ Martin Luther (1483–1546)

WHAT A DIFFERENCE!

Therefore, if anyone is in Christ, he is a new creation; old things have passed away, and look, new things have come.

2 Corinthians 5:17

There is a most intimate connection between his life before and after conversion...the life in sin and the life in the beauty of holiness are both conditioned by the same character and disposition, by similar circumstances and influences. Wherefore, to bring about our final perfection the Holy Spirit must influence the previous development, the formation of character, and the disposition of the whole person...since our personal life is only a manifestation of human life in general, it follows that the Holy Spirit must have been active also in the creation of man...

And finally, as the disposition of man as such is connected with the host of heaven and earth, His work must touch the formation of this also... Hence the Spirit's work reaches as far as the influences that affect man in the attaining of his destiny or in the failure to attain it... In the departure of the redeemed soul every one acknowledges a work of the Holy Spirit... Yet the Scripture teaches not only that we are born again by the power of the Spirit of God, but that: "by the Word of the LORD were the heavens made, and all the host of them by the breath [Spirit] of his mouth.

~ Abraham Kuyper (1837–1920)

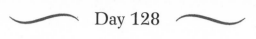
HE SEEKS US

For the Son of Man has come to seek and to save the lost.

Luke 19:10

It is simply and only a question of becoming acquainted with God, and getting to know what He is, and what He does, and what He feels. Comfort and peace never come from anything we know about ourselves, but only and always from what we know about Him. We may spend our days in what we call our religious duties, and we may fill our devotions with fervor, and still may be miserable. Nothing can set our hearts at rest but a real acquaintance with God; for, after all, everything in our salvation must depend upon Him in the last instance; and, according as He is worthy or not of our confidence, so must necessarily be our comfort.

If we were planning to take a dangerous voyage, our first question would be as to the sort of captain we were to have. Our common sense would tell us that if the captain were untrustworthy, no amount of trustworthiness on our part would make the voyage safe; and it would be his character and not our own that would be the thing of paramount importance to us.

~ Hannah Whitall Smith (1832–1911)

PERSONAL OIL

But the foolish ones said to the sensible ones, "Give us some of your oil, because our lamps are going out."

Matthew 25:8

No one can give of his oil to another…A man can give light, but he cannot give oil. The latter is the gift of God alone. "The wise answered, saying, Not so; lest there be not enough for us and you but go ye rather to them that sell and buy for yourselves. And while they went to buy, the bridegroom came and they that were ready went in with him to the marriage; and the door was shut." It is of no use looking to Christian friends to help us or prop us up. No use in flying hither and thither for some one to lean upon…our creed, or our sacraments.

We want oil. Not from man, not from the church, not from the saints, not from the fathers. We must get it from God; and He, blessed be His name, gives freely. "The Gift of God is eternal life, through Jesus Christ our Lord." No man can believe, or get life for another. Each must have to do with God for himself. The link which connects the soul with Christ is intensely individual. There is no such thing as second-hand faith. A man may teach us religion, or theology, or the letter of Scripture; but he cannot give us oil; he cannot give us faith; he cannot give us life. "It is the gift of God." Precious little word, "gift."

∼ C. H. Mackintosh (1820–1896)

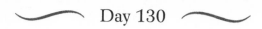
IT'S UP TO THE PARENTS!

*Teach a youth about the way he should go; even when he is old he will
not depart from it.*

Proverbs 22:6

The world is old, and we have the experience of nearly six thousand
years to help us. We live in days when there is a mighty zeal for
education in every quarter. We hear of new schools rising on all
sides. We are told of new systems, and new books for the young, of
every sort and description. And still for all this, the vast majority
of children are manifestly not trained in the way they should go,
for when they grow up to man's estate, they do not walk with God.
The plain truth is, the Lord's commandment in our text is not regarded; and therefore the Lord's promise in our text is not fulfilled.

I know that you cannot convert your child. I know well that
they who are born again are born, not of the will of man, but of
God. But I know also that God says expressly, "Train up a child
in the way he should go," and that He never laid a command on
man which He would not give man Grace to perform…It is just
in the going forward that God will meet us. The path of obedience
is the way in which He gives the blessing. We have only to do as
the servants were commanded at the marriage feast in Cana, to fill
the water pots with water, and we may safely leave it to the Lord to
turn that water into wine.

~ J. C. Ryle (1816–1900)

PRECIOUS CHRIST

So honor will come to you who believe, but for the unbelieving, The stone that the builders rejected—this One has become the cornerstone.

1 Peter 2:7

Unto believers Jesus Christ is precious. In Himself He is of inestimable preciousness, for He is the very God of very God. He is, moreover, perfect man without sin. The precious gopher wood of his humanity is overlaid with the pure gold of his divinity. He is a mine of jewels, and a mountain of gems. He is altogether lovely, but, alas! this blind world seeth not His beauty. The painted harlotries of that which, Madam Bubble, the world can see, and all men wonder after her.

This life, its joy, its lust, its gains, its honours—these have beauty in the eye of the unregenerate man, but in Christ he sees nothing which he can admire. He hears his name as a common word, and looks upon his cross as a thing in which he has no interest, neglects his gospel, despises his Word, and, perhaps, vents fierce spite upon his people. But not so the believer. The man who has been brought to know that Christ is the only foundation upon which the soul can build its eternal home, he who has been taught that Jesus Christ is the first and the last, the Alpha and the Omega, the author and the finisher of faith, thinks not lightly of Christ. He calls him all his salvation and all his desire; the only glorious and lovely one.

~ Charles Spurgeon (1834–1892)

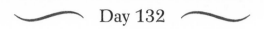
TO CHRIST WE OWE
OUR RIGHTEOUSNESS

For just as through one man's disobedience the many were made sinners, so also through the one man's obedience the many will be made righteous.

Romans 5:19

"Through the obedience of the One shall the many be made righteous." These words tell us what we owe to Christ. As in Adam we were made sinners, in Christ we are made righteous. The words tell us, too, to what in Christ it is we owe our righteousness. As Adam's disobedience made us sinners, the obedience of Christ makes us righteous. To the obedience of Christ we owe everything. Among the treasures of our inheritance in Christ this is one of the richest… You are familiar with the blessed truth of justification by faith…

The object of Christ's life of obedience was threefold: (1) As an Example, to show us what true obedience was. (2) As our Surety, by His obedience to fulfill all righteousness for us. (3) As our Head, to prepare a new and obedient nature to impart to us. So He died, too, to show us that His obedience means a readiness to obey to the uttermost, to die for God; that it means the vicarious endurance and atonement of the guilt of our disobedience; that it means a death to sin as an entrance to the life of God for Him and for us.

～ Andrew Murray (1828–1917)

EFFECTIVE PRAYER

If only I knew how to find Him, so that I could go to His throne. I would plead my case before Him and fill my mouth with arguments.

Job 23:3–4

Put these three things together, the deep spirituality which recognizes prayer as being real conversation with the invisible God—much distinctness which is the reality of prayer, asking for what we know we want—and much fervency, believing the thing to be necessary, and therefore resolving to obtain it if it can be had by prayer, and above all these, complete submission, leaving it still with the Master's will—commingle all these, and you have a clear idea of what it is to order your cause before the Lord. Still prayer itself is an art which only the Holy Ghost can teach us. He is the giver of all prayer. Pray for prayer—pray till you can pray; pray to be helped to pray, and give not up praying because you cannot pray, for it is when you think you cannot pray that you are most praying. Sometimes when you have no sort of comfort in your supplications, it is then that your heart all broken and cast down is really wrestling and truly prevailing with the Most High.

— Charles Haddon Spurgeon (1834–1892)

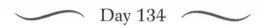

SERMON ON THE MOUNT

When He saw the crowds, He went up on the mountain, and after He sat down, His disciples came to Him. Then He began to teach them…

Matthew 5:1–2

Consider the sermon which our Lord Jesus Christ spoke on the mount, as we read it in the Gospel according to Matthew…so far as regards the highest morals, a perfect standard of the Christian life: and this we do not rashly venture to promise, but gather it from the very words of the Lord Himself. For the sermon itself is brought to a close in such a way, that it is clear there are in it all the precepts which go to mould the life.

For thus He speaks: "Therefore, whosoever heareth these words of mine, and doeth them, I will liken him unto a wise man, which built his house upon a rock: and the rain descended, and the floods came, and the winds blew, and beat upon that house; and it fell not: for it was founded upon a rock. And every one that heareth these words of mine, and doeth them not, I will liken unto a foolish man, which built his house upon the sand: and the rain descended, and the floods came, and the winds blew, and beat upon that house; and it fell: and great was the fall of it." Since, therefore, He has not simply said, "Whosoever heareth my words," but has made an addition, saying, "Whosoever heareth these words of mine," He has sufficiently indicated…that these sayings which He uttered on the mount so perfectly guide the life of those who may be willing to live according to them, that they may justly be compared to one building upon a rock.

〜 St. Augustine (345–430)

JOY

"I have spoken these things to you so that My joy may be in you and your joy may be complete."

John 15:11

Joy, which was the small publicity of the pagan, is the gigantic secret of the Christian… I open again the strange small book from which all Christianity came; and I am again haunted by a kind of confirmation. The tremendous figure which fills the Gospels towers in this respect, as in every other, above all the thinkers who ever thought themselves tall. His pathos was natural, almost casual. The Stoics, ancient and modern, were proud of concealing their tears. He never concealed His tears; He showed them plainly on His open face at any daily sight, such as the far sight of His native city. Yet He concealed something.

Solemn supermen and imperial diplomatists are proud of restraining their anger. He never restrained His anger. He flung furniture down the front steps of the Temple, and asked men how they expected to escape the damnation of Hell. Yet He restrained something. I say it with reverence; there was in that shattering personality a thread that must be called shyness. There was something that He hid from all men when He went up a mountain to pray. There was something that He covered constantly by abrupt silence or impetuous isolation. There was some one thing that was too great for God to show us when He walked upon our earth; and I have sometimes fancied that it was His mirth.

~ Gilbert K. Chesterton (1874–1936)

REPENTANCE

Therefore repent and turn back, so that your sins may be wiped out, that seasons of refreshing may come from the presence of the Lord.

Acts 3:19

Our Lord denounced dreadful woes against the self-righteous Pharisees; so ministers must cut and hack them, and not spare; but say woe, woe, woe to all those that will not submit to the righteousness of Jesus Christ! I could almost say this is the last stroke the Lord Jesus gave Paul. I mean in turning him to real Christianity; for having given him a blow as a persecutor and injurious, He then brought him out of himself by revealing His person and office as a Saviour. "I am Jesus."

Hence says the apostle, "I count all things but loss—that I may win Christ, and be found in Him; not having my own righteousness, which is of the law, but that which is through the faith of Christ; the righteousness which is of God by faith."…to be washed in His blood; to be clothed in His glorious imputed righteousness: the consequence of this imputation, or application of a Mediator's righteousness to the soul, will be a conversion from sin to holiness…. They that are truly converted to Jesus, and are justified by faith in the Son of God, will take care to evidence their conversion, not only by the having grace implanted in their hearts, but by that grace diffusing itself through every faculty of the soul, and making an universal change in the whole man.

~ George Whitefield (1714–1770)

DEAD WORKS

And if a righteous person is saved with difficulty, what will become of the ungodly and the sinner?

1 Peter 4:18

Must a regenerate Christian daily pour out to God so many ardent prayers and utter so many agonizing supplications, shed so many bitter tears, be so distressed and concerned respecting his sins, find it necessary to strive so manfully against them, and in addition be compelled to endure so many temptations and afflictions; and can you, by one heartless sigh to God and a little superficial service, become an heir of salvation? Oh, no! But, do you ask, are there none then saved who do not experience such a conflict? No, none!…

Let it not be supposed, however, that this conflict is the meritorious cause of the salvation of the righteous. Oh, no! That is to be attributed to pure sovereign grace, but it is the way to salvation, for God leads His children through conflict and conquest. You will possibly say, "If this be so narrow a way, I should dread to enter upon it; for who could always live thus?" But know, O man, that it is but for a time, and that the sufferings of this present time are not to be compared with the glory which shall hereafter be revealed to the children of God (Romans 8:18). Is the labor great? The reward is still greater. Is the contest severe? The victory is glorious. Though the battle endure for awhile, the glorious issue is certain.

~ Theodorus J. Frelinghuysen (1691–1748)

MEDITATION

"My kingdom is not of this world," said Jesus. "If My kingdom were of this world, My servants would fight, so that I wouldn't be handed over to the Jews. As it is, My kingdom does not have its origin here."

John 18:36

"The kingdom of God is within you," says the Lord. Turn, then, to God with all your heart. Forsake this wretched world and your soul shall find rest. Learn to despise external things, to devote yourself to those that are within, and you will see the kingdom of God come unto you, that kingdom which is peace and joy in the Holy Spirit, gifts not given to the impious. Christ will come to you offering His consolation, if you prepare a fit dwelling for Him in your heart, whose beauty and glory, wherein He takes delight, are all from within. His visits with the inward man are frequent, His communion sweet and full of consolation, His peace great, and His intimacy wonderful indeed.

Therefore, faithful soul, prepare your heart for this Bridegroom that He may come and dwell within you; He Himself says: "If any one love Me, he will keep My word, and My Father will love him, and We will come to him, and will make Our abode with him." Give place, then, to Christ, but deny entrance to all others, for when you have Christ you are rich and He is sufficient for you. He will provide for you. He will supply your every want, so that you need not trust in frail, changeable men. Christ remains forever, standing firmly with us to the end.

～ Thomas à Kempis (1380–1471)

COMMUNION WITH GOD

But if we walk in the light as He Himself is in the light, we have fellowship with one another, and the blood of Jesus His Son cleanses us from all sin.

1 John 1:7

The communion of saints is twofold: 'tis their communion with God and communion with one another (1 John 1:3). That ye also may have fellowship with us, and truly our fellowship is with the Father and with His Son, Jesus Christ. Communion is a common partaking of good, either of excellency or happiness, so that when it is said the saints have communion or fellowship with the Father and with the Son, the meaning of it is that they partake with the Father and the Son of their good, which is either their excellency and glory (2 Peter 1:4), Ye are made partakers of the Divine nature (Heb. 12:10). That we might be partakers of His holiness (John 17:22–23). And the glory which Thou hast given Me I have given them, that they may be one, even as we are one, I in them and Thou in Me; or of their joy and happiness: (John 17:13) That they might have My joy fulfilled in themselves. But the Holy Ghost being the love and joy of God is His beauty and happiness, and it is in our partaking of the same Holy Spirit that our communion with God consists (2 Cor. 13:14). They are not different benefits but the same...for the Holy Ghost is that love and grace...

~ Jonathan Edwards (1703–1758)

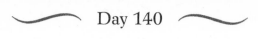
COME UNTO ME

Come to Me, all of you who are weary and burdened, and I will give you rest.

Matthew 11:28

No one ought to think that it is difficult to come to Him, though it sounds difficult and is really difficult at the beginning, and in separating oneself from and dying to all things. But when a man has once entered upon it, no life is lighter or happier or more desirable; for God is very zealous to be at all times with man, and teaches him that He will bring him to Himself if man will but follow.

Man never desires anything so earnestly as God desires to bring a man to Himself, that he may know Him. God is always ready, but we are very unready; God is near to us, but we are far from Him; God is within, but we are without; God is at home, but we are strangers. The prophet saith: God guideth the redeemed through a narrow way into the broad road, so that they come into the wide and broad place; that is to say, into true freedom of the spirit, when one has become a spirit with God. May God help us to follow this course, that He may bring us to Himself.

～ Johannes Eckhart (1260–1327)

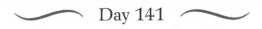
IN HIS PRESENCE

Therefore, confess your sins to one another and pray for one another, so that you may be healed. The urgent request of a righteous person is very powerful in its effect.

James 5:16

God is, by grace and benediction, specially present in holy places, and in the solemn assemblies of His servants. If holy people meet in grots and dens of the earth when persecution or a public necessity disturbs the public order, circumstance, and convenience, God fails not to come thither to them; but God is also, by the same or a greater reason, present there where they meet ordinarily by order and public authority; there God is present ordinarily, that is, at every such meeting.

God will go out of His way to meet His saints when themselves are forced out of their way of order by a sad necessity; but else, God's usual way is to be present in those places where His servants are appointed ordinarily to meet. But His presence there signifies nothing but a readiness to hear their prayers, to bless their persons, to accept their offices, and to like even the circumstance of orderly and public meeting. For thither the prayers of consecration, the public authority separating it, and God's love of order, and the reasonable customs of religion, have in ordinary, and in a certain degree, fixed this manner of His presence, and He loves to have it so.

— Jeremy Taylor (1613–1667)

DIRECT COMMUNICATION

How sweet Your word is to my taste—sweeter than honey in my mouth.

Psalm 119:103

If it were announced upon reliable authority that on a certain date in the near future an angel from heaven would visit New York and would deliver a sermon upon the invisible world, the future destiny of man, or the secret of deliverance from the power of sin, what an audience he would command! There is no building in that city large enough to accommodate the crowd which would throng to hear him. If upon the next day, the newspapers were to give a verbatim report of his discourse, how eagerly it would be read!

And yet, we have between the covers of the Bible not merely an angelic communication but a Divine revelation. How great then is our wickedness if we undervalue and despise it! And yet we do.

— A. W. Pink (1886–1952)

PRAYER

Therefore, I want the men in every place to pray, lifting up holy hands without anger or argument.

1 Timothy 2:8

God's command to "pray without ceasing" is founded on the necessity we have of His grace to preserve the life of God in the soul, which can no more subsist one moment without it, than the body can without air. Whether we think of; or speak to, God, whether we act or suffer for Him, all is prayer, when we have no other object than His love, and the desire of pleasing Him. All that a Christian does, even in eating and sleeping, is prayer, when it is done in simplicity, according to the order of God, without either adding to or diminishing from it by his own choice.

Prayer continues in the desire of the heart, though the understanding be employed on outward things. In souls filled with love, the desire to please God is a continual prayer. As the furious hate which the devil bears us is termed the roaring of a lion, so our vehement love may be termed crying after God. God only requires of his adult children, that their hearts be truly purified, and that they offer Him continually the wishes and vows that naturally spring from perfect love. For these desires, being the genuine fruits of love, are the most perfect prayers that can spring from it.

～ John Wesley (1703–1788)

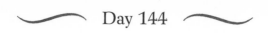

CHRISTIAN LIFE

More than that, I also consider everything to be a loss in view of the surpassing value of knowing Christ Jesus my Lord. Because of Him I have suffered the loss of all things and consider them filth, so that I may gain Christ.

Philippians 3:8

I insist not that the life of the Christian shall breathe nothing but the perfect Gospel, though this is to be desired, and ought to be attempted. I insist not so strictly on evangelical perfection, as to refuse to acknowledge as a Christian any man who has not attained it. In this way all would be excluded from the Church, since there is no man who is not far removed from this perfection, while many, who have made but little progress, would be undeservedly rejected. What then?

Let us set this before our eye as the end at which we ought constantly to aim. Let it be regarded as the goal towards which we are to run. For you cannot divide the matter with God, undertaking part of what His Word enjoins, and omitting part at pleasure. For, in the first place, God uniformly recommends integrity as the principal part of His worship, meaning by integrity real singleness of mind, devoid of gloss and fiction, and to this is opposed a double mind; as if it had been said, that the spiritual commencement of a good life is when the internal affections are sincerely devoted to God, in the cultivation of holiness and justice.

~ John Calvin (1509–1564)

BE SPECIFIC

Now this is the confidence we have before Him: Whenever we ask anything according to His will, He hears us. And if we know that He hears whatever we ask, we know that we have what we have asked Him for.

1 John 5:14–15

There is no need for us to go beating about the bush, and not telling the Lord distinctly what it is that we crave at His hands. Nor will it be seemly for us to make any attempt to use fine language; but let us ask God in the simplest and most direct manner for just the things we want.

I believe in business prayers. I mean prayers in which you take to God one of the many promises which He has given us in His Word, and expect it to be fulfilled as certainly as we look for the money to be given us when we go to the bank to cash a check. We should not think of going there, lolling over the counter chattering with the clerks on every conceivable subject except the one thing for which we had gone to the bank, and then coming away without the coin we needed; but we should lay before the clerk the promise to pay the bearer a certain sum, tell him in what form we wish to take the amount, count the cash after him, and then go on our way to attend to other business. That is just an illustration of the method in which we should draw supplies from the Bank of Heaven.

— C. H. Spurgeon (1834–1892)

OUT OF AND INTO

*But He brought us from there in order to lead us in and give us the
land that He swore to our fathers.*

Deuteronomy 6:23

After Israel had crossed the river, the Captain of the Lord's host
had to come and encourage Joshua, promising to take charge of the
army and remain with them. You need the power of God's Spirit
to enable you to overcome sin and temptation. You need to live in
His fellowship—in His unbroken fellowship, without which you
cannot stand or conquer. If you are to venture today, say by faith
"My God, I know that Jesus Christ is willing to be the Captain of
my salvation, and to conquer every enemy for me, He will keep me
by faith and by His Holy Spirit; and though it be dark to me, and
as if the waters would pass over my soul, and though my condition
seem hopeless, I will walk forward, for God is going to bring me in
to-day, and I am going to follow Him. My God, I follow Thee now
into the promised land." Perhaps some have already entered in,
and the angels have seen them, while they have been reading these
solemn words. Is there anyone still hesitating because the waters of
Jordan look threatening and impassable? Oh! Come, beloved soul;
come at once, and doubt not.

~ Andrew Murray (1828–1917)

THE RISEN CHRIST

Jesus said to her, "I am the resurrection and the life. The one who believes in Me, even if he dies, will live."

John 11:25

The risen Christ lingered on earth long enough fully to satisfy His adherents of the truth of His resurrection. They were not easily convinced. The apostles treated the reports of the holy women with scornful incredulity; Thomas doubted the testimony of the other apostles; and some of the five hundred to whom He appeared on a Galilean mountain doubted their own eyesight, and only believed when they heard His voice. The loving patience with which He treated these doubters showed that, though His bodily appearance was somewhat changed, He was still the same in heart as ever.

This was pathetically shown too by the places which He visited in His glorified form. They were the old haunts where He has prayed and preached, labored and suffered—the Galilean mountain, the well-beloved lake, the Mount of Olives, the village of Bethany, and, above all, Jerusalem, the fatal city which had murdered her own Son, but which He could not cease to love. Yet there were obvious indications that He belonged no more to this lower world. There was a new reserve about His risen humanity.... His glorified humanity was received up into that world to which it rightfully belonged.

～ James Stalker (1848–1927)

GOD'S EXCELLENCE

So He became higher in rank than the angels, just as the name He inherited is superior to theirs.

Hebrews 1:4

Intellectual pleasures consist in the beholding of spiritual excellencies and beauties, but the glorious excellency and beauty of God are far the greatest. God's excellence is the supreme excellence. When the understanding of the reasonable creature dwells here, it dwells at the fountain, and swims in a boundless, bottomless ocean. The love of God is also the most suitable entertainment of the soul of man, which naturally desires the happiness of society, or of union with some other being. The love of so glorious a being is infinitely valuable, and the discoveries of it are capable of ravishing the soul above all other love.

It is suitable to the nature of an intelligent being also, as it is that kind of delight that reason approves of. There are many other delights in which men indulge themselves, which, although they are pleasing to the senses and inferior powers, yet are contrary to reason. Reason opposes the enjoyment of them, so that unless reason be suppressed and stifled, they cannot be enjoyed without a war in the soul. Reason, the noblest faculty, resists the inferior rebellious powers. And the more reason is in exercise, the more will it resist, and the greater will be the inward war and opposition.

~ Jonathan Edwards (1703–1758)

CARNAL CHRISTIANS

So He became higher in rank than the angels, just as the name He inherited is superior to theirs.

1 Corinthians 3:1

Based upon the work of the Son of God on the Cross of Calvary, in which the sinner for whom He died was identified with the Substitute who died for him, the redeemed and regenerate believer is called to "reckon," or account himself "dead to sin," because "our old man was crucified with Him." The Holy Spirit of God dwelling in his spirit can then carry out to its ultimate issue the Divine purpose that the "body of sin"—i.e., the whole continent of sin in the whole of fallen man may be " destroyed " or abolished, as the man on his part steadily and faithfully refuses to "let sin reign" … the "babe in Christ" knows this that the "flesh" ceases to dominate, and have control, and he rises in spirit into real union with the Ascended Lord—alive unto God in Christ Jesus.

The "babe in Christ"…ceases to fulfill the desires of the flesh, and henceforth gives his spirit, indwelt by the Spirit of God, the domination of his entire being. It does not mean that he may not again lapse into the walk "after the flesh," but as long as he gives his mind to the "things of the Spirit," and reckons himself continually "dead indeed unto sin," he, "by the Spirit," steadfastly "makes to die" the "doings of the body" and walks in newness of life.

～ Jessie Penn Lewis (1861–1927)

O LORD, OUR FATHER, THANKS TO THEE

O Lord, our Father, thanks to Thee
In this new year we render,
For every evil had to flee
Before Thee, our Defender.
Our life was nourished, we were fed
With rich supplies of daily bread,
And peace reigned in our borders.
Lord Jesus Christ, our thanks to Thee
In this new year we render;
Thy reign hath kept Thy people free,
Hath shown Thy mercies tender.
Thou hast redeemed us with Thy blood,
Thou art our Joy, our only Good,
In life and death our Savior.
Lord Holy Ghost, our thanks to Thee
In this new year we render,
For Thou hast led our eyes to see
Thy truth in all its splendor
And thus enkindled from above
Within our hearts true faith and love
And other Christian virtues.
Our faithful God, we cry to Thee:
Still bless us with Thy favor,
Blot out all our iniquity,
And hide our sins forever.
Grant us a happy, good new year
And, when the hour of death draws near,
A peaceful, blest departure. Amen.

~ Cyriacus Schneegass (1546–1597)

CONFORMED TO HIS IMAGE

For our momentary light affliction is producing for us an absolutely incomparable eternal weight of glory.

2 Corinthians 4:17

In choosing us in Christ before the foundation of the world, our Heavenly Father also had in His eternal plan the sphere of service with which He intended to entrust us. In doing so, surely He had in mind that through our reaction in all the testing of Christian work and through our faithfulness or lack of it in the opportunities that He is pleased to give us, we are fashioned into the likeness of His dear Son…

What a day it will be when the Lord welcomes us home! Indeed, it will be worth it all when we see Jesus. We will understand then, as we can never understand now, that the very wounds which so often have been inflicted upon us have been the means of conforming us to the image of the Lord Jesus Christ, and of making Him all the more precious to us. Circumstances which we have resented, situations which we have found desperately difficult, have all been the means in the hands of God of driving the nails into the self-life which so easily complains. His dealing causes us to rejoice in the midst of affliction, "For our light affliction, which is but for a moment, worketh for us a far more exceeding and eternal weight of glory."

~ Alan Redpath (1907–1989)

INDWELLING AND OUTGOING WORKS OF GOD

The heavens were made by the word of the LORD, and all the stars, by the breath of His mouth.

Psalm 33:6

Regarding the permanently indwelling works of God that do not relate to the creature, but flow from the mutual relation of the Father, the Son, and the Holy Spirit, the distinctive characteristics of the three Persons must be kept in view. But with those that are to become manifest, relating to the creature, this distinction disappears. Here the rule applies that all indwelling works are activities of the divine Being without distinction of Persons.

To illustrate: In the home there are two kinds of activities, one flowing from the mutual relation of parents and children, another pertaining to the social life. In the former the distinction between parents and children is never ignored; in the latter, if the relation be normal, neither the father nor the children act alone, but the family as a whole. Even so in the holy, mysterious economy of the divine Being, every operation of the Father upon the Son and of both upon the Holy Spirit is distinct; but in every outgoing act it is always the one divine Being, the thoughts of whose heart are for all His creatures. On that account the natural man knows no more than that he has to do with a God.

~ Abraham Kuyper (1837–1920)

GOD WITH US

Where can I go to escape Your Spirit? Where can I flee from Your presence?

Psalm 139:7

There are times in our lives when delirium makes us utterly unaware of the presence of our most careful and tender nurses. A child in delirium will cry out in anguish for its mother, and will harrow her heart by its piteous lamentations and appeals, when all the while she is holding its fevered hand, and bathing its aching head, and caring for it with all the untold tenderness of a mother's love. The darkness of disease has hidden the mother from the child, but has not hidden the child from the mother. And just so it is with our God and us. The darkness of our doubts or our fears, of our sorrows or our despair, or even of our sins, cannot hide us from Him, although it may, and often does, hide Him from us. He has told us that the darkness and the light are both alike to Him; and if our faith will only lay hold of this as a fact, we will be enabled to pass through the darkest seasons in quiet trust, sure that all the while, though we cannot see nor feel Him, our God is caring for us, and will never leave nor forsake us.

~ Hannah Whitall Smith (1832–1911)

VENGEANCE IS MINE!

Do not be conquered by evil, but conquer evil with good.

Romans 12:21

When two goats meet upon a narrow bridge over deep water, how do they behave? Neither of them can turn back again, neither can pass the other, because the bridge is too narrow; if they should thrust one another, they might both fall into the water and be drowned; nature, then, has taught them, that if the one lays himself down and permits the other to go over him, both remain without hurt. Even so people should rather endure to be trod upon, than to fall into debate and discord one with another.

A Christian, for the sake of his own person, neither curses nor revenges himself; but faith curses and revenges itself…we must distinguish God and man, the person and cause. In what concerns God and His cause, we must have no patience, nor bless; as for example, when the ungodly persecute the Gospel, this touches God and His cause, and then we are not to bless or to wish good success, but rather to curse the persecutors and their proceedings… faith's cursing, which, rather than it would suffer God's Word to be suppressed and heresy maintained, would have all creatures go to wreck; for through heresy we lose God Himself. But individuals personally ought not to revenge themselves, but to suffer all things, and according to Christ's doctrine and the nature of love, to do good to their enemies.

～ Martin Luther (1483–1546)

AN APOSTLE'S SUPREME AMBITION

My goal is to know Him and the power of His resurrection and the
fellowship of His sufferings, being conformed to His death,

Philippians 3:10

It is important in understanding the Apostle to realize that he was not thinking of conformity to Christ's death as the end of all else. His real meaning was that he should increase in the knowledge of Christ, know the power of His resurrection and the fellowship of His sufferings by becoming conformed to His death. His death… was behind…and the spiritual history of the believer is a working back to what that death meant. It meant the end of the "old man," crucifixion to the world mind and will; the closing of the door to a whole system which was not Christ-centered and Christ- governed.

All this had been stated and presented in Paul's earlier letters… The meaning of Christ's death—Paul taught—was to be the inner history of the believer, and this would work out—progressively—in the power of His resurrection and the fellowship of His sufferings. So that, by being conformed to His death, he would come to the fuller knowledge of Him and of that Divine power. It is ever so. The all-governing passion opens the way for the effectual, and effectuating power, by the essential basis, through the progressive principle of conformity to His death.

∼ T. Austin-Sparks (1888–1971)

THE MAN AFTER GOD'S OWN HEART

After removing him, He raised up David as their king and testified about him: "I have found David the son of Jesse, a man loyal to Me, who will carry out all My will."

Acts 13:22

No man can be making much of his life who has not a very definite conception of what he is living for. And if you ask, at random, a dozen men what is the end of their life, you will be surprised to find how few have formed to themselves more than the most dim idea. The question of the summum bonum has ever been the most difficult for the human mind to grasp. What shall a man do with his life? What is life for? Why is it given?

These have been the one great puzzle for human books and human brains; and ancient philosophy and medieval learning and modern culture alike have failed to tell us what these mean... The general truth of these words is simply this: that the end of life is to do God's will... It may seem too bright and beautiful, for all things fair have soon to come to an end. And if any cloud could cross the true Christian's sky it would be when he thought that this ideal life might cease. But God, in the riches of His forethought, has rounded off this corner of his life with a great far-reaching text, which looks above the circumstance of time, and projects his life into the vast eternity beyond. "He that doeth the will of God abideth for ever" (1 John 2:17).

~ Henry Drummond (1851–1897)

MY HEAVENLY FRIEND

No one has greater love than this, that someone would lay down his life for his friends.

John 15:13

The precious Lord Jesus Christ is our friend. Oh, let us seek to realize this! It is not merely a religious phrase or statement, but truly He is our friend. He is the Brother "born for adversity," the one who "sticks closer than a brother." Who will never leave and never forsake us…He is willing not merely to grant this for a few months, or a year or two, but to the very end of our earthly pilgrimage. David, in Psalm 23 says: "Yea, though I walk through the valley of the shadow of death, I will fear no evil, for Thou art with me." Oh, how precious this is. For this "Lovely One" is coming again, and soon. Soon He will come again; and then He will take us home and there we shall be forever with Him. Oh, how precious is that bright and glorious prospect. Here again the practical point is to appropriate this to ourselves. "He is coming to take me—poor, guilty, worthless, hell-deserving me—He is coming to take me to Himself." And to the degree in which we enter into these glorious things, the joys of heaven have already commenced!

～ George Muller (1483–1586)

HIS CREATED BEAUTY

The Lord will send His faithful love by day; His song will be with me in the night—a prayer to the God of my life.

Psalm 42:8

Had I been alive in Adam's stead, how should I have admired the Glories of the World! What a confluence of Thoughts and wonders, and joys, and thanksgivings would have replenished me in the sight of so magnificent a theatre, so bright a dwelling place; so great a temple, so stately a house replenished with all kind of treasure, raised out of nothing and created for me and for me alone. Shall I now despise them?

When I consider the heavens which Thou hast made, the moon and stars, which are the works of Thy fingers: what is man that Thou art mindful of him, or the son of man that Thou visiteth him! Thou hast made him a little lower than the angels, and crowned him with glory and honour. O what love must that needs be, that prepared such a palace! Attended with what power! With what wisdom illuminated! Abounding with what zeal! And how glorious must the King be, that could out of nothing erect such a curious, so great, and so beautiful a fabric! It was glorious while new: and is as new as it was glorious.

— Thomas Traherne (1636–1674)

BY GRACE I'M SAVED, GRACE FREE AND BOUNDLESS

By grace I'm saved, grace free and boundless; My soul, believe and doubt it not. Why stagger at this word of promise? Hath Scripture ever falsehood taught? Nay; then this word must true remain; By grace thou, too, shalt heav'n obtain.

By grace! None dare lay claim to merit; Our works and conduct have no worth. God in His love sent our Redeemer, Christ Jesus, to this sinful earth; His death did for our sins atone, And we are saved by grace alone.

By grace! Oh, mark this word of promise When thou art by thy sins opprest, When Satan plagues thy troubled conscience, And when thy heart is seeking rest. What reason cannot comprehend God by His grace to thee doth send.

By grace God's Son, our only Savior, Came down to earth to bear our sin. Was it because of thine own merit That Jesus died thy soul to win? Nay, it was grace, and grace alone, That brought Him from His heavenly throne.

By grace! This ground of faith is certain; So long as God is true, it stands. What saints have penned by inspiration, What in His Word our God commands, What our whole faith must rest upon, Is Grace alone, grace in His Son.

By grace to timid hearts that tremble, In tribulation's furnace tried, By grace, despite all fear and trouble, The Father's heart is open wide. Where could I help and strength secure If grace were not my anchor sure?

~ Christian L. Scheidt (1709–1761)

SWEET FLOWERS OF THE MARTYR BAND

Sweet flowerets of the martyr band,
Plucked by the tyrant's ruthless hand
Upon the threshold of the morn,
Like rosebuds by a tempest torn;
First victims for the incarnate Lord,
A tender flock to feel the sword;
Beside the very altar gay,
With palm and crown, ye seemed to play.
Ah, what availed King Herod's wrath?
He could not stop the Savior's path.
Alone, while others murdered lay,
In safety Christ is borne away.
O Lord, the Virgin-born,
to Thee Eternal praise and glory be,
Whom with the Father we adore
And Holy Ghost forevermore. Amen.

~ Aurelius C. Prudentius (348–413)

GOD IS…

The Lord reigns! He is robed in majesty; The Lord is robed, enveloped in strength. The world is firmly established; it cannot be shaken.

Psalm 93:1

Admitting that Jesus was indeed the God-man, the hope is vain of either escaping or explaining the mystery which invests Him; for He presents the phenomenon of history, original, unique, solitary; no being like Him, before or after. Here is a combination heretofore supposed to be contradictory and impossible! God is infinite; space cannot contain Him, nor time limit Him. Man is finite, fenced in by definite bounds.

How can the unlimited and limited combine and unite? All our previous notions of things are contradicted in the God-man. God is omnipresent; yet here is God, submitting to the laws and limits of a human body, which can occupy but one place at any one time, and must, by the law of locomotion, take time for a transfer from one place to place. God is omniscient; yet here is being claiming equality with Jehovah, yet affirming that there are some things which as a man, and even as the Messiah, He knows not. God is omnipresent; yet the God-man says He "can do nothing of Himself," and that it is God dwelling in Him that "doeth the works."

⌁ Arthur T. Pierson (1867–1911)

I'M IN THE LORD'S ARMY!

David spoke to the men who were standing with him: "What will be done for the man who kills that Philistine and removes this disgrace from Israel? Just who is this uncircumcised Philistine that he should defy the armies of the living God?"

I Samuel 17: 26

To Saul and his soldiers, God was an absentee—a name, but little else. They believed that He had done great things for His people in the past, and that at some future time, in the days of the Messiah… Keenly sensitive to the defiance of the Philistine, and grieved by the apathy of his people, David…felt that God was alive. He had lived alone with Him in the solitude of the hills, till God had become one of the greatest and most real facts of his young existence…he was sublimely conscious of the presence of the living God amid the clang of the camp.

This is what we need. To live so much with God, that when we come amongst men, whether in the bazaars of India or the market-place of an English town, we may be more aware of His over-shadowing presence than of the presence or absence of any one. Lo, God is here! This place is hallowed ground! But none can realize this by the act of the will. We can only find God everywhere when we carry Him everywhere…If our faith can but make Him a passage, along which He shall come, there is no Goliath He will not quell; no question He will not answer; no need He will not meet.

~ F. B. Meyer (1847–1929)

EASTER MONDAY

All the prophets testify about Him that through His name everyone who believes in Him will receive forgiveness of sins.

Acts 10:43

Peter, by way of proving conclusively to the world that this one Lord, as he names Him, Jesus of Nazareth, is the true Messiah promised of old in the Scriptures, says: "To him bear all the prophets witness." The prophets plainly speak of such a person, one to be born of David's flesh and blood, in the city of Bethlehem, who should suffer, die and rise again, accomplishing just what this Jesus has accomplished and even proven by miraculous signs.

Therefore, truly the Jews and the non-Christians have no reason to doubt concerning Christ, no reason to await the coming of another... Peter, citing the testimony of the prophets, indicates the nature of Christ's kingdom as not external power; not temporal dominion like that of earthly lords, kings, and emperors; not dominion over countries or control of people, property and temporal concerns; but a spiritual, eternal kingdom, a kingdom in the hearts of men, an authority over, and power opposed to, sin, everlasting death and hell, a power able to redeem us from those things and bestow upon us salvation. Salvation is ours, Peter teaches, through the preaching of the Gospel, and is received by faith. Faith is the obedience every man must render unto the Lord. By faith he makes himself subject to Christ and partaker of His grace and blessings.

～ Martin Luther (1483–1586)

WEEPING MARY

For they still did not understand the Scripture that He must rise from the dead. Then the disciples went home again. But Mary stood outside facing the tomb, crying. As she was crying, she stooped to look into the tomb. She saw two angels in white sitting there, one at the head and one at the feet, where Jesus' body had been lying. They said to her, "Woman, why are you crying?" "Because they've taken away my Lord," she told them, "and I don't know where they've put Him."

John 20:9–13

For as yet they did not know the Scripture, that He must rise again from the dead. Then the disciples went away again to their own homes. But Mary stood outside by the tomb weeping, and as she wept she stooped down and looked into the tomb. And she saw two angels in white sitting, one at the head and the other at the feet, where the body of Jesus had lain...Here is a woman more forward in seeking Christ nor [than] all His eleven disciples are. Because she get not her errand that she was seeking, she could not get Christ, and therefore she will not leave, nor give over, but will wait on and seek Him.

A soul that is in love with Christ, they never get their errand till they get Christ Himself. Ye that are seeking Christ, never give over seeking till ye meet with Him, for they shall at last meet with Him who lie at His door, seeking, as this woman did, who say, "I shall lie still at Thy door, let me die there if Thou likest, and albeit it should come to that, I shall die, or I go away and meet not with Him." Ye may know the ardent desire of a soul after Christ can be satisfied with nothing but Himself.

〜 Samuel Rutherford (1600–1661)

TRUSTING GOD

Again, I will trust in Him. And again, Here I am with the children God gave Me.

Hebrews 2:13

I have discovered, through personal experience and from biblical example, that human effort, self-assertion, positive thinking, and willpower are of little use in the quest for godliness. Throughout my years at elementary school, I was a straight "C" student. I barely squeaked through high school, and was forced to abandon any hopes I had of going to college, because of a lack of discipline. Instead of school, I told my family, "I'm going surfing," and for the next four years, lived the life of a California beach bum, regularly blowing out my brains on drugs.

At age twenty-one, a longhaired, broken, burned-out freak with barely enough discipline to hold down a job, I landed at the foot of the Cross, and was gloriously saved. Since that time, God, through His mercy and grace, has helped me to discipline my life—not because I had any natural endowment of stick-to itiveness, but because His Holy Spirit came and took up residence in my life when I surrendered to Him and trusted Him. Trust, spelled with a capital "T," is the key. If we want to better our devotional life, we must trust Him....All of God's dealings with man, Christian and non-Christian, are for one purpose: to bring us to a point where we can trust Him.

~ Danny Lehmann (1964 –)

HOPE IS YOUR WORD

The longer you read the Bible, the more you will like it; it will grow sweeter and sweeter; and the more you get into the spirit of it, the more you will get into the spirit of Christ.

William Romaine

Your word is a lamp for my feet and a light on my path. I have solemnly sworn to keep Your righteous judgments. I am severely afflicted; LORD, give me life through Your word. LORD, please accept my willing offerings of praise, and teach me Your judgments.

My life is constantly in danger, yet I do not forget Your instruction. The wicked have set a trap for me, but I have not wandered from Your precepts. I have Your decrees as a heritage forever; indeed, they are the joy of my heart. I am resolved to obey Your statutes to the very end. I hate those who are double-minded, but I love Your instruction. You are my shelter and my shield; I put my hope in Your word.

~ Psalm 119:105–114 (King David)

REALITY

The one who commits sin is of the Devil, for the Devil has sinned from the beginning. The Son of God was revealed for this purpose: to destroy the Devil's works.

1 John 3:18

God looks for reality… He, blessed be His name, did not love us in word or in tongue, but in deed and in truth; and He looks for a response from us—a response clear, full, and distinct; a response coming out in a life of good works, a life yielding mellow clusters of the "fruits of righteousness which are by Christ Jesus, to the glory and praise of God."… Ought we not diligently to seek to promote love and good works? And how can this be most effectually accomplished?

Surely by walking in love ourselves, and faithfully treading the path of good works in our own private life. For ourselves, we confess we are thoroughly sick of hollow profession. High truth on the lips and low practice in daily life, is one of the crying evils of our day. We talk of grace; but fail in common righteousness—fail in the plainest moral duties in our daily private life. We boast of our "position" and our "standing"; but we are deplorably lax as to our "condition" and "state." May the Lord, in His infinite goodness, stir up all hearts to more thorough earnestness, in the pursuit of good works, so that we may more fully adorn the doctrine of God our Savior in all things!

~ C. H. Mackintosh (1820–1896)

SAVED SAINTS

To all who are in Rome, loved by God, called as saints. Grace to you and peace from God our Father and the Lord Jesus Christ.

Romans 1:7

The scripture knows no Christians but saints, who in all things act as becometh saints. But now if the scripture saint did not mean a man that escheweth all evil, and was holy in all his conversation, saint and no saint would have only such difference, as one carnal man will always have from another. Preachers and writers comfort the half Christians with telling them, that God requires not a perfect, sinless obedience, but accepts the sincerity of our weak endeavors instead of it. Here, if ever, the blind lead the blind.

For St. Paul, comparing the way of salvation to a race, says, "In a race all run, but ONE obtaineth the prize: so run that ye may obtain." Now if Paul had seeing eyes, must not they be blind who teach, that God accepts of all that run in the religious race, and requires not that any should obtain the prize…The first God accepts, that is, bears with. But why or how? Not because he seeks or requires no more, but he bears with them, because though at a great distance from, they are, or may be making towards that perfection, or new creature, which he absolutely requires, which is the fullness of the stature of Christ, and is that which Paul says, is the ONE that obtains the prize.

～ William Law (1686–1761)

CHRISTIAN CONTENTMENT DESCRIBED

I don't say this out of need, for I have learned to be content in whatever circumstances I am.

Philippians 4:11

These words are brought in by Paul as a clear argument to persuade the Philippians that he did not seek after great things in the world, and that he sought not "theirs" but "them." He did not long for great wealth. His heart was taken up with better things. "I do not speak", he says, "in respect of want, for whether I have or have not, my heart is fully satisfied, I have enough: I have learned in whatsoever state I am, therewith to be content." "I have learned"—Contentment in every condition is a great art, a spiritual mystery. It is to be learned, and to be learned as a mystery. And so in verse 12 he affirms: "I know how to be abased, and I now how to abound: everywhere and in all things I am instructed." The word which is translated "instructed" is derived from the word that signifies "mystery"; it is just as if he had said, "I have learned the mystery of this business."

Contentment is to be learned as a great mystery, and those who are thoroughly trained in this art, which is like Samson"s riddle to a natural man, have learned a deep mystery. "I have learned it"—I do not have to learn it now, nor did I have the art at first; I have attained it, though with much ado, and now, by the grace of God, I have become the master of this art.

~ Jeremiah Burroughs (1599–1646)

THINGS THAT CORRUPT

Be serious! Be alert! Your adversary the Devil is prowling around like a roaring lion, looking for anyone he can devour.

                                                            1 Peter 5:8

Be thoroughly acquainted with your temptations and the things that may corrupt you—and watch against them all day long. You should watch especially the most dangerous of the things that corrupt, and those temptations that either your company or business will unavoidably lay before you.

Watch against the master sins of unbelief: hypocrisy, selfishness, pride, flesh pleasing and the excessive love of earthly things. Take care against being drawn into earthly mindedness and excessive cares, or covetous designs for rising in the world, under the pretence of diligence in your calling. At first these things will be very difficult, while sin has any strength in you, but once you have grasped a continual awareness of the poisonous danger of any one of these sins, your heart will readily and easily avoid them.

                          ∼ Richard Baxter (1615–1691)

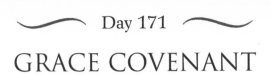
GRACE COVENANT

He has made us competent to be ministers of a new covenant, not of the letter, but of the Spirit. For the letter kills, but the Spirit produces life.

2 Corinthians 3:6

When one person assigns a stipulated work to another person with the promise of a reward upon the condition of the performance of that work, there is a covenant. Nothing can be plainer than that all this is true in relation to the Father and the Son. The Father gave the Son a work to do; He sent Him into the world to perform it, and promised Him a great reward when the work was accomplished. Such is the constant representation of the Scriptures. We have, therefore, the contracting parties, the promise, and the condition.

These are the essential elements of a covenant. Such being the representation of Scripture, such must be the truth to which we are bound to adhere. It is not a mere figure, but a real transaction, and should be regarded and treated as such if we would understand aright the plan of salvation. In Psalm 40, expounded by the Apostle as referring to the Messiah, it is said, "Lo, I come: in the volume of the book it is written of me, I delight to do thy will," i.e., to execute thy purpose, to carry out thy plan. Christ came, therefore, in execution of a purpose of God, to fulfill a work which had been assigned Him.

~ Charles Hodge (1797–1887)

HEADING GOD'S CALL

He told them: "The harvest is abundant, but the workers are few. Therefore, pray to the Lord of the harvest to send out workers into His harvest. Now go; I'm sending you out like lambs among wolves."

Luke 10:2–3

A young Christian once came to me, and told me that for some time she had been giving the Lord her profession and prayers and money, but now she wanted to give Him her life. She wanted to go right into the fight. In other words, she wanted to go to His assistance in the sea.

As when a man from the shore, seeing another struggling in the water, takes off those outer garments that would hinder his efforts and leaps to the rescue, so will you who still linger on the bank, thinking and singing and praying about the poor perishing souls, rush to the rescue of this multitude of dying men and women. Does the surging sea look dark and dangerous? Unquestionably it is so. He who beckons you from the sea however, knows what it will mean, and knowing, He still calls to you and bids to you to come. You must do it! You cannot hold back. Now what will you do?

~ William Booth (1829–1912)

THE RELATION OF THE WILL OF GOD TO SANCTIFICATION

For this is God's will, your sanctification: that you abstain from sexual immorality.

1 Thessalonians 4:3

We take our doctrines from the Bible and our assurance from Christ. But for want of the living bright reality of His presence in our hearts we search the world all round for impulses. We search religious books for impulses, and tracts and sermons, but in vain… "I am Alpha and Omega, the beginning and the end." "Christ is all and in all." The beginning of all things is in the will of God. The end of all things is in sanctification through faith in Jesus Christ. "By the which will ye are sanctified."

Between these two poles all spiritual life and Christian experience run. And no motive outside Christ can lead a man to Christ. If your motive to holiness is not as high as Christ it cannot make you rise to Christ. For water cannot rise above its level. "Beware, therefore, lest any man spoil you through philosophy and vain deceit, after the tradition of men, after the rudiments of the world, and not after Christ. For in Him dwelleth all the fullness of the Godhead bodily. And ye are complete in Him which is the head of all principality and power" (1 Cor. 1:30). "As ye have therefore received the Lord Jesus, so walk ye in Him."

~ Henry Drummond (1818–1888)

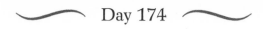
FAITH OR EXPERIENCE?

. . . the Son of God, who loved me, and gave himself for me.

Galatians 2:20 KJV

We should battle through our moods, feelings, and emotions into absolute devotion to the Lord Jesus. We must break out of our own little world of experience into abandoned devotion to Him. Think who the New Testament says Jesus Christ is, and then think of the despicable meagerness of the miserable faith we exhibit by saying, "I haven't had this experience or that experience!" Think what faith in Jesus Christ claims and provides; He can present us faultless before the throne of God, inexpressibly pure, absolutely righteous, and profoundly justified. How dare we talk of making a sacrifice for the Son of God! We are saved from hell and total destruction, and then we talk about making sacrifices!

We must continually focus and firmly place our faith in Jesus Christ, not a "prayer meeting" Jesus Christ, or a "book" Jesus Christ, but the New Testament Jesus Christ, who is God Incarnate, and who ought to strike us dead at His feet. Our faith must be in the One from whom our salvation springs. Jesus Christ wants our absolute, unrestrained devotion to Himself. We can never experience Jesus Christ, or selfishly bind Him in the confines of our own hearts. Our faith must be built on strong determined confidence in Him. It is because of our trusting in experience that we see the steadfast impatience of the Holy Spirit against unbelief. All of our fears are sinful, and we create our own fears by refusing to nourish ourselves in our faith. How can anyone who is identified with Jesus Christ suffer from doubt or fear! Our lives should be an absolute hymn of praise resulting from perfect, irrepressible, triumphant belief.

~ Oswald Chambers (1874–1917)

LOVEST THOU ME?

Your eyes saw me when I was formless; all my days were written in Your book and planned before a single one of them began.

Psalm 139:16

God deserves to be loved very much...because He loved us first, He infinite and we nothing, loved us, miserable sinners, with a love so great and so free...the measure of our love to God is to love immeasurably. For since our love is toward God, who is infinite and immeasurable, how can we bound or limit the love we owe Him? Besides, our love is not a gift but a debt. And since it is the Godhead who loves us...since it is He who loves us, I say, can we think of repaying Him grudgingly? "I will love Thee, O Lord, my strength. The Lord is my rock and my fortress and my deliverer, my God, my strength, in whom I will trust" (Psalm 18:1).

He is all that I need, all that I long for. My God and my help, I will love Thee for Thy great goodness... I cannot love Thee as Thou deservest to be loved, for I cannot love Thee more than my own feebleness permits. I will love Thee more when Thou deemest me worthy to receive greater capacity for loving; yet never so perfectly as Thou hast deserved of me. Yet Thou recordest in that book all who do what they can, even though they cannot do what they ought.

~ Bernard of Clairvaux (1090–1153)

GOD'S EXISTENCE

In the year that King Uzziah died, I saw the Lord seated on a high and lofty throne, and His robe filled the temple.

Isaiah 6:1

When we know that something exists, it still remains to inquire into the manner of its existence, in order to know what it is. But we cannot inquire into the manner in which God exists. We can inquire only into the manner in which He does not exist, since we cannot know of God what He is, but only what He is not.

We must therefore consider how God does not exist, how we know Him, and how we name Him. The manner in which God does not exist can be shown by excluding what is in—of the simple nature of God compatible with God, such as composition, movement, and the like. We shall therefore inquire into the simple nature of God which repels composition. We shall also inquire into the divine perfection, since the simple natures of corporeal things are imperfect.

~ Thomas Aquinas (1225–1274)

FOR THE BEAUTY OF THE EARTH

For the beauty of the earth, For the glory of the skies;

For the love which from our birth,

Over and around us lies; Lord of all, to Thee we raise

This, our hymn of grateful praise.

For the wonder of each hour, Of the day and of the night;

Hill and vale and tree and flow'r,

Sun and moon, and stars of light;

Lord of all, to Thee we raise

This, our hymn of grateful praise.

For the joy of ear and eye,

For the heart and mind's delight;

For the mystic harmony,

Linking sense to sound and sight;

Lord of all, to Thee we raise

This, our hymn of grateful praise.

For the joy of human love,

Brother, sister, parent, child;

Friends on Earth and friends above,

For all gentle thoughts and mild;

Lord of all, to Thee we raise

This, our hymn of grateful praise.

For Thy church that evermore,

Lifteth holy hands above; Off'ring up on ev'ry shore,

Her pure sacrifice of love;

Lord of all, to Thee we raise

This, our hymn of grateful praise. Amen.

~ Folliott S. Pierpont (1835–1917)

THE HANDS OF THE FATHER

A third time he said to them, "Why? What has this man done wrong? I have found in Him no grounds for the death penalty. Therefore, I will have Him whipped and then release Him."

Luke 23:22

We may commend any brother, any sister, to the common father-hood. And there will be moments when, filled with that spirit which is the Lord, nothing will ease our hearts of their love but the commending of all men, all our brothers, all our sisters, to the one Father. Nor shall we ever know that repose in the Father's hands, that rest of the Holy Sepulchre, which the Lord knew when the agony of death was over, when the storm of the world died away behind His retiring spirit, and He entered the regions where there is only life, and therefore all that is not music is silence, (for all noise comes of the conflict of Life and Death)—we shall never be able, I say, to rest in the bosom of the Father, till the fatherhood is fully revealed to us in the love of the brothers.

For He cannot be our father save as He is their father; and if we do not see Him and feel Him as their father, we cannot know him as ours. Never shall we know Him aright until we rejoice and exult for our race that He is the Father. He that loveth not his brother whom he hath seen, how can he love God whom he hath not seen? To rest, I say, at last, even in those hands into which the Lord commended His spirit, we must have learned already to love our neighbour as ourselves.

~ George MacDonald (1824–1905)

FALSE RELIGIONS

Jesus told him, "I am the way, the truth, and the life. No one comes to the Father except through Me."

John 14:6

The world today is a world of religion. Christ came to save men from sin and religion. Adam was the founder of the first religion. Upon being caught in sin in the garden, rather than cry to God for mercy, he sewed fig leaves together to cover his nakedness. He relied on his works rather than God's grace. From that day to this, man has been incurably religious. He continues to invent religions, thinking in this way to cover his spiritual nakedness.

As the fig leaves of Adam's time did not cover sin, so all the religious acts of man today cannot atone for sin. Religion can only leave a sinner hoping. Salvation makes the sinner sure. Of course, many people are sincerely religious, but they are sincerely wrong. We do not condemn them, but in the Gospel we show them a better way—the only way. God's way!… You have a divine Saviour who has given you victory over sin and eternal life. The heathen are marching blindly on to death. If you were heathen, you would be on that march.

∼ Dick Hillis (1913–2005)

OUR NAMES RECORDED THERE

The heavens, indeed the highest heavens, belong to the LORD your God, as does the earth and everything in it.

Deuteronomy 10:14

We are told that one time just before sunrise, two men got into a dispute about what part of the heavens the sun would first appear in. They became so excited over it that they began to fight, and beat each other over the head so badly that when the sun arose neither of them could see it. So there are persons who go on disputing about heaven until they dispute themselves out of it, and more who dispute over hell until they dispute themselves into it.

The Hebrews in their writings tell us of three distinct heavens. The air—the atmosphere about the earth—is one heaven; the firmament where the stars are is another, and above that is the heaven of heavens, where God's throne is, and the mansions of the Lord are—those mansions of light and peace which are the abode of the blessed, the homes of the Redeemer and the redeemed...the heaven where Christ is...the place we read of in Deuteronomy.

~ Dwight L. Moody (1837–1899)

BEHOLD THE SURE FOUNDATION-STONE

Behold the sure Foundation-stone
Which God in Zion lays
To build our heavenly hopes upon
And His eternal praise.
Chosen of God, to sinners dear,
Let saints adore the name;
They trust their whole salvation here,
Nor shall they suffer shame.
The foolish builders, scribe and priest,
Reject it with disdain;
Yet on this rock the Church shall rest
And envy rage in vain.
What though the gates of hell withstood
Yet must this building rise.
'Tis Thine own work, Almighty God,
And wondrous in our eyes.

~ Isaac Watts (1674–1748)

HAVING A HUMBLE OPINION OF SELF

"...he that followeth me shall not walk in darkness, but shall have the light of life."

John 8:12 KJV

Every man naturally desires knowledge; but what good is knowledge without fear of God? Indeed a humble rustic who serves God is better than a proud intellectual who neglects his soul to study the course of the stars. He who knows himself well becomes mean in his own eyes and is not happy when praised by men. If I knew all things in the world and had not charity, what would it profit me before God Who will judge me by my deeds? Shun too great a desire for knowledge, for in it there is much fretting and delusion. Intellectuals like to appear learned and to be called wise. Yet there are many things the knowledge of which does little or no good to the soul, and he who concerns himself about other things than those which lead to salvation is very unwise.

Many words do not satisfy the soul; but a good life eases the mind and a clean conscience inspires great trust in God. The more you know and the better you understand, the more severely will you be judged, unless your life is also the more holy. Do not be proud, therefore, because of your learning or skill. Rather, fear because of the talent given you. If you think you know many things and understand them well enough, realize at the same time that there is much you do not know. Hence, do not affect wisdom, but admit your ignorance. Why prefer yourself to anyone else when many are more learned, more cultured than you?

～ Thomas à Kempis (1380–1471)

ALL THE WAY MY SAVIOUR LEADS ME

All the way my Saviour leads me;
What have I to ask beside?
Can I doubt His faithful mercies,
Who through life has been my guide?
Heav'nly peace, divinest comfort,
Here by faith in Him do dwell;
For I know whate'er befall me,
Jesus doeth all things well.
All the way my Saviour leads me,
Cheers each winding path I tread;
Gives me strength for every trial,
Feeds me with the living bread.
Though my weary steps may falter,
And my soul athirst may be,
Gushing from the Rock before me,
Lo, a spring of joy I see.
All the way my Saviour leads me,
O the fullness of His love!
Perfect rest in me is promised,
In my Father's house above;
When my spirit, clothed immortal,
Wings its flight to realms of day,
This my song through endless ages:
"Jesus led me all the way."

~ Fanny J. Crosby (1820–1915)

LOVE THY NEIGHBOUR

The second is like it: Love your neighbor as yourself.

Matthew 22:39

It is possible to love our neighbour as ourselves. Our Lord never spoke hyperbolically, although, indeed, that is the supposition on which many unconsciously interpret His words, in order to be able to persuade themselves that they believe them. We may see that it is possible before we attain to it; for our perceptions of truth are always in advance of our condition. True, no man can see it perfectly until he is it; but we must see it, that we may be it.

A man who knows that he does not yet love his neighbour as himself may believe in such a condition, may even see that there is no other goal of human perfection, nothing else to which the universe is speeding, propelled by the Father's will. Let him labour on, and not faint at the thought that God's day is a thousand years: his millennium is likewise one day—yea, this day, for we have him, The Love, in us, working even now the far end… A man must not choose his neighbour; he must take the neighbour that God sends him. In him, whoever he be, lies, hidden or revealed, a beautiful brother. The neighbour is just the man who is next to you at the moment, the man with whom any business has brought you in contact.

~ George MacDonald (1824–1905)

HOW TO BE HAPPY

You love Him, though you have not seen Him. And though not seeing Him now, you believe in Him and rejoice with inexpressible and glorious joy.

1 Peter 1:8

The text tells us that the way to obtain this "inexpressible and glorious joy," the way to be inexpressibly happy at all times and under all circumstances, is just by believing on the unseen Christ Jesus. What does it mean to believe on Jesus Christ? There is no mystery at all about that. It simply means to put confidence in Jesus Christ to be what He claims to be and what He offers Himself to be to us, to put confidence in Him as the One who died in our place; to put confidence in Him as the One who was raised from the dead and who now has "all power in heaven and on earth," and therefore is able to keep us day by day, and give us victory over sin; and to put confidence in Him as our absolute Lord and Master, and therefore to surrender our thoughts and wills and lives entirely to His control; and worship and adore Him. It is wonderful the joy that comes to him who thus believes on Jesus Christ. But one must really believe on Jesus Christ to have this joy.

～ R. A. Torrey (1856–1926)

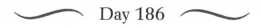
THE GOLDEN MILESTONE OF THE AGES

Earth, earth, earth, hear the word of the LORD!

Jeremiah 22:29

The Bible is the Golden Milestone of the ages. It has been for thousands of years the grand center of all the noblest thought, purest love, and holiest life of the world… From this great book proceeds the inspiration of the best literature, the most unselfish philanthropy, the most faultless morality, which the world has ever known.

Whence came the Bible? Is this the accidental point of all this convergence; or is it the designed focus of all this light, love, and life? Was this golden pillar erected by one infinitely more august than the foremost of Caesars, to be the center and source of all human progress? Did God put the Bible in the very Forum of the nations, that by all paths men might, in the honest search after truth, find in this their goal; and that, from this, as a starting point, every true lover of God and man might proceed in his noble career of service? This is the decisive test. No literary excellence, no scientific accuracy, No perfection, as a book, could atone for one vital error in ethical teaching or moral percept, in a volume which claims the high dignity of being a guide to the human soul, in matters of faith and life, doctrine, and duty!

~ Arthur T. Pierson (1867–1911)

NO ROOM FOR NEUTRALITY

But if it doesn't please you to worship Yahweh, choose for yourselves today the one you will worship: the gods your fathers worshiped beyond the Euphrates River or the gods of the Amorites in whose land you are living. As for me and my family, we will worship Yahweh.

Joshua 24:15

Neutrality is no longer feasible or desirable where the peace of the world is involved and the freedom of its peoples, and the menace to that peace and freedom lies in the existence of autocratic governments backed by organized force which is controlled wholly by their will, not by the will of their people. We have seen the last of neutrality in such circumstances. We are at the beginning of the age in which it will be insisted that the same standards of conduct and of responsibility for wrong done shall be observed among nations and their governments that are observed among the individual citizens of civilized states…

A steadfast concert for peace can never be maintained except by a partnership of democratic nations. No autocratic government could be trusted to keep faith within it or observe its covenants… Only a free peoples can hold their purpose and their honor steady to a common end and prefer the interests of mankind to any narrow interest of their own.

~ Woodrow Wilson (1856–1924)

THE UNERRING WORD OF GOD

Your word is a lamp for my feet and a light on my path.

Psalm 119:105

Nature is full of wants with corresponding supplies; of appetites or cravings with their gratifications and satisfactions. The wing of the bird tells of the air on which it may float; the fin of the fish, of the water through which it may glide; the ball of the joint, of the socket; the eye is a prophecy of the light, and the ear of sound. So universal is this correspondence that wherever we find a craving, and adaptation, or a lack, we look with unerring certainty for something else filling the craving, meeting the adaptation, supplying the lack.

Emerson closed a protracted argument with a literary skeptic in these forcible words: "Sir, I hold that God, who keeps His word with the birds and fishes in all their migratory instinct, will keep His word with man." And Bryant, in his "Lines to a Waterfowl," with great beauty, points out the lesson taught by this wonderful correspondence and correlation, in these lines: He who, from zone to zone, Guides, through the boundless sky, thy certain flight, In the long way that I must tread along, Will lead my steps aright! The Bible declares and exhibits such an object, exactly adapted to fill and fulfill all this need.

∼ Arthur T. Pierson (1867–1911)

A REMARKABLE BOOK

The heavens declare the glory of God, and the sky proclaims the work of His hands.

Psalm 19:1

One of the princes of men…Chrysostom…whose virtues made him the admiration and terror of the corrupt court of Eudoxia— such a man…has given to the Bible its very name, " "O Biblos"— the Book! In every work we see the workman—his skill! In handling tools, his inventive genius in planning, his taste in arranging and adoring. The artist breathes in his canvas and speaks in the marble. If there be a work of God, we expect it to express and exhibit Him.

You go to St. Peter's Cathedral; you stand beneath that vast dome, prepared to feel a sense of awe at the grand proportions and exquisite decorations—for Michael Angelo designed and adorned it. And when, in the hush of midnight, you look up into the dome of heaven and see thousands of lamps that burn for whole millenniums unconsumed, and shine at a distance beyond calculation— when you remember that streaming banner of light, the "Milky Way," is myriads of stars, in close ranks, like countless warriors, so that you see only the lines of light flashing from their silver helmets, you are prepared to believe that God planned that concave, and wrote His own name on it in letters of light. "The heavens declare the glory of God, and the firmament sheweth His handiwork."

~ Arthur T. Pierson (1867–1911)

HELPLESS WITHOUT GOD

Therefore let us approach the throne of grace with boldness, so that we may receive mercy and find grace to help us at the proper time.

Hebrews 4:16

A dear friend of mine who was quite a lover of the chase, told me the following story: "Rising early one morning," he said, "I heard the baying of a score of deerhounds in pursuit of their quarry. Looking away to a broad, open field in front of me, I saw a young fawn making its way across, and giving signs, moreover, that its race was well-nigh run. Reaching the rails of the enclosure, it leaped over and crouched within ten feet from where I stood. A moment later two of the hounds came over, when the fawn ran in my direction and pushed its head between my legs. I lifted the little thing to my breast, and, swinging round and round, fought off the dogs. I felt, just then, that all the dogs in the West could not, and should not capture that fawn after its weakness had appealed to my strength." So is it, when human helplessness appeals to Almighty God. Well do I remember when the hounds of sin were after my soul, until, at last, I ran into the arms of Almighty God.

~ A. C. Dixon (1854–1925)

THE LORD, MY STRENGTH

The LORD is my strength and my song; He has become my salvation. This is my God, and I will praise Him, my father's God, and I will exalt Him.

Exodus 15:2

Who am I, and what is my nature? What evil is there not in me and my deeds; or if not in my deeds, my words; or if not in my words, my will? But Thou, O Lord, art good and merciful, and thy right hand didst reach into the depth of my death and didst empty out the abyss of corruption from the bottom of my heart…now I did not will to do what I willed, and began to will to do what Thou didst will.

But where was my free will during all those years and from what deep and secret retreat was it called forth in a single moment, whereby I gave my neck to thy "easy yoke" and my shoulders to thy "light burden," O Christ Jesus, "my Strength and my Redeemer"? …Thou didst cast them away, and in their place Thou didst enter in Thyself—sweeter than all pleasure, though not to flesh and blood; brighter than all light, but more veiled than all mystery; more exalted than all honor, though not to them that are exalted in their own eyes. Now was my soul free from the gnawing cares… scratching the itch of lust. And I prattled like a child to thee, O Lord my God—my light, my riches, and my salvation.

⌐ St. Augustine (345–440)

THE NECESSITY OF PRAYER

Then you will delight in the Almighty and lift up your face to God.

Job 22:26

It is the initial quality in the heart of any man who essays to talk to the Unseen. He must, out of sheer helplessness, stretch forth hands of faith. He must believe, where he cannot prove. In the ultimate issue, prayer is simply faith, claiming its natural yet marvelous prerogatives—faith taking possession of its illimitable inheritance. True godliness is just as true, steady, and persevering in the realm of faith as it is in the province of prayer. Moreover: when faith ceases to pray, it ceases to live.

Faith does the impossible because it brings God to undertake for us, and nothing is impossible with God. How great—without qualification or limitation—is the power of faith! If doubt be banished from the heart, and unbelief made stranger there, what we ask of God shall surely come to pass, and a believer hath vouchsafed to him "whatsoever he saith." Prayer projects faith on God, and God on the world. Only God can move mountains, but faith and prayer move God. In His cursing of the fig-tree our Lord demonstrated His power. Following that, He proceeded to declare, that large powers were committed to faith and prayer, not in order to kill but to make alive, not to blast but to bless.

~ Edward M. Bounds (1835–1913)

FAITH

For we walk by faith, not by sight.

2 Corinthians 5:7

A work of grace in the soul discovereth itself, either to him that hath it, or to standers-by. To him that hath it, thus: It gives him conviction of sin, especially the defilement of his nature, and the sin of unbelief, for the sake of which he is sure to be damned, if he findeth not mercy at God's hand, by faith in Jesus Christ. This sight and sense of things worketh in him sorrow and shame for sin. He findeth, moreover, revealed in him the Saviour of the world, and the absolute necessity of closing with him for life; at the which he findeth hungerings and thirstings after him; to which hungerings, etc., the promise is made.

Now, according to the strength or weakness of his faith in his Saviour, so is his joy and peace, so is his love to holiness, so are his desires to know him more, and also to serve him in this world. But though, I say it discovereth itself thus unto him, yet it is but seldom that he is able to conclude that this is a work of grace; because his corruptions now, and his abused reason, make his mind to misjudge in this matter: therefore in him that hath this work there is required a very sound judgment, before he can with steadiness conclude that this is a work of grace.

— John Bunyan (1628–1688)

A SUDDEN CHANGE

But the fruit of the Spirit is love, joy, peace, patience, kindness, goodness, faith, gentleness, self-control. Against such things there is no law.

Galatians 5:22–23

Spiritual joy is a sweet and delightful passion, arising from the apprehension and feeling of some good, whereby the soul is supported under present troubles, and fenced against future fear. Joy is not a fancy, or conceit; but is rational, and arises from the feeling of some good, as the sense of God's love and favour.

Joy is so real a thing that it makes a sudden change in a person; and turns mourning into melody. As in the spring-time, when the sun comes to our horizon, it makes a sudden alteration in the face of the universe: the birds sing, the flowers appear, the fig-tree puts forth her green figs; every thing seems to rejoice and put off its mourning, as being revived with the sweet influence of the sun; so when the Sun of Righteousness arises on the soul, it makes a sudden alteration, and the soul is infinitely rejoiced with the golden beams of God's love.

⁓ Thomas Watson (1874–1956)

WHAT A FRIEND
WE HAVE IN JESUS

What a friend we have in Jesus,
All our sins and griefs to bear;
What a privilege to carry
Ev'rything to God in prayer!
O what peace we often forfeit,
O what needless pain we bear.
Just because we do not carry
Ev'rything to God in prayer.

Have we trials and temptations?
Is there trouble anywhere?
We should never be discouraged;
Take it to the Lord in prayer.
Can we find a friend so faithful,
Who will all our sorrows share?
Jesus knows our ev'ry weakness;
Take it to the Lord in prayer.

Are we weak and heavy-laden,
Cumbered with a load of care?
Precious Saviour, still our refuge;
Take it to the Lord in prayer.
Do thy friends despise, forsake thee?
Take it to the Lord in prayer;
In His arms He'll take and shield thee,
Thou wilt find a solace there.

~ Joseph Scriven (1819–1886)

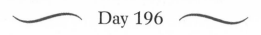
HOLDING ON

Wait for the LORD; be strong and courageous. Wait for the LORD.

Psalm 27:14

God's will, then, is as great as God, as high as heaven, yet as easy as love. For love knows no hardness, and feels no yoke. It desires no yielding to its poverty in anything it loves. Let God be greater, and His will sterner, love will be stronger and obedience but more true. Let not God come down to me, slacken truth for me, make His will weaker for me: my interests, as subject, are safer with my King, are greater with the greatness of my King—only give me love, pure, burning love and loyalty to Him, and I shall climb from law to law through grace and glory, to the place beside the throne where the angels do His will. There are two ways, therefore, of looking at God's will—one looking at the love side of it, the other at the law; the one ending in triumph, the other in despair; the one a liberty, the other a slavery. And you might illustrate this in a simple way, to make it finally clear—for this is the hardest point to hold—in some such way as this.

~ Henry Drummond (1851–1897)

CARRY YOUR CROSS

Summoning the crowd along with His disciples, He said to them, "If anyone wants to be My follower, he must deny himself, take up his cross, and follow Me."

Mark 8:34

The cross which my Lord bids me take up and carry may assume different shapes. I may have to content myself with a lowly and narrow sphere, when I feel that I have capacities for much higher work. I may have to go on cultivating year after year, a field which seems to yield me no harvests whatsoever.

There are many crosses, and every one of them is sore and heavy. None of them is likely to be sought out by me of my own accord. But never is Jesus so near me as when I lift my cross, and lay it submissively on my shoulder, and give it the welcome of a patient and unmurmuring spirit. He draws close, to ripen my wisdom, to deepen my peace, to increase my courage, to augment my power to be of use to others, through the very experience which is so grievous and distressing, and then I grow under the load.

～ Alexander Smellie (1857–1923)

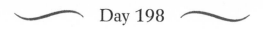

DESIRE FOR RIGHTEOUSNESS

Those who hunger and thirst for righteousness are blessed, for they will be filled.

Matthew 5:6

It is written of our blessed Lord, "Thou hast loved righteousness, and hated iniquity; therefore God, even thy God, hath anointed thee with the oil of gladness above thy fellows." It is the purpose of God that we, as we are indwelt by the Spirit of His Son, should likewise love righteousness and hate iniquity.

I see that there is a place for us in Christ Jesus where we are no longer under condemnation but where the heavens are always open to us. I see that God has a realm of divine life opening up to us where there are boundless possibilities, where there is limitless power, where there are untold resources, where we have victory over all the power of the devil. I believe that, as we are filled with the desire to press on into this life of true holiness, desiring only the glory of God, there is nothing that can hinder our true advancement.

~ Smith Wigglesworth (1859–1947)

OH, WORSHIP THE KING

Oh, worship the King All glorious above:
Oh, gratefully sing His power and His love,
Our Shield and Defender, The Ancient of Days,
Pavilioned in splendor and girded with praise!
Oh, tell of His might, Oh, sing of His grace,
Whose robe is the light, Whose canopy space!
His chariots of wrath The deep thunder-clouds form,
And dark is His path On the wings of the storm.
This earth, with its store Of wonders untold,
Almighty, Thy power Hath founded of old,
Hath stablished it fast By a changeless decree,
And round it hath cast, Like a mantle, the sea.
Thy bountiful care What tongues can recite?
It breathes in the air, It shines in the light,
It streams from the hills, It descends to the plain,
And sweetly distils In the dew and the rain.
Frail children of dust And feeble as frail,
In Thee do we trust Nor find Thee to fail.
Thy mercies, how tender, How firm to the end,
Our maker, Defender, Redeemer, and Friend!
O measureless Might, Ineffable Love,
While angels delight To hymn Thee above,
Thy humbler creation, Though feeble their lays,
With true adoration Shall sing to Thy praise.

〜 Robert Grant (1779–1838)

THE GLORY OF GOD

We have also obtained access through Him by faith into this grace in which we stand, and we rejoice in the hope of the glory of God.

Romans 5:2

There were, indeed, in the first times of the church, sums of proud, doting, brain-sick persons, who vented many foolish imaginations about him, which issued at length in Arianism, in whose ruins they were buried. The gates of hell in them prevailed not against the rock on which the church is built. But as it was said of Caesar, "He alone went soberly about the destruction of the commonwealth"; so we now have great numbers who oppose the Person and glory of Christ, under a pretence of sobriety of reason, as they vainly plead.

Yea, the disbelief of the mysteries of the Trinity, and the incarnation of the Son of God—the sole foundation of Christian religion—is so diffused in the world, as that it has almost devoured the power and vitals of it. And not a few, who dare not yet express their minds, do give broad intimations of their intentions and good-will towards Him, in making them the object of their scorn and reproach who desire to know nothing but Him, and Him crucified. God, in His appointed time, will effectually vindicate His honour and glory from the vain attempts of men of corrupt minds against them.

~ John Owen (1616–1683)

HOLY SPIRIT WORK

So he answered me… "Not by strength or by might, but by My Spirit,"
says the LORD *of Hosts.*

Zechariah 4:6

The redeemed are not sanctified without Christ, who is made to them sanctification; hence the work of the Spirit must embrace the Incarnation of the Word and the work of the Messiah. But the work of Messiah involves preparatory working in the Patriarchs and Prophets of Israel, and later activity in the Apostles…Likewise this revelation involves the conditions of man's nature and the historical development of the race; hence the Holy Spirit is concerned in the formation of the human mind and the unfolding of the spirit of humanity…man's condition depends on that of the earth…and no less on the actions of spirits, be they angels or demons from other spheres…the Spirit's work must touch the entire host of heaven and earth.

To avoid a mechanical idea of His work as tho it began and ended at random…it must not be determined nor limited till it extends to all the influences that affect the sanctification of the Church. The Holy Spirit is God, therefore sovereign; hence He cannot depend on these influences, but completely controls them. For this He must be able to operate them; so His work must be honored in all the host of heaven, in man and in his history, in the preparation of Scripture, in the Incarnation of the Word, in the salvation of the elect.

~ Abraham Kuyper (1837–1920)

O PERFECT LIFE OF LOVE

O perfect life of love!
All, all, is finished now,
All that He left His throne above
To do for us below.
No work is left undone
Of all the Father willed;
His toil, His sorrows, one by one,
The Scriptures have fulfilled.
No pain that we can share
But He has felt its smart;
All forms of human grief and care
Have pierced that tender heart.
And on His thorn-crowned head
And on His sinless soul
Our sins in all that guilt were laid
That He might make us whole.
In perfect love He dies;
For me He dies, for me.
O all-atoning Sacrifice,
I cling by faith to Thee.
In every time of need,
Before the judgment-throne,
Thy works, O Lamb of God, I'll plead,
Thy merits, not mine own.
Yet work, O Lord, in me
As Thou for me hast wrought,
And let my love the answer be
To grace Thy love has brought.

~ Henry W. Baker (1821–1877)

GOD'S CALL

Deeply hurt, Hannah prayed to the L<small>ORD</small> and wept with many tears.

1 Samuel 1:10

We may know God's call when it grows in intensity. If an impression comes into your soul, and you are not quite sure of its origin, pray over it; above all, act on it so far as possible, follow in the direction in which it leads—and as you lift up your soul before God, it will wax or wane. If it wanes at all, abandon it. If it waxes follow it, though all hell attempt to stay you. We may test God's call by the assistance of godly friends. The aged Eli perceived that the Lord had called the child, and gave him good advice as to the manner in which he should respond to it. Our special gifts and the drift of our circumstances will also assuredly concur in one of God's calls.

We may test God's call by its effect on us. Does it lead to self-denial? Does it induce us to leave the comfortable bed and step into the cold? Does it drive us forth to minister to others? Does it make us more unselfish, loving, tender, modest, humble! Whatever is to the humbling of our pride, and the glory of God, may be truly deemed God's call. Be quick to respond, and fearlessly deliver the message the Lord has given you.

~ F. B. Meyer (1847–1929)

LIKE CHRIST

Elijah was a man with a nature like ours; yet he prayed earnestly that it would not rain, and for three years and six months it did not rain on the land.

James 5:17

If for one moment we are left to ourselves, we may take a step which may shatter our influence, and forever after put us into a very different position from that which might have been ours if only we had remained true. As children, we may be forgiven; as servants we are never reinstated or trusted quite as we were once.

It is noteworthy that the Bible saints often fail just where we would have expected them to stand. Abraham was the father of those who believe; but his faith failed him when he went down to Egypt and lied to Pharaoh about his wife. Moses was the meekest of men; but he missed Canaan because he spoke unadvisedly with his lips. John was the apostle of love, yet in a moment of intolerance he wished to call down fire out of heaven. So Elijah, who might have been supposed to be superior to all human weakness, shows himself to be indeed "a man subject to like passions as are we."

～ F. B. Meyer (1847–1929)

ALIVE IN CHRIST

Therefore do not let sin reign in your mortal body, so that you obey its desires. And do not offer any parts of it to sin as weapons for unrighteousness. But as those who are alive from the dead, offer yourselves to God, and all the parts of yourselves to God as weapons for righteousness.

Romans 6:12–13

"Present yourselves unto God, as alive from the dead." This defines for us the point at which consecration begins. For what is here referred to is not the consecration of anything belonging to the old creation, but only of that which has passed through death to resurrection. The "presenting" spoken of is the outcome of my knowing my old man to be crucified. Knowing, reckoning, presenting to God: that is the Divine order.

When I really know I am crucified with Him, then spontaneously I reckon myself dead; and when I know that I am raised with Him from the dead, then likewise I reckon myself "alive unto God in Christ Jesus," for both the death and the resurrection side of the Cross are to be accepted by faith. When this point is reached, giving myself to Him follows. In resurrection He is the source of my life—indeed He is my life; so I cannot but present everything to Him, for all is His, not mine… Presenting myself to God means that henceforth I consider my whole life as now belonging to the Lord.

～ Watchman Nee (1903–1972)

JOYFUL OBEDIENCE

Therefore, submit to God. But resist the Devil, and he will flee from you. Draw near to God, and He will draw near to you. Cleanse your hands, sinners, and purify your hearts, double-minded people!

James 4:7–8

It is a very great thing to obey, to live under a superior and not to be one's own master, for it is much safer to be subject than it is to command. Many live in obedience more from necessity than from love. Such become discontented and dejected on the slightest pretext; they will never gain peace of mind unless they subject themselves wholeheartedly for the love of God. Go where you may, you will find no rest except in humble obedience to the rule of authority. Dreams of happiness expected from change and different places have deceived many.

~ Thomas à Kempis (1380–1471)

O GOD, BE WITH US

O God, be with us, for the night is falling;
For Thy protection we to Thee are calling;
Beneath Thy shadow to our rest we yield us;
Thou, Lord, wilt shield us.
May evil fancies flee away before us;
Till morning cometh, watch, O Father, o'er us;
In soul and body Thou from harm defend us,
Thine angel send us.
While we are sleeping, keep us in Thy favor;
When we awaken, let us never waver
All day to serve Thee,
Thy due praise pursuing In all our doing.
Through Thy Beloved soothe the sick and weeping
And bid the captive lose his grief in sleeping;
Widows and orphans, we to Thee commend them,
Do Thou befriend them.
We have no refuge, none on earth to aid us,
Save Thee, O Father, who Thine own hast made us.
But Thy dear presence will not leave them lonely
Who seek Thee only.
Thy name be hallowed and Thy kingdom given,
Thy will among us done as 'tis in heaven;
Feed us, forgive us, from all ill deliver Now and forever.

~ Petrus Herbert (1533–1571)

IN THE BEGINNING GOD CREATED!
(PART 1)

In the beginning God created the heavens and the earth.

Genesis 1:1

I stop struck with admiration at this thought. What shall I first say? Where shall I begin my story? Shall I show forth the vanity of the Gentiles? Shall I exalt the truth of our faith? The philosophers of Greece have made much ado to explain nature, and not one of their systems has remained firm and unshaken, each being overturned by its successor. It is vain to refute them; they are sufficient in themselves to destroy one another. Those who were too ignorant to rise to a knowledge of a God, could not allow that an intelligent cause presided at the birth of the Universe; a primary error that involved them in sad consequences.

Some had recourse to material principles and attributed the origin of the Universe to the elements of the world. Others imagined that atoms, and indivisible bodies, molecules and ducts, form, by their union, the nature of the visible world. Atoms reuniting or separating, produce births and deaths and the most durable bodies only owe their consistency to the strength of their mutual adhesion: a true spider's web woven by these writers who give to heaven, to earth, and to sea so weak an origin and so little consistency! It is because they knew not how to say "In the beginning God created the heaven and the earth."

～ Henry Wace (1836–1924)

IN THE BEGINNING GOD CREATED!
(PART 2)

What a glorious order! He first establishes a beginning, so that it might not be supposed that the world never had a beginning. Then He adds "Created" to show that which was made was a very small part of the power of the Creator. In the same way that the potter, after having made with equal pains a great number of vessels, has not exhausted either His art or His talent; thus the Maker of the Universe, whose creative power, far from being bounded by one world, could extend to the infinite, needed only the impulse of His will to bring the immensities of the visible world into being.

If then the world has a beginning, and if it has been created, enquire who gave it this beginning, and who was the Creator: or rather, in the fear that human reasonings may make you wander from the truth, Moses has anticipated enquiry by engraving in our hearts, as a seal and a safeguard, the awful name of God: "In the beginning God created"—It is He, beneficent Nature, Goodness without measure, a worthy object of love for all beings endowed with reason, the beauty the most to be desired, the origin of all that exists, the source of life, intellectual light, impenetrable wisdom, it is He who "in the beginning created heaven and earth."

～ Henry Wace (1836–1924)

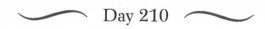

THE REALITY OF PRAYER

During His earthly life, He offered prayers and appeals with loud cries and tears to the One who was able to save Him from death, and He was heard because of His reverence.

Hebrews 5:7

The word "Prayer" expresses the largest and most comprehensive approach unto God. It gives prominence to the element of devotion. It is communion and intercourse with God. It is enjoyment of God. It is access to God. "Supplication" is a more restricted and more intense form of prayer, accompanied by a sense of personal need, limited to the seeking in an urgent manner of a supply for pressing need. "Supplication" is the very soul of prayer in the way of pleading for some one thing, greatly needed, and the need intensely felt. "Intercession" is an enlargement in prayer, a going out in broadness and fullness from self to others. Primarily, it does not centre in praying for others, but refers to the freeness, boldness and childlike confidence of the praying. It is the fullness of confiding influence in the soul's approach to God, unlimited and unhesitating in its access and its demands. This influence and confident trust is to be used for others. Prayer always, and everywhere is an immediate and confiding approach to, and a request of, God the Father. In the prayer universal and perfect, as the pattern of all praying, it is "Our Father, Who art in Heaven"…Strong, tool, and touching and tearful, was His praying.

⁓ Edward M. Bounds (1835–1913)

THE ESSENTIALS OF PRAYER

The sacrifice of the wicked is detestable to the LORD, but the prayer of the upright is His delight.

Proverbs 15:8

Prayer has to do with the entire man. Prayer takes in man in his whole being, mind, soul, and body. It takes the whole man to pray, and prayer affects the entire man in its gracious results. As the whole nature of man enters into prayer, so also all that belongs to man is the beneficiary of prayer. All of man receives benefits in prayer. The whole man must be given to God in praying. The largest results in praying come to him who gives himself, all of himself, all that belongs to himself, to God.

This is the secret of full consecration, and this is a condition of successful praying, and the sort of praying which brings the largest fruits. The men of olden times who wrought well in prayer, who brought the largest things to pass, who moved God to do great things, were those who were entirely given over to God in their praying. God wants, and must have, all that there is in man in answering his prayers. He must have whole-hearted men through whom to work out His purposes and plans concerning men. God must have men in their entirety. No double-minded man need apply. No vacillating man can be used. No man with a divided allegiance to God, and the world and self, can do the praying that is needed.

— Edward M. Bounds (1835–1913)

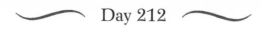
WHAT HAVE YOU DONE?

Worship the LORD your God, and He will bless your bread and your water. I will remove illnesses from you.

Exodus 23:25

If men used as much care in uprooting vices and implanting virtues as they do in discussing problems, there would not be so much evil and scandal in the world, or such laxity in religious organizations. On the day of judgment, surely, we shall not be asked what we have read but what we have done; not how well we have spoken but how well we have lived. Tell me, where now are all the masters and teachers whom you knew so well in life and who were famous for their learning?…During life they seemed to be something; now they are seldom remembered…

If only their lives had kept pace with their learning, then their study and reading would have been worth while. How many there are who perish because of vain worldly knowledge and too little care for serving God. They became vain in their own conceits because they chose to be great rather than humble. He is truly great who has great charity. He is truly great who is little in his own eyes and makes nothing of the highest honor. He is truly wise who looks upon all earthly things as folly that he may gain Christ. He who does God's will and renounces his own is truly very learned…

⌒ Thomas à Kempis (1380–1471)

HIS GLORIOUS GOSPEL

You bring darkness, and it becomes night, when all the forest animals stir.

Psalm 104:20

We of this nation have long enjoyed the light of the glorious gospel among us; it has shone in much clearness upon this sinful island, for more than a whole century of happy years: but the longest day has an end, and we have cause to fear our bright sun is going down upon us; for the shadows in England are grown greater than the substance, which is one sign of approaching night (Jer. 6:4). "The beasts of prey creep out of their dens and coverts," which is another sign of night at hand (Ps. 104:20). "And the workmen come home apace from their labours, and go to rest," which is as sad a sign as any of the rest (Job 7:1–2; Isa. 57: 1–2).

Happy were it, if, in such a juncture as this, every man would make it his work and business to secure himself in Christ from the storm of God's indignation, which is ready to fall upon these sinful nations. It is said of the Egyptians, when the storm of hail was coming upon the land, "He that feared the word of the Lord made his servants and cattle flee into the houses" (Exod. 9:20). It is but an odd sight to see the prudence of an Egyptian out-vying the wisdom and circumspection of a Christian.

~ John Flavel (1630–1691)

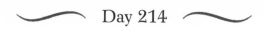

WHERE GOD DWELLS

Wait for the LORD and keep His way, and He will exalt you to inherit the land. You will watch when the wicked are destroyed.

Psalm 37:34

Charity and Righteousness: these two lay the foundation of the kingdom of the soul where God would dwell. And this foundation is humility. These three virtues prop and bear the whole weight and the whole edifice of all the other virtues and of all transcendence. For charity always confronts man with the unfathomable goodness of God, from which it has flowed forth, that thereby he may live worthily and remain steadfast before God, and grow in true humility and all other virtues.

And righteousness places man face to face with the eternal truth of God, that he may know truth, and become enlightened, and may fulfill all virtue without erring. But humility brings man face to face with the most high mightiness of God, that he may always remain little and lowly, and may surrender himself to God, and may not stand upon his selfhood. This is the way in which a man should hold himself before God, that thereby he may grow continually in new virtues.

〜 John of Ruysbroeck (1293–1381)

NEVER ALONE

"Teaching them to observe everything I have commanded you. And remember, I am with you always, to the end of the age."

Matthew 28:20

How is He with us? Not outwardly, every illiterate man knows; not inwardly, says many a learned doctor, because a Christ within us is as gross enthusiasm…as the light within us. How then shall the faith of the common Christian find any comfort in these words of Christ's promise, unless the spirit brings him into a remembrance and belief, that Christ is in him, and with him, as the vine is with and in the branch. Christ says, "Without me ye can do nothing"; and also, "If any man loves me, my Father will love him, and we will come unto him, and make our abode with him."

Now if without Him we can do nothing, then all the love that a man can possibly have for Christ, must be from the power and life of Christ in him, and from such a love, so begotten, man has the Father and the Son dwelling and making their abode in him. What higher proof, or fuller certainty can there be, that the whole work of redemption in the soul of man is and can be nothing else, but the inward, continual, immediate operation of Father, Son, and Holy Spirit, raising up again their own first life in the soul, to which our first father died?

～ William Law (1686–1761)

ALL HAIL THE POWER OF JESUS' NAME

All hail the power of Jesus' name!
Let angels prostrate fall;
Bring forth the royal diadem
And crown Him Lord of all.
Crown Him, ye martyrs of our God,
Who from His altar call;
Extol the Stem of Jesse's rod
And crown Him Lord of all.
Ye seed of Israel's chosen race,
Ye ransomed from the Fall,
Hail Him who saves you by His grace
And crown Him Lord of all.
Hail Him, ye heirs of David's line,
Whom David Lord did call,
The God incarnate, Man divine,
And crown Him Lord of all.
Sinners, whose love can ne'er forget
The wormwood and the gall,
Go, spread your trophies at His feet
And crown Him Lord of all.
Let every kindred, every tribe,
On this terrestrial ball
To Him all majesty ascribe
And crown Him Lord of all.
Oh, that with yonder sacred throng
We at His feet may fall!
We'll join the everlasting song
And crown Him Lord of all.

～ Edward Perronet (1726–1792)

SEE, THE CONQUEROR MOUNTS IN TRIUMPH

See, the Conqueror mounts in triumph; See the King in royal state, Riding on the clouds, His chariot, To His heavenly palace gate! Hark, the choirs of angel voices Joyful alleluias sing, And the portals high are lifted To receive their heavenly King. Who is this that comes in glory With the trump of jubilee? Lord of battles, God of armies—He hath gained the victory. He who on the cross did suffer, He who from the grave arose, He hath vanquished sin and Satan; He by death hath spoiled His foes. While He lifts His hands in blessing He is parted from His friends; While their eager eyes behold Him, He upon the clouds ascends. He who walked with God and pleased Him, Preaching truth and doom to come, He, our Enoch, is translated To His everlasting home.

Now our heavenly Aaron enter With His blood within the veil; Joshua now is come to Canaan, And the kings before Him quail. Now He plants the tribes of Israel In their promised resting-place; Now our great Elijah offers Double portion of His grace. Thou hast raised our human nature On the clouds to God's right hand; There we sit in heavenly places, There with Thee in glory stand.

Jesus reigns, adored by angels; Man with God is on the throne. Mighty Lord, in Thine ascension We by faith behold our own. Glory be to God the Father; Glory be to God the Son, Dying, risen, ascending for us, Who the heavenly realm hath won. Glory to the Holy Spirit! To One God in Persons Three Glory both in earth and heaven, Glory, endless glory, be.

~ Christopher Wordsworth (1807–1885)

THE CROOK IN THE LOT

Consider the work of God, for who can straighten out what He has made crooked?

Ecclesiastes 7:13

Everybody's lot in this world has some crook in it. Complainers are apt to make odious comparisons. They look about, and take a distant view of the condition of others, can discern nothing in it but what is straight, and just to one's wish; so they pronounce their neighbor's lot wholly straight. But that is a false verdict; there is no perfection here; no lot out of heaven without a crook. For, as to "all the works that are done under the sun, behold, all is vanity and vexation of spirit. That which is crooked cannot be made straight."

Who would have thought but that Haman's lot was very straight, while his family was in a flourishing condition, and he prospering in riches and honor, being prime minister of state in the Persian court, and standing high in the king's favor? Yet there was, at the saline time, a crook in his lot, which so galled him, that "all this availed him nothing." Every one feels for himself, when he is pinched, though others do not perceive it. Nobody's lot, in this world, is wholly crooked; there are always some straight and even parts in it. Indeed, when men's passions, having gotten up, have cast a mist over their minds, they are ready to say, all is wrong with them, nothing right. But, though in hell that tale is and ever will be true, yet it is never true in this world. For there, indeed, there is not a drop of comfort allowed; but here it always holds good, that "it is of the Lord's mercies we are not consumed."

~ Thomas Boston (1677–1732)

MY TIMES ARE IN THY HANDS
(FROM PSALM 31:15)

Father, I know that all my life Is portioned out for me, And the changes that are sure to come, I do not fear to see; But I ask Thee for a present mind Intent on pleasing Thee. I ask Thee for a thoughtful love, Through constant watching wise, To meet the glad with joyful smiles, And to wipe the weeping eyes; And a heart at leisure from itself, To soothe and sympathize. I would not have the restless will That hurries to and fro, Seeking for some great thing to do, Or secret thing to know; I would be treated as a child, And guided where I go.

Wherever in the world I am, In whatsoe'er estate, I have a fellowship with hearts To keep and cultivate; And a work of lowly love to do For the Lord on whom I wait. So I ask Thee for the daily strength, To none that ask denied, And a mind to blend with outward life While keeping at Thy side; Content to fill a little space, If Thou be glorified. And if some things I do not ask, In my cup of blessing be, I would have my spirit filled the more With grateful love to Thee—more careful—not to serve Thee much, But to please Thee perfectly.

There are briers besetting every path, That call for patient care; There is a cross in every lot, And an earnest need for prayer; But a lowly heart that leans on Thee Is happy anywhere. In a service which Thy will appoints, There are no bonds for me; For my inmost heart is taught "the truth" That makes Thy children "free;" And a life of self–renouncing love, Is a life of liberty.

~ Anna L. Waring (1823–1910)

INSTANT OBEDIENCE

Then Abraham took his son Ishmael and all the slaves born in his house or purchased with his money—every male among the members of Abraham's household—and he circumcised the flesh of their foreskin on that very day, just as God had said to him.

Genesis 17:23

Instant obedience is the only kind of obedience there is; delayed obedience is disobedience. Every time God calls us to any duty, He is offering to make a covenant with us; doing the duty is our part, and He will do His part in special blessing.

The only way we can obey is to obey "in the selfsame day," as Abraham did. To be sure, we often postpone a duty and then later on do it as fully as we can. It is better to do this than not to do it at all. But it is then, at the best, only a crippled, disfigured, half-way sort of duty-doing; and a postponed duty never can bring the full blessing that God intended, and that it would have brought if done at the earliest possible moment. It is a pity to rob ourselves, along with robbing God and others, by procrastination. "In the selfsame day" is the Genesis way of saying, "Do it now."

~ Charles G. Trumbull (1875–1941)

PRAYERS FROM THE HEART
(PART 1)

O God, You led Your holy apostles to ordain ministers in every place: Grant that Your Church, under the guidance of the Holy Spirit, may choose suitable persons for the ministry of Word and Sacrament, and may uphold them in their work for the extension of your kingdom; through Him who is the Shepherd and Bishop of our souls, Jesus Christ our Lord, who lives and reigns with You and the Holy Spirit, one God, for ever and ever. Amen

Almighty and everlasting God, by whose Spirit the whole body of your faithful people is governed and sanctified: Receive our supplications and prayers, which we offer before You for all members of Your holy Church, that in their vocation and ministry they may truly and devoutly serve You; through our Lord and Savior Jesus Christ, who lives and reigns with You, in the unity of the Holy Spirit, one God, now and for ever. Amen

Almighty God, unto whom all hearts are open, all desires known, and from whom no secrets are hid: Cleanse the thoughts of our hearts by the inspiration of thy Holy Spirit, that we may perfectly love Thee, and worthily magnify Thy holy Name; through Christ our Lord. Amen

～ William Wilberforce (1759–1833)

PRAYERS FROM THE HEART
(PART 2)

Lord God Almighty, You have made all the peoples of the earth for Your glory, to serve You in freedom and in peace: Give to the people of our country a zeal for justice and the strength of forbearance, that we may use our liberty in accordance with Your gracious will; through Jesus Christ our Lord, who lives and reigns with You and the Holy Spirit, one God, for ever and ever. Amen

Almighty God, who created us in Your image: Grant us grace fearlessly to contend against evil and to make no peace with oppression; and, that we may reverently use our freedom, help us to employ it in the maintenance of justice in our communities and among the nations, to the glory of Your holy Name; through Jesus Christ our Lord, who lives and reigns with You and the Holy Spirit, one God, now and for ever. Amen

Almighty God, the fountain of all wisdom: Enlighten by Your Holy Spirit those who teach and those who learn, that, rejoicing in the knowledge of Your truth, they may worship You and serve You from generation to generation; through Jesus Christ our Lord, who lives and reigns with You and the Holy Spirit, one God, for ever and ever. Amen

~ William Wilberforce (1759–1833)

PRAYERS FROM THE HEART
(PART 3)

O God of unchangeable power and eternal light: Look favorably on Your whole Church, that wonderful and sacred mystery; by the effectual working of Your providence, carry out in tranquility the plan of salvation; let the whole world see and know that things which were cast down are being raised up, and things which had grown old are being made new, and that all things are being brought to their perfection by Him through whom all things were made, Your Son Jesus Christ our Lord; who lives and reigns with You, in the unity of the Holy Spirit, one God, for ever and ever. Amen

Almighty and most merciful Father, we have erred and strayed from Thy ways like lost sheep, we have followed too much the devices and desires of our/own hearts, we have offended against Thy holy laws, we have left undone those things which we ought to/have done, and we have done those things which we ought not to/have done. But Thou, O Lord, have mercy upon us, spare Thou those who confess their faults, restore thou those who are penitent, according to Thy promises declared unto mankind in Christ Jesus our Lord; and grant, O most merciful Father, for His sake, that we may hereafter live a godly, righteous, and sober life, to the glory of Thy holy Name. Amen

~ William Wilberforce (1759–1833)

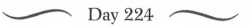
THE TRUTH OF GOD: THE CHRISTIAN LIFE WAS IN THE FIRST PLACE OBEDIENCE

By obedience to the truth having purified yourselves for sincere love of the brothers, love one another earnestly from a pure heart,

1 Peter 1:22

In Paul's Epistle to the Romans, we, have, the opening and closing verses the expression, "the obedience of faith among all nations"(1:5; 16:26), as that for which he was made an apostle. He speaks of what God had wrought "to make the Gentiles obedient." He teaches that, as the obedience of Christ makes us righteous, we become the servants of obedience unto righteousness. As disobedience in Adam and in us was the one thing that wrought death, so obedience, in Christ and in us, is the one thing that the gospel makes known as the way of restoration to God and His favor.

We all know how James warns us not to be hearers of the Word only but doers, and expounds how Abraham was justified, and his faith perfected, by his works. In Peter's first epistle we have only to look at the first chapter, to see the place obedience has in his system. In 1:2 he speaks to the "Elect, in sanctification of the Spirit, unto obedience and blood-sprinkling of Jesus Christ," and so points us to obedience as the eternal purpose of the Father, as the great object of the work of the Spirit, and a chief part of the salvation of Christ…"As children of obedience," born of it, marked by it, subject to it, "be ye holy in all manner of conversation." Obedience is the very starting point of true holiness.

⁓ Andrew Murray (1828–1917)

AFFECTIONS

A woman of Samaria came to draw water. "Give Me a drink," Jesus said to her.

John 4:7

The more a true saint loves God with a gracious love, the more he desires to love Him, and the more uneasy is he at his want of love to Him; the more he hates sin, the more he desires to hate it, and laments that he has so much remaining love to it; the more he mourns for sin, the more he longs to mourn for sin; the more his heart is broke, the more he desires it should be broke; the more he thirsts and longs after God and holiness, the more he longs to long, and breathe out his very soul in longings after God: the kindling and raising of gracious affections is like kindling a flame…So that the spiritual appetite after holiness, and an increase of holy affections is much more lively and keen in those that are eminent in holiness, than others, and more when grace and holy affections are in their most lively exercise, than at other times…

The most that the saints have in this world, is but a taste…it is only an earnest of their future inheritance in their hearts. The most eminent saints in this state are but children, compared with their future, which is their proper state of maturity and perfection…

~ Jonathan Edwards (1703–1758)

HOW TO KNOW THE WILL OF GOD

"If anyone wants to do His will, he will understand whether the teaching is from God or if I am speaking on My own."

John 7:17

It requires a well-kept life to do the will of God, and even a better kept life to will to do His will. To be willing is a rarer grace than to be doing the will of God. For he who is willing may sometimes have nothing to do, and must only be willing to wait: and it is easier far to be doing God's will than to be willing to have nothing to do—it is easier far to be working for Christ than it is to be willing to cease. No, there is nothing rarer in the world to-day than the truly willing soul, and there is nothing more worth coveting than the will to will God's will.

There is no grander possession for any Christian life than the transparently simple mechanism of a sincerely obeying heart. And if we could keep the machinery clear, there would be lives in thousands doing God's will on earth even as it is done in Heaven. There would be God in many a man's career whose soul is allowed to drift—a useless thing to God and the world—with every changing wind of life, and many a noble Christian character rescued from wasting all its virtues on itself and saved for work for Christ.

~ Henry Drummond (1851–1897)

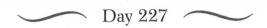
CARNAL OR SPIRITUAL?

And he went outside and wept bitterly.

Luke 22:62

These words indicate the turning point in the life of Peter—a crisis. There is often a question about the life of holiness. Do you grow into it? Or do you come into it by a crisis suddenly? Peter has been growing for three years under the training of Christ, but he had grown terribly downward, for the end of his growing was, he denied Jesus. And then there came a crisis. After the crisis he was a changed man, and then he began to grow aright.

We must indeed grow in grace, but before we can grow in grace we must be put right...Just as the Lord Jesus gave the Holy Spirit to Peter, He is willing to give the Holy Spirit to you. Are you willing to receive Him? Are you willing to give up yourself entirely as an empty, helpless vessel, to receive the power of the Holy Spirit, to live, to dwell, and to work in you every day? Dear believer, God has prepared such a beautiful and such a blessed life for every one of us, and God as a Father is waiting to see why you will not come to Him and let Him fill you with the Holy Ghost. Are you willing for it?

~ Andrew Murray (1828–1917)

TRUST, NO MATTER WHAT!

You would call, and I would answer You. You would long for the work of Your hands.

Job 14:15

This was a noble expression, which has been appropriated by thousands in every subsequent age. In every friendship there is a probation, during which we narrowly watch the actions of another, as indicating the nature of his soul; but after awhile we get to such intimate knowledge and confidence, that we read and know his inner secret. We have passed from the outer court into the Holy Place of fellowship. We seem familiar with every nook and cranny of our friend's nature. And then it is comparatively unimportant how he appears to act; we know him. So it is in respect of God.

At first we know Him through the testimony of others, and on the evidence of Scripture; but as time passes, with its everdeepening experiences of what God is, with those opportunities of converse that arise during years of prayer and communion, we get to know Him as He is and to trust Him implicitly. If He seem to forget and forsake us, it is only in appearance. His heart is yearning over us more than ever. God cannot do a thing which is not perfectly loving and wise and good. Oh to know Him thus! "Leaving the final issue In His hands Whose goodness knows no change, whose love is sure, Who sees, foresees, who cannot judge amiss."

～ F. B. Meyer (1847–1929)

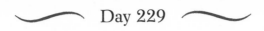

COSTLY GRACE

"Whoever does not bear his own cross and come after Me cannot be My disciple."

Luke 14:27

Costly grace is the treasure hidden in the field; for the sake of it a man will gladly go and sell all that he has. It is the pearl of great price to buy which the merchant will sell all his goods. It is the kingly rule of Christ, for whose sake of one will pluck out the eye which causes him to stumble; it is the call of Jesus Christ at which the disciple leaves his nets and follows Him.

Such grace is *costly* because it calls us to follow, and it is *grace* because it calls us to follow *Jesus Christ*. It is costly because it costs a man his life, and it is grace because it gives a man the only true life. It is costly because it condemns sin, and grace because it justifies the sinner. Grace is costly because it compels a man to submit to the yoke of Christ and follow Him; it is grace because Jesus says: "my yoke is easy and my burden light."

~ Dietrich Bonhoeffer (1906–1945)

HOW DO YOU LIVE?

A man's steps are established by the LORD, and He takes pleasure in his way.

Psalm 37:23

If men used as much care in uprooting vices and implanting virtues as they do in discussing problems, there would not be so much evil and scandal in the world, or such laxity in religious organizations. On the day of judgment, surely, we shall not be asked what we have read but what we have done; not how well we have spoken but how well we have lived. Tell me, where now are all the masters and teachers whom you knew so well in life and who were famous for their learning?…During life they seemed to be something; now they are seldom remembered…If only their lives had kept pace with their learning, then their study and reading would have been worth while.

How many there are who perish because of vain worldly knowledge and too little care for serving God. They became vain in their own conceits because they chose to be great rather than humble. He is truly great who has great charity. He is truly great who is little in his own eyes and makes nothing of the highest honor. He is truly wise who looks upon all earthly things as folly that he may gain Christ. He who does God's will and renounces his own is truly very learned…

～ Thomas à Kempis (1380–1471)

THE CHARIOTS OF GOD
(PART 1)

Laying the beams of His palace on the waters above, making the clouds
His chariot, walking on the wings of the wind,...

Psalm 104:3

The baby carried in the chariot of its mother's arms rides triumphantly through the hardest places, and does not even know they are hard. And how much more we, who are carried in the chariot of the "arms of God"!

Get into your chariot, then. Take each thing that is wrong in your lives as God's chariot for you. No matter who the builder of the wrong may be, whether men or devils, by the time it reaches your side it is God's chariot for you, and is meant to carry you to a heavenly place of triumph. Shut out all the second causes, and find the Lord in it. Say, "Lord, open my eyes that I may see, not the visible enemy, but thy unseen chariots of deliverance." Accept His will in the trial, whatever it may be, and hide yourself in His arms of love. Say, "Thy will be done; Thy will be done!" over and over. Shut out every other thought but the one thought of submission to His will and of trust in His love. Make your trial thus your chariot, and you will find your soul "riding upon the heavens" with God in a way you never dreamed could be.

~ Hannah Whitall Smith (1832–1911)

THE CHARIOTS OF GOD
(PART 2)

I have not a shadow of doubt that if all our eyes were opened today we would see our homes, and our places of business, and the streets we traverse, filled with the "chariots of God." There is no need for any one of us to walk for lack of chariots. That cross inmate of your household, who has hitherto made life a burden to you, and who has been the Juggernaut car to crush your soul into the dust, may henceforth be a glorious chariot to carry you to the heights of heavenly patience and longsuffering. That misunderstanding, that mortification, that unkindness, that disappointment, that loss, that defeat, all these are chariots waiting to carry you to the very heights of victory you have so longed to reach.

Mount into them, then, with thankful hearts, and lose sight of all second causes in the shining of His love who will "carry you in His arms" safely and triumphantly over it all.

~ Hannah Whitall Smith (1832–1911)

A PRAYER FOR OUR CHILDREN

Come, children, listen to me; I will teach you the fear of the LORD.

Psalm 34:11

O almighty and most merciful Father, who hast promised children as a reward to the righteous, and hast given them to me as a testimony of thy mercy, and an engagement of my duty, be pleased to be a Father unto them, and give them healthful bodies, understanding souls, and sanctified spirits, that they may be thy servants and thy children all their days.

Let a great mercy and providence lead them through the dangers and temptations and ignorances of their youth, that they may never run into folly and the evils of an unbridled appetite. So order the accidents of their lives, that by good education, careful tutors, holy example, innocent company, prudent counsel, and thy restraining grace, their duty to thee may be secured in the midst of a crooked and untoward generation. Amen.

~ Jeremy Taylor (1613–1667)

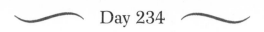

GOD'S MERCY

So then it does not depend on human will or effort but on God who shows mercy.

Romans 9:16

Mercy then is to be found alone in Jesus Christ. Again, the righteousness of the law is to be obtained only by faith of Jesus Christ; that is, in the Son of God is the righteousness of the law to be found; for He, by His obedience to His Father, is become the end of the law for righteousness. And for the sake of His legal righteousness (which is also called the righteousness of God, because it was God in the flesh of the Lord Jesus that did accomplish it), is mercy, and grace from God extended to whoever dependeth by faith upon God by this Jesus His righteousness for it. And hence it is, that we so often read, that this Jesus is the way to the Father; that God, for Christ's sake, forgiveth us; that by the obedience of one many are made righteous, or justified; and that through this man is preached to us the forgiveness of sins; and that by Him all that believe are justified from all things from which they could not be justified by the law of Moses.

~ John Bunyan (1628–1688)

LOVE

Now these three remain: faith, hope, and love. But the greatest of these is love.

1 Corinthians 13:13

You can take nothing greater to the heathen world than the impress and reflection of the Love of God upon your own character. That is the universal language. It will take you years to speak in Chinese, or in the dialects of India. From the day you land, that language of Love, understood by all, will be pouring forth its unconscious eloquence. It is the man who is the missionary, it is not his words. His character is his message.

In the heart of Africa, among the great Lakes, I have come across black men and women who remembered the only white man they ever saw before—David Livingstone; and as you cross his footsteps in that dark continent, men's faces light up as they speak of the kind Doctor who passed there years ago. They could not understand him; but they felt the Love that beat in his heart. Take into your new sphere of labor, where you also mean to lay down your life, that simple charm, and your lifework must succeed. You can take nothing greater, you need take nothing less. It is not worth while going if you take anything less. You may take every accomplishment; you may be braced for every sacrifice; but if you give your body to be burned, and have not Love, it will profit you and the cause of Christ nothing.

~ Henry Drummond (1851–1897)

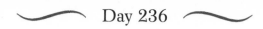

CHRISTIANITY IN THE WORLD

Because whatever has been born of God conquers the world. This is the victory that has conquered the world: our faith.

1 John 5:4

It is the Son of Man before whom the nations of the world shall be gathered. It is in the presence of Humanity that we shall be charged. And the spectacle itself, the mere sight of it, will silently judge each one. Those will be there whom we have met and helped: or there, the unpitied multitude whom we neglected or despised. No other Witness need be summoned. No other charge than lovelessness shall be preferred. Be not deceived.

The words which all of us shall one Day hear, sound not of theology but of life, not of churches and saints but of the hungry and the poor, not of creeds and doctrines but of shelter and clothing, not of Bibles and prayer-books but of cups of cold water in the name of Christ. Thank God the Christianity of today is coming nearer the world's need. Live to help that on. Thank God men know better, by a hairsbreadth, what religion is, what God is, who Christ is, where Christ is. Who is Christ? He who fed the hungry, clothed the naked, visited the sick. And where is Christ? Where?— whoso shall receive a little child in My name receiveth Me. And who are Christ's? Every one that loveth is born of God.

∼ Henry Drummond (1851–1897)

ALTOGETHER LOVELY

His mouth is sweetness. He is absolutely desirable. This is my love, and this is my friend, young women of Jerusalem.

Song of Solomon 5:16

Our Lord Jesus makes sinners lovely. In their natural state, men are deformed and hideous to the eye of God; and as they have no love to God, so He has no delight in them. He is weary of them, and is grieved that He made men upon the earth. The Lord is angry with the wicked every day. Yet, when our Lord Jesus comes in, and covers these sinful ones with His righteousness, and, at the same time, infuses into them His life, the Lord is well pleased with them for His Son's sake.

Even in heaven, the infinite Jehovah sees nothing which pleases Him like His Son. The Father from eternity loved His Only-begotten, and again and again He hath said of Him, "This is My beloved Son, in whom I am well pleased." What higher encomium can be passed upon Him? Our Lord's loveliness appears in every condition: in the manger, or in the temple; by the well, or on the sea; in the garden, or on the cross; in the tomb, or in the resurrection; in His first, or in His second coming. He is not as the herb, which flowers only at one season; or as the tree, which loses its leaves in winter; or as the moon, which waxes and wanes; or as the sea, which ebbs and flows. In every condition, and at every time, "He is altogether lovely."

~ Charles H. Spurgeon (1834–1892)

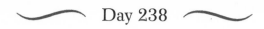
GOD WANTS HOLY MEN

Now may the God of peace Himself sanctify you completely. And may your spirit, soul, and body be kept sound and blameless for the coming of our Lord Jesus Christ.

1 Thessalonians 5:23

Holiness is wholeness, and so God wants holy men, men whole-hearted and true, for His service and for the work of praying. These are the sort of men God wants for leaders of the hosts of Israel, and these are the kind out of which the praying class is formed… Man is one in all the essentials and acts and attitudes of piety. Soul, spirit, and body are to unite in all things pertaining to life and godliness. The body, first of all, engages in prayer, since it assumes the praying attitude in prayer.

Prostration of the body becomes us in praying as well as prostration of the soul. The attitude of the body counts much in prayer, although it is true that the heart may be haughty and lifted up, and the mind listless and wandering, and the praying a mere form, even while the knees are bent in prayer…The entire man must pray. The whole man, life, heart, temper, mind, are in it. Each and all join in the prayer exercise. Doubt, double-mindedness, division of the affections, are all foreign to the closet character and conduct, undefiled, made whiter than snow, are mighty potencies, and are the most seemly beauties for the closet hour, and for the struggles of prayer.

~ Edward M. Bounds (1835–1913)

AND CAN IT BE?

And can it be that I should gain
An int'rest in the Savior's blood?
Died He for me who caused His pain?
For me, who Him to death pursued?
Amazing love! How can it be
That Thou, my God, shouldst die for me?
'Tis mystery all! The Immortal dies!
Who can explore His strange design?
In vain the first-born seraph tries
To sound the depths of love divine!
'Tis mercy all! let earth adore,
Let angel-minds inquire no more.
He left His father's throne above
So free, so infinite His grace!
Emptied Himself of all but love
And bled for Adam's helpless race!
'Tis mercy all, immense and free
For O my God, it found out me.
Long my imprisoned spirit lay
Fast bound in sin and nature's night.
Thine eye diffused a quick'ning ray:
I woke—the dungeon flamed with light!
My chains fell off, my heart was free
I rose, went forth and followed Thee.
No condemnation now I dread
Jesus, and all in Him, is mine!
Alive in Him, my living Head
And clothed in righteousness divine
Bold I approach the 'ternal throne
And claim the crown thru Christ my own.

~ Charles Wesley (1707–1788)

EXAMINE YOURSELVES

Now faith is the reality of what is hoped for, the proof of what is not seen.

Hebrews 11:1

The Holy Spirit has Paul write to each of us, "Examine yourselves, whether ye be in the faith" (2 Corinthians 13:5a), and the recommendation is certainly not out of order at the very inception of this series of studies…"without faith it is impossible to please him" (Hebrews 11:6a)…true faith must be based solely upon scriptural FACTS, for "faith cometh by hearing, and hearing by the word of God" (Romans 10:17). Unless our faith is established upon facts, it is no more than conjecture, superstition, speculation, or presumption. Hebrews 11:1 leaves no question about this: "Faith is the substance of things hoped for, the evidence of things not seen."

Faith standing on the FACTS of the Word of God substantiates and gives evidence of things not seen. And everyone knows that evidence must be founded upon facts. All of us started on this principle when we were born again—our belief stood directly upon the eternal fact of the redeeming death and resurrection of our Lord and Savior Jesus Christ (1 Corinthians 15:1–4). This is the faith by which we began, and it is the same faith by which we are to "stand" and "walk" and "live." "As ye have therefore received Christ Jesus the Lord, so walk ye in him."

⌒ Miles Stanford (1914 –1999)

ARE YOUR DAYS GETTING BETTER?

The righteous thrive like a palm tree and grow like a cedar tree in Lebanon.

Psalm 92:12

Seeing that, in this earthly prison of the body, no man is supplied with strength sufficient to hasten in his course with due alacrity, while the greater number are so oppressed with weakness, that hesitating, and halting, and even crawling on the ground, they make little progress, let every one of us go as far as his humble ability enables him, and prosecute the journey once begun.

No one will travel so badly as not daily to make some degree of progress. This, therefore, let us never cease to do, that we may daily advance in the way of the Lord; and let us not despair because of the slender measure of success. How little soever the success may correspond with our wish, our labour is not lost when to-day is better than yesterday, provided with true singleness of mind we keep our aim, and aspire to the goal, not speaking flattering things to ourselves, nor indulging our vices, but making it our constant endeavour to become better, until we attain to goodness itself. If during the whole course of our life we seek and follow, we shall at length attain it, when relieved from the infirmity of flesh we are admitted to full fellowship with God.

~ John Calvin (1509–1564)

THE ART OF MANFISHING

"Follow Me," He told them, "and I will make you fish for people!"

Matthew 4:19

O power and life from God in ordinances is sweet. Seek it for thyself, and seek it for thy hearers. Acknowledge thine own weakness and uselessness without it, and so cry incessantly for it, that the Lord may drive the fish into the net, when thou art spreading it out. Have an eye to this power, when thou art preaching; and think not thou to convert men by the force of reason: if thou do, thou wilt be beguiled.

What an honorable thing is it to be fishers of men! How great an honor shouldst thou esteem it, to be a catcher of souls! We are workers together with God, says the apostle. If God has ever so honored thee, O that thou knewest it that thou mightst bless His holy name, that ever made such a poor fool as thee to be a co-worker with Him. God has owned thee to do good to those who were before caught. O my soul, bless Thou the Lord. Lord, what am I, or what is my father's house, that Thou hast brought me to this?

⌒ Thomas Boston (1677–1732)

COME, SINNERS, TO THE GOSPEL FEAST
(LUKE 14:16–24)

Come, sinners, to the gospel feast, Let every soul be Jesus' guest;
Ye need not one be left behind, For God hath bidden all mankind.
Sent by my Lord, on you I call, The invitation is to ALL:

Come, all the world; come, sinner, thou! All things in Christ
are ready now. Come, all ye souls by sin opprest, Ye restless wander-
ers after rest, Ye poor, and maimed, and halt, and blind, In Christ
a hearty welcome find.

Come, and partake the gospel feast; Be saved from sin; in
Jesus rest; O taste the goodness of your God, And eat His flesh, and
drink His blood! Ye vagrant souls, on you I call; (O that my voice
could reach you all!)

Ye all may now be justified, Ye all may live, for Christ hath
died. My message as from God receive, Ye all may come to Christ,
and live; O let His love your hearts constrain, Nor suffer Him to
die in vain! His love is mighty to compel; His conquering love consent to feel, Yield to His love's resistless power, And fight against
your God no more.

See Him set forth before your eyes, That precious, bleeding
sacrifice! His offered benefits embrace, And freely now be saved by
grace. This is the time; no more delay! This is the acceptable day,
Come in, this moment, at His call, And live for Him who died
for all.

~ Charles Wesley (1707–1788)

CHRISTIAN DEVELOPMENT PROCESS

But grow in the grace and knowledge of our Lord and Savior Jesus Christ. To Him be the glory both now and to the day of eternity. Amen.

2 Peter 3:18

Since the Christian life matures and becomes fruitful by the principle of growth, rather than by struggle and "experiences," much time is involved. Unless we see and acquiesce to this, there is bound to be constant frustration, to say nothing of resistance to our Father's development processes for us…

A. H. Strong illustrates, "A student asked the President of his school whether he could not take a shorter course than the one prescribed. 'Oh yes,' replied the President, 'but then it depends upon what you want to be. When God wants to make an oak, He takes an hundred years, but when He wants to make a squash, He takes six months.'…Growth is not a uniform thing in the tree or in the Christian, In some single months there is more growth than in all the year besides. During the rest of the year, however, there is solidification, without which the green timber would be useless. The period of rapid growth, when woody fiber is actually deposited between the bark and the trunk, occupies but four to six weeks."

There are no shortcuts to reality!… Unless the time factor is acknowledged from the heart, there is always danger of turning to the false enticement of a shortcut via the means of "experiences," and "blessings," where one becomes pathetically enmeshed in the vortex of ever-changing "feelings," adrift from the moorings of scriptural facts.

~ Miles Stanford (1914 –1999)

OUR DUAL PROBLEM: SINS AND SIN
(PART 1)

If we confess our sins, He is faithful and righteous to forgive us our sins and to cleanse us from all unrighteousness.

1 John 1:9

No matter how many sins I commit, it is always the one sin principle that leads to them. I need forgiveness for my sins, but I need also deliverance from the power of sin. The former touches my conscience, the latter my life. I may receive forgiveness for all my sins, but because of my sin I have, even then, no abiding peace of mind. When God's light first shines into my heart my one cry is for forgiveness, for I realize I have committed sins before Him; but when once I have received forgiveness of sins I make a new discovery, namely, the discovery of sin, and I realize not only that I have committed sins before God but that there is something wrong within.

I discover that I have the nature of a sinner. There is an inward inclination to sin, a power within that draws to sin. When that power breaks out I commit sins. I may seek and receive forgiveness, but then I sin once more. So life goes on in a vicious circle of sinning and being forgiven and then sinning again. I appreciate the blessed fact of God's forgiveness, but I want something more than that: I want deliverance. I need forgiveness for what I have done, but I need also deliverance from what I am.

~ Watchmen Nee (1903–1972)

GOD'S DUAL REMEDY:
THE BLOOD AND THE CROSS
(PART 2)

They are justified freely by His grace through the redemption that is in Christ Jesus. God presented Him as a propitiation through faith in His blood, to demonstrate His righteousness, because in His restraint God passed over the sins previously committed.

Romans 3:24–25

Thus in the first eight chapters of Romans two aspects of salvation are presented to us: firstly, the forgiveness of our sins, and secondly, our deliverance from sin. But now, in keeping with this fact, we must notice a further difference. In the first part of Romans 1 to 8, we twice have reference to the Blood of the Lord Jesus, in chapter 3:25 and in chapter 5:9. In the second, a new idea is introduced in chapter 6:6, where we are said to have been "crucified" with Christ.

The argument of the first part gathers round that aspect of the work of the Lord Jesus which is represented by "the Blood" shed for our justification through "the remission of sins." This terminology is however not carried on into the second section, where the argument centers now in the aspect of His work represented by "the Cross," that is to say, by our union with Christ in His death, burial and resurrection. This distinction is a valuable one. We shall see that the Blood deals with what we have done, whereas the Cross deals with what we are. The Blood disposes of our sins, while the Cross strikes at the root of our capacity for sin.

~ Watchman Nee (1903–1972)

GROWING IN CHRIST

I pursue as my goal the prize promised by God's heavenly call in Christ Jesus.

Philippians 3:14

Graham Scroggie affirmed: "Spiritual renewal is a gradual process. All growth is progressive, and the finer the organism, the longer the process. It is from measure to measure: thirtyfold, sixtyfold, an hundredfold. It is from stage to stage: 'first the blade, then the ear, and after that, the full corn in the ear.' And it is from day to day. How varied these are! There are great days, days of decisive battles, days of crisis in spiritual history, days of triumph in Christian service, days of the right hand of God upon us. But there are also idle days, days apparently useless, when even prayer and holy service seem a burden. Are we, in any sense, renewed in these days? Yes, for any experience which makes us more aware of our need of God must contribute to spiritual progress, unless we deny the Lord who bought us."

It takes time to get to know ourselves; it takes time and eternity to get to know our Infinite Lord Jesus Christ. Today is the day to put our hand to the plow, and irrevocably set our heart on His goal for us—that we "may know him, and the power of his resurrection, and the fellowship of his sufferings, being made conformable unto his death" (Phil. 3:10).

~ Miles Stanford (1914–1999)

GOD'S TEMPLE, WE ARE

Only be on your guard and diligently watch yourselves, so that you don't forget the things your eyes have seen and so that they don't slip from your mind as long as you live. Teach them to your children and your grandchildren.

Deuteronomy 4:9

Every living creature possesses within himself, by the gift of God, the Ordainer of all things, certain resources for self protection. Investigate nature with attention, and you will find that the majority of brutes have an instinctive aversion from what is injurious; while, on the other hand, by a kind of natural attraction, they are impelled to the enjoyment of what is beneficial to them. Wherefore also God our Teacher has given us this grand injunction, in order that what brutes possess by nature may accrue to us by the aid of reason, and that what is performed by brutes unwittingly may be done by us through careful attention and constant exercise of our reasoning faculty.

We are to be diligent guardians of the resources given to us by God, ever shunning sin as brutes shun poisons…Take heed to thyself, that thou mayest be able to discern between the noxious and the wholesome… Look well around thee, that thou mayest be delivered "as a gazelle from the net and a bird from the snare." It is because of her keen sight that the gazelle cannot be caught in the net. It is her keen sight that gives her her name. And the bird, if only she take heed, mounts on her light wing far above the wiles of the hunter.

～ Henry Wace (1836–1924)

THE PRAYER OF ST. FRANCIS

Take delight in the LORD, and He will give you your heart's desires.

Psalm 37:4

A PRAYER FOR PEACE, GROWTH, AND RECOVERY

Lord, make me an instrument of Your peace.

Where there is hatred, let me sow love;

Where there is injury, pardon;

Where there is doubt, faith;

Where there is despair, hope;

Where there is darkness, light;

Where there is sadness, joy.

O Divine Master, grant that I may not so much

seek to be consoled as to console;

To be understood as to understand;

To be loved as to love.

For it is in giving that we receive.

It is in pardoning that we are pardoned.

It is in dying that we are born to eternal life.

~ St. Francis of Assisi (1182–1226)

UNION WITH GOD

He brought me up from a desolate pit, out of the muddy clay, and set my feet on a rock, making my steps secure.

Psalm 40:2

We should be indeed purely, simply, and wholly at one with the one eternal Will of God, or altogether without will, so that the created will should flow out into the eternal Will and be swallowed up and lost in it, so that the eternal Will alone should do and leave undone in us. Now observe what may be of use to us in attaining this object. Religious exercises cannot do this, nor words, nor works, nor any creature or work done by a creature.

We must therefore give up and renounce all things, suffering them to be what they are, and enter into union with God. Yet the outward things must be; and sleeping and waking, walking and standing still, speaking and being silent, must go on as long as we live…when God Himself dwells in a man; as we plainly see in the case of Christ. Moreover, where there is this union, which is the outflow of the Divine light and dwells in its beams, there is no spiritual pride nor boldness of spirit, but unbounded humility and a lowly broken heart; there is also an honest and blameless walk, justice, peace, contentment, and every virtue… Be well assured of this.

～ Johannes Eckhart (1260–1327)

PRAYER AS DESIRING SOMEONE'S GOOD

Even before they call, I will answer; while they are still speaking, I will hear.

Isaiah 65:24

Prayer is expressed through various modes. There are petitions and intercessions; sometimes agony, tear, and fasting. I am especially intrigued by the prayer that comes wafting into our mind, that tugs at our heart as an inward desire to pray a particular blessing upon some individual, whether a loved one or a stranger. Often we have no way to trace the efficacy of such prayers. But over the years I have occasionally discovered that such "inward desire" prayers for others have been answered in a definite way.

I was reminded of one such incident when coming upon the March 8, 1988 entry in my journal. I was working at the Des Moines, Iowa post office. A number of weeks prior to the journal entry I had a quiet, easy, simple inward desire to pray for a woman that I knew only slightly upon seeing her working at a distance. My prayer desire was that she would seek and find God, supposing her to be a woman of the world and without any special interest in things spiritual. Several weeks later I happened to be working near her and heard her carrying on a conversation with a Christian man. She related that she had recently come to Christ, was attending church, and attempting to read and understand the Bible.

~ Raymond V. Banner (1937–)

METHOD OF GRACE IN THE GOSPEL REDEMPTION

He who calls you is faithful, who also will do it.

1 *Thessalonians* 5:24

It is…a great design of the enemy of mankind, to corrupt persons of eminent rank and quality both in religion and morality; and by their influence and example, to infect and poison the whole body politic; and his success herein deserves to be greatly lamented and bewailed. Persons of eminency are more especially obliged to shun base and sordid actions. Hierom professed he saw nothing desirable in nobility, except this, that such persons are bound by a certain kind of necessity, not to degenerate from the probity, or stain the glory of their ancestors.

But alas! how many in our times have not only exposed Christianity to contempt, but obscured the glory of their own families, and the kingdom in which they had their birth and breeding…In this general corruption it is very hard to escape infection; many are compelled to be evil, lest they should be accounted vile, and incur the offence of God, to avoid the slights and censures of men…It was an excellent apology that Tertullian made for the Christians of his time, against the Gentiles "Wherein (saith he) do we offend you, if we believe there are other pleasures? if we will not partake with, you in your delights, it is only for our own injury: we reject your pleasures, and you are not delighted with ours."

— John Flavel (1630–1691)

OUR DAILY HOMILY

"No, my lord," Hannah replied. "I am a woman with a broken heart. I haven't had any wine or beer; I've been pouring out my heart before the LORD.

1 Samuel 1:15

Is your face darkened by the bitterness of your soul? Perhaps the enemy has been vexing you sorely; or there is an unrealized hope, an unfulfilled purpose. in your life; or, perchance, the Lord seems to have forgotten you. Poor sufferer, there is nothing for it but to pour out your soul before the Lord. Empty out its contents in confession and prayer. God knows it all; yet tell Him, as if He knew nothing. "Ye people, pour out your hearts before Him. God is a refuge for us." "In everything, by prayer and supplication make your requests known unto God."

As we pour out our bitterness, God pours in His peace. Weeping goes out of one door whilst joy enters at another. We transmit the cup of tears to the Man of Sorrows, and He hands it back to us filled with the blessings of the new covenant. Some day you will come to the spot where you wept and prayed, bringing your offering of praise and thanksgiving.

⌒ F. B. Meyer (1847–1929)

WE WILL BE PERFECT!

God—His way is perfect; the word of the LORD is pure. He is a shield to all who take refuge in Him.

Psalm 18:30

We may consider the state of our minds in glory. The faculties of our souls shall then be made perfect, Hebrews 12:23, "The spirits of just men made perfect." (1.) Freed from all the clogs of the flesh, and all its influence upon them, and restraint of their powers in their operation (2.) Perfectly purified from all principles of instability and variety—of all inclinations unto things sensual and carnal, and all contrivances of self-preservation or advancement—being wholly transformed into the image of God in spirituality and holiness.

And to take in the state of our bodies after the resurrection; even they also, in all their powers and senses, shall be made entirely subservient unto the most spiritual actings of our minds in their highest elevation by the light of glory. Hereby shall we be enabled and fitted eternally to abide in the contemplation of the glory of Christ with joy and satisfaction. The understanding shall be always perfected with the vision of God, and the affections cleave inseparably to him—which is blessedness…It is Christ alone who is the likeness and image of God. When we awake in the other world, with our minds purified and rectified, the beholding of Him shall be always satisfying unto us.

~ John Owen (1616–1683)

THE ACCESSION

The voice that from the glory came To tell how Moses died unseen, And waken Joshua's spear of flame To victory on the mountains green, Its trumpet tones are sounding still, When Kings or Parents pass away, They greet us with a cheering thrill Of power and comfort in decay. Behind the soft bright summer cloud That makes such haste to melt and die, Our wistful gaze is oft allow'd A glimpse of the unchanging sky: Let storm and darkness do their worst; For the lost dream the heart may ache, The heart may ache, but may not burst: Heaven will not leave thee nor forsake.

One rock amid the weltering floods, One torch in a tempestuous night, One changeless pine in fading woods: Such is the thought of Love and Might, True Might and ever-present Love, When Death is busy near the throne, And Sorrow her keen sting would prove On Monarchs orphan'd and alone In that lorn hour and desolate, Who could endure a crown? but He, Who singly bore the world's sad weight, Is near, to whisper, "Lean on Me: "Thy days of toil, thy nights of care, "Sad lonely dreams in crowded hall, "Darkness within, while pageants glare "Around—the Cross supports them all.

"O Promise of undying Love! While Monarchs seek thee for repose, Far in the nameless mountain cove Each pastoral heart thy bounty knows. Ye, who in place of shepherds true Come trembling to their awful trust, Lo here the fountain to imbue With strength and hope your feeble dust. Not upon Kings or Priests alone The power of that dear word is spent; It chants to all in softest tone The lowly lesson of Content: Heaven's light is pour'd on high and low; To high and low Heaven's Angel spake; "Resign thee to thy weal or woe; I ne'er will leave thee nor forsake."

~ John Keble (1792–1866)

MEANINGFUL PRAYER

I call on You, God, because You will answer me; listen closely to me; hear what I say.

Psalm 17:6

Stop a moment and think. Is it not often the case, when men stand up to pray in public, or kneel down to pray in private, that they are thinking far more of what they are asking for than they are of the great God who made heaven and earth, and who has all power? Is it not often the case that in our prayers our thoughts are wandering off everywhere? We take the name of God on our lips, but there is no real conscious approach to God in our hearts.

If there is to be any power in our prayer, if our prayer is to get anything, the first thing to be sure of when we pray is that we really have come into the presence of God, and are really speaking to Him. Oh, let those two words, "to God," "to God," "to God," sink deep into your heart; and from this time on never pray, never utter one syllable of prayer, until you are sure that you have come into the presence of God and are really talking to Him.

～ R. A. Torrey (1856–1928)

COME AND DINE

Again, he sent out other slaves, and said, "Tell those who are invited: Look, I've prepared my dinner; my oxen and fattened cattle have been slaughtered, and everything is ready. Come to the wedding banquet."

Matthew 22:4

Let the King of Heaven and Earth say this to you. In honor of His Son He has prepared a great supper. There the Son bears His human nature. There are all the children of men, dear and precious to the Father, and He has caused them to be invited to the great festival of the Divine love. He is prepared to receive and honor them there as guests and friends. He will feed them with His heavenly food. He will bestow upon them the gifts and energies of everlasting life.

O my soul, thou also hast received this heavenly invitation. To be asked to eat with the King of Glory: how it behooves thee to embrace and be occupied with this honor. How desirous must you be to prepare yourself for this feast. How you must long that you should be in dress and demeanor, and language and disposition, all that may be rightly expected of one who is invited to the court of the King of kings. Glorious invitation! I think of the banquet itself and what it has cost the great God to prepare it…I think of the blessing of the banquet. The dying are fed with the power of a heavenly life, the lost are restored to their places in the Father's house, those that thirst after God are satisfied with God Himself and with His love. Glorious invitation!

— Andrew Murray (1828–1917)

ACCEPTANCE

Therefore, since we have been declared righteous by faith, we have peace with God through our Lord Jesus Christ.

Romans 5:1

There are two questions that every believer must settle as soon as possible. The one is, Does God fully accept me? and, If so, upon what basis does He do so? This is crucial. What devastation often permeates the life of one, young or old, rich or poor, saved or unsaved, who is not sure of being accepted, even on the human level. Yet so many believers, whether "strugglers" or "vegetators," move through life without this precious fact to rest and build upon: "Having predestinated us unto the adoption of children by Jesus Christ to himself, according to the good pleasure of his will, to the praise of the glory of his grace, wherein he hath made us accepted in the beloved" (Ephesians 1:5–6).

Every believer is accepted by the Father, in Christ. The peace is God's toward us, through His Beloved Son—upon this, our peace is to be based. God is able to be at peace with us through our Lord Jesus Christ, "having made peace by the blood of his cross" (Colossians 1:20). And we must never forget that His peace is founded solely on the work of the cross, totally apart from anything whatsoever in or from us, since "God commendeth his love toward us, in that, while we were yet sinners, Christ died for us" (Romans 5:8).

〜 Miles Stanford (1914–1999)

TOWARD THE GOAL

I pursue as my goal the prize promised by God's heavenly call in Christ Jesus.

Philippians 3:14

Seeing that, in this earthly prison of the body, no man is supplied with strength sufficient to hasten in his course with due alacrity, while the greater number are so oppressed with weakness, that hesitating, and halting, and even crawling on the ground, they make little progress, let every one of us go as far as his humble ability enables him, and prosecute the journey once begun. No one will travel so badly as not daily to make some degree of progress. This, therefore, let us never cease to do, that we may daily advance in the way of the Lord; and let us not despair because of the slender measure of success.

How little soever the success may correspond with our wish, our labour is not lost when to-day is better than yesterday, provided with true singleness of mind we keep our aim, and aspire to the goal, not speaking flattering things to ourselves, nor indulging our vices, but making it our constant endeavour to become better, until we attain to goodness itself. If during the whole course of our life we seek and follow, we shall at length attain it, when relieved from the infirmity of flesh we are admitted to full fellowship with God.

～ John Calvin (1509–1564)

CALL TO LEADERSHIP
(PART 1)

So that you may walk worthy of the Lord, fully pleasing to Him,
bearing fruit in every good work and growing in the knowledge of God.

Colossians 1:10

Thou'lt think and with great confidence too, that thou art in a condition, to guide Souls in the way of the Spirit, and perhaps, that may be secret Vanity, spiritual Pride, and plain Blindness; seeing besides, that this high employment requires supernatural Light, total abstraction, and other qualities...the Grace of a Call is also necessary, without which all is but vanity, confidence and self-conceit; because, tho' it be a holy and good thing to guide Souls, and conduct them to Contemplation; yet how know'st thou that God would have thee so employed?

And though thou knowest (which yet is not easy) that thou hast great Light and Experience, yet what evidence hast thou that the Lord would have thee to be of that Profession? This Ministry is of such importance that it is not our parts to take it upon us, until it please God...otherwise it would be a heavy prejudice to us, though it might be profitable to our Neighbour. What availeth it us to gain the whole World to God, if our own Soul thereby suffer detriment?

~ Miguel de Molinos (1628–1696)

CALL TO LEADERSHIP
(PART 2)

Howsoever evident it may be to thee, that thy Soul is endowed with internal light and experience; the best thing still that thou canst do, is to keep quiet and resigned in thine own nothingness, until God call thee for the Good of Souls: That belongs only to him, who knows thy sufficiency and abstraction: It is not thy part to make that judgment, neither to press into that Ministry...if thou are governed by thine own opinion and judgment, in an affair of so high concern, self-love will blind, undo, and deceive thee.

If then experience, light, and sufficiency are not sufficient, without the grace of a Call to qualifie one for that employment, how must it be without sufficiency? how must it be without internal light? without due experience, which are gifts not communicated to all Souls; but to abstracted and resigned Souls, and to such as have advanced to perfect annihilation, by the way of terrible tribulation, and passive purgation...

O how many self confident men by their own judgment and opinion, undertake this Ministry; and instead of pleasing God...are filled with Earth, Straw, and Self-conceit! Be quiet and Resigned, renounce thy own Judgment and Desire, sink down into the Abyss of thy own Insufficiency and Nothingness; for there only thou'lt find God, the true Light, thy Happiness, and greatest Perfection.

~ Miguel de Molinos (1628–1696)

EVERY MAN'S NEED OF A REFUGE

Each will be like a shelter from the wind, a refuge from the rain, like streams of water in a dry land and the shade of a massive rock in an arid land.

Isaiah 32:2

Christ is a hiding-place from the wrath to come. Now, of course, I cannot prove that from experience, for it lies in the future; but I can prove it by an argument that is unanswerable. That argument is this: the Christ that has power to save men from the power of sin now certainly has power to save them from the consequences of sin hereafter. Is not that a good argument? Let me add, that any religion that is not saving you from the power of sin to-day will not save you from the consequences of sin in eternity. There is a lot of religion in this world that is absolutely, worthless. People tell you that they are Christians and that they are religious. They are saying their prayers, and doing all sorts of things.

I will ask you a question: "Have you got that kind of faith in Jesus Christ that is saving you from the power of sin today?" If you have, you have that kind of faith in Jesus Christ that will save you from the consequences of sin hereafter. But if you have that kind of faith in Jesus Christ which after all is not faith, which it not saving you now, you have that kind of faith in Jesus Christ that won't save you from the penalty of sin hereafter.

Friends, Jesus Christ is a refuge, a hiding-place from experience and its accusations, from the power of sin within, from the power of Satan, from the wrath to come, from all that man needs a hiding-place from. Who will come to this hiding-place…

~ R. A. Torrey (1856–1928)

WE WILL SERVE THE LORD!

...As for me and my house, we will serve the Lord.

Joshua 24:15 KJV

It is true indeed, visit our churches, and you may perhaps see something of the form of godliness still subsisting amongst us; but even that is scarcely to be met with in private houses. So that were the blessed angels to come, as in the patriarchal age, and observe our spiritual economy at home, would they not be tempted to say as Abraham to Abimilech, "Surely, the fear of God is not in this place?" (Gen. 20:11 KJV).

How such a general neglect of family-religion first began to overspread the Christian world, is difficult to determine. As for the primitive Christians, I am positive it was not so with them: No, they had not so learned Christ, as falsely to imagine religion was to be confined solely to their assemblies for public worship; but, on the contrary, behaved with such piety and exemplary holiness in their private families, that St. Paul often styles their house a church: "Salute such a one, says he, and the church which is in his house." And, I believe, we must for ever despair of seeing a primitive spirit of piety revived in the world, till we are so happy as to see a revival of primitive family religion; and persons unanimously resolving with good old Joshua, in the words of the text, "As for me and my house, we will serve the Lord."

~ George Whitefield (1714–1770)

THE SHADOW OF THE ROCK

Because You are my helper; I will rejoice in the shadow of Your wings.

Psalm 63:7

Guarded by Omnipotence, the chosen of the Lord are always safe; for as they dwell in the holy place, hard by the mercy-seat, where the blood was sprinkled of old, the pillar of fire by night, the pillar of cloud by day, which ever hangs over the sanctuary, covers them also. The shadow of a rock is remarkably cooling, and so was the Lord Jesus eminently comforting to us.

The shadow of a rock is more dense, more complete, and more cool than any other shade; and so the peace which Jesus gives passeth all understanding, there is none like it. No chance beam darts through the rock-shade, nor can the heat penetrate as it will do in a measure through the foliage of a forest. Jesus is a complete shelter, and blessed are they who are "under His shadow." Let them take care that they abide there, and never venture forth to answer for themselves, or to brave the accusations of Satan. As with sin, so with sorrow of every sort: the Lord is the Rock of our refuge. No sun shall smite us, nor, any heat, because we are never out of Christ. The saints know where to fly, and they use their privilege.

~ Charles H. Spurgeon (1834–1892)

THE CHILD IN THE MIDST

Whoever welcomes one little child such as this in My name welcomes Me. And whoever welcomes Me does not welcome Me, but Him who sent Me.

Mark 9:37

What is the kingdom of Christ? A rule of love, of truth—a rule of service. The king is the chief servant in it. "The kings of the earth have dominion: it shall not be so among you." "The Son of Man came to minister." "My Father worketh hitherto, and I work." The great Workman is the great King, labouring for his own. So he that would be greatest among them, and come nearest to the King himself, must be the servant of all. It is like king like subject in the kingdom of heaven.

No rule of force, as of one kind over another kind. It is the rule of kind, of nature, of deepest nature—of God. If, then, to enter into this kingdom, we must become children, the spirit of children must be its pervading spirit throughout, from lowly subject to lowliest king. The lesson added by St Luke to the presentation of the child is: "For he that is least among you all, the same shall be great." And St Matthew says: "Whosoever shall humble himself as this little child, the same is greatest in the kingdom of heaven." Hence the sign that passes between king and subject. The subject kneels in homage to the kings of the earth: the heavenly king takes his subject in his arms. This is the sign of the kingdom between them. This is the all-pervading relation of the kingdom.

~ George MacDonald (1824–1905)

THE PRESENCE OF CHRIST

Immediately Jesus spoke to them. "Have courage! It is I. Don't be afraid."

Matthew 14:27

Think, first, of the presence of Christ lost. You know the disciples loved Christ, clung to Him, and with all their failings, they delighted in Him. But what happened? The Master went up into the mountain to pray, and sent them across the sea all alone without Him; there came a storm, and they toiled, rowed, and laboured, but the wind was against them, they made no progress, they were in danger of perishing, and how their hearts said, "Oh, if the Master only were here!" But His presence was gone. They missed Him.

Once before, they had been in a storm, and Christ had said, "Peace, be still," and all was well; but here they are in darkness, danger, and terrible trouble, and no Christ to help them. Ah, isn't that the life of many a believer at times? I get into darkness, I have committed sin, the cloud is on me, I miss the face of Jesus; and for days and days I work, worry, and labour; but it is all in vain, for I miss the presence of Christ. Oh, beloved, let us write that down, —the presence of Jesus lost is the cause of all our wretchedness and failure.

~ Andrew Murray (1828–1917)

PEACE WITH GOD

You will keep the mind that is dependent on You in perfect peace, for it is trusting in You.

Isaiah 26:3

There is Peace that comes from submission; tranquility of spirit, which is the crown and reward of obedience; repose, which is the very smile upon the face of faith, and all these things are given unto us along with the Grace and Mercy of our God. And the man that possesses this is at Peace with God, and at Peace with himself, so he may bear in his heart that singular blessing of a perfect tranquility and quiet amidst the distractions of duty, of sorrows, of losses, and of cares.

"In everything by prayer and supplication with thanksgiving let your requests be known unto God; and the Peace of God which passeth all understanding shall keep your hearts and minds in Christ Jesus." And he who is thus at friendship with God, and in harmony with himself, and at rest from sorrows and cares, will surely find no enemies amongst men with whom he must needs be at war, but will be a son of Peace, and walk the world, meeting in them all a friend and a brother. So all discords may be quieted; even thought still we have to fight the good fight of faith, we may do, like Gideon of old, build an altar to "Jehovah Shalom," the God of Peace.

~ Alexander Maclaren (1826–1910)

CROWN HIM WITH MANY CROWNS

Crown Him with many crowns
The Lamb upon His throne;
Hark how the heavenly anthem drowns
All music but its own. Awake, my soul, and sing
Of Him who died for thee
And hail Him as thy matchless King
Through all eternity.
Crown Him the Virgin's Son, The God incarnate born,
Whose arm those crimson trophies won
Which now His brow adorn; Fruit of the mystic rose,
As of that rose the stem; The root whence mercy ever flows,
The Babe of Bethlehem. Crown Him the Lord of Love.
Behold His hands and side, Rich wounds, yet visible above,
In beauty glorified. No angel in the sky
Can fully bear that sight,
But downward bends his wondering eye
At mysteries so bright! Crown Him the Lord of Life
Who triumphed o'er the grave
And rose victorious in the strife For those He came to save.
His glories now we sing Who died and rose on high,
Who died eternal life to bring And lives that death may die.
Crown Him the Lord of Heaven, Enthroned in worlds above,
Crown Him the King to whom is given
The wondrous name of Love.
Crown Him with many crowns As thrones before Him fall;
Crown Him, ye kings, with many crowns For He is King of all.

~ Matthew Bridges (1800–1894)

STAND UP FOR CHRIST

What then are we to say about these things? If God is for us, who is against us?

Romans 8:31

It is much easier to stand up for Christ than to be identified with Him. Most leaders of God's young people are strong for Christ, but they are not yet "weak with Christ." His weakness they fear and refuse, yet it is this very weakness that opens the door to Heaven's power. Little wonder that without this power there is such a scramble for the help of the world, the patronage of its princes, the loan of its resources, and the use of its wisdom. Remember, the early church employed none of these. Come to Corinth and listen to the apostle Paul. Facing that carnal and conceited world, he knew that he did not have "what it takes." Hear him confess, "I was with you in weakness and in fear, and in much trembling…That your faith should not stand in the wisdom of men, but in the power of God…I determined to know anything among you, save Jesus Christ, and Him crucified" (1 Cor. 2:3, 5).

~ L. E. Maxwell (1895–1984)

A FOUNTAIN OF JOY

You love Him, though you have not seen Him. And though not seeing Him now, you believe in Him and rejoice with inexpressible and glorious joy.

1 Peter 1:8

Happiness is caused by things that happen around me, and circumstances will mar it; but joy flows right on through trouble; joy flows on through the dark; joy flows in the night as well as in the day; joy flows all through persecution and opposition. It is an unceasing fountain bubbling up in the heart; a secret spring the world can't see and doesn't know anything about.

The Lord gives His people perpetual joy when they walk in obedience to Him. Joy is love exalted; peace is love in repose; long-suffering is love enduring; gentleness is love in society; goodness is love in action; faith is love on the battlefield; meekness is love in school; and temperance is love in training. The world does not understand theology or dogma, but it understands love and sympathy.

$\sim$ Dwight L. Moody (1837–1899)

PROOF FULFILLED

"Don't assume that I came to destroy the Law or the Prophets. I did not come to destroy but to fulfill."

Matthew 5:17

Every sacrifice lit…pointed as with flaming fingers to Calvary's cross! Nay all the centuries moved as in solemn procession to lay their tributes upon Golgotha. But that age of grand fulfillment was also the age of grander prophecies…. But the prophecies, fulfilled and fulfilling before our eyes, become a new miracle…adapted to prove omniscience as unmistakably as the miracles of two thousand years ago proved omnipotence. Scripture is seen by us as a colossal wheel, compassing all history with its gigantic and awful rim, and full of the eyes that tell of one who sees all things!

…We have before our very eyes some of the most awe-inspiring proofs of our holy religion. Disciples, who saw His miracles and had evidence of the senses, left us their witness to Christ. But, of many prophecies, they had only the record, while we have the evidence of or very senses to their fulfillment…. But he who can see prophecy fulfilled and not believe, is not to be persuaded by any other miracle…The Christian religion is the only religion that has ever dared to rest its claim upon either miracle or prophecy. The appeal to such supernatural signs is so bold, that its audacity is one proof of its genuineness.

Arthur T. Pierson (1867–1911)

GOD'S WORLD

In the beginning God created the heavens and the earth.

Genesis 1:1

The WORLD is not this little Cottage of Heaven and Earth. Though this be fair, it is too small a Gift. When God made the World He made the Heavens, and the Heavens of Heavens, and the Angels, and the Celestial Powers. These also are parts of the World: So are all those infinite and eternal Treasures that are to abide for ever, after the Day of Judgment. Neither are these, some here, and some there, but all every where, and at once to be enjoyed.

The WORLD is unknown, till the Value and Glory of it is seen: till the Beauty and the Serviceableness of its parts is considered. When you enter into it, it is an illimited field of Variety and Beauty: where you may lose yourself in the multitude of Wonders and Delights. But it is an happy loss to lose oneself in admiration at one's own Felicity: and to find GOD in exchange for oneself: Which we then do when we see Him in His Gifts, and adore His Glory.

~ Thomas Traherne (1636–1674)

UNSEEN

From ancient times no one has heard, no one has listened, no eye has seen any God except You, who acts on behalf of the one who waits for Him.

Isaiah 64:4

It was necessary for man's salvation that there should be a doctrine founded on revelation, as well as the philosophical sciences discovered by human reason. It was necessary, in the first place, because man is ordained to God as his end, who surpasses the comprehension of reason.

Men must have some foreknowledge of the end to which they ought to direct their intentions and actions. It was therefore necessary that some things which transcend human reason should be made known through divine revelation. It was necessary also that man should be instructed by divine revelation even in such things concerning God as human reason could discover. For such truth about God as could be discovered by reason would be known only by the few, and that after a long time, and mixed with many errors.

Now the whole salvation of man, which lies in God, depends on the knowledge of this truth. It was therefore necessary that men should be instructed in divine things through divine revelation, in order that their salvation might come to pass the more fittingly and certainly. It was necessary, therefore, that there should be a sacred doctrine given through revelation, as well as the philosophical sciences discovered by reason.

∼ Thomas Aquinas (1225–1274)

THE INFINITE CHRIST

Surely You desire integrity in the inner self, and You teach me wisdom deep within.

Psalm 51:6

Why are love, knowledge, wisdom, and goodness said to be infinite and eternal in God, capable of no increase or decrease, but always in the same highest state of existence? Why is His power eternal and omnipotent, His presence not here, or there, but everywhere The same? No reason can be assigned, but because nothing that is temporary, limited, or bounded can be in God. It is His nature to be that which He is, and all that He is, in an infinite, unchangeable degree, admitting neither higher, nor lower, neither here nor there, but always and everywhere in the same unalterable state of infinity.

If therefore wrath, rage, and resentment could be in the Deity itself, it must be an unbeginning, boundless, never-ceasing wrath, capable of no more, or less, no up or down, but always existing, always working, and breaking forth in the same strength, and everywhere equally burning in the height and depth of the abyssal Deity. There is no medium here; there must be either all or none, either no possibility of wrath, or no possibility of its having any bounds...For nothing can have any existence in God, but in the way and manner as His eternity, infinity, and omnipotence have their existence in Him. Have you anything to object to this?

∼ William Law (1686–1761)

MARTIN LUTHER WRITES
(PART 1)

Cannons and firearms are cruel and damnable machines. I believe them to have been the direct suggestion of the devil. Against the flying ball no valor avails; the soldier is dead, ere he sees the means of his destruction. If Adam had seen in a vision the horrible instruments his children were to invent, he would have died of grief.

War is one of the greatest plagues that can afflict humanity; it destroys religion, it destroys states, it destroys families. Any scourge, in fact, is preferable to it. Famine and pestilence become as nothing in comparison with it. Pestilence is the least evil of the three, and 'twas therefore David chose it, willing rather to fall into the hands of God than into those of pitiless man.

Great people and champions are special gifts of God, whom He gives and preserves: they do their work, and achieve great actions, not with vain imaginations, or cold and sleepy cogitations, but by motion of God. Even so 'twas with the prophets, St Paul, and other excelling people, who accomplished their work by God's special grace. The Book of Judges also shows how God wrought great matters through one single person.

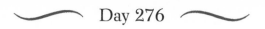
MARTIN LUTHER WRITES
(PART 2)

A valiant and brave soldier seeks rather to preserve one citizen than to destroy a thousand enemies, as Scipio the Roman said; therefore an upright soldier begins not a war lightly, or without urgent cause. True soldiers and captains make not many words, but when they speak, the deed is done.

They who take to force, give a great blow to the Gospel, and offend many people; they fish before the net, etc. The prophet Isaiah and St Paul say: "I will grind him (antichrist) to powder with the rod of my mouth, and will slay him with the spirit of my lips." With such weapons we must beat the pope. Popedom can neither be destroyed nor preserved by force; for it is built upon lies; it must therefore be turned upside down and destroyed with the word of truth. It is said: "Preach thou, I will give strength."

Every great champion is not fitted to govern; he that is a soldier, looks only after victories, how he may prevail, and keep the field; not after policy, how people and countries may be well governed. Yet Scipio, Hannibal, Alexander, Julius and Augustus Caesars looked also after government, and how good rule might be observed.

THANKFULNESS

If only they were wise, they would figure it out; they would understand their fate.

Deuteronomy 32:29

That which has the greatest tendency to excite the generality of fallen men to praise and thanksgiving, is a sense of God's private mercies, and particular benefits bestowed upon ourselves. For as these come nearer our own hearts, so they must be more affecting: and as they are peculiar proofs, whereby we may know, that God does in a more especial manner favor us above others, so they cannot but sensibly touch us; and if our hearts are not quite frozen, like coals of a refiner's fire, they must melt us down into thankfulness and love.

It was a consideration of the distinguishing favor God had shown to His chosen people Israel, and the frequent and remarkable deliverance wrought by Him in behalf of "those who go down to the Sea in ships, and occupy their business in great matters," that made the holy Psalmist break out so frequently as he does in this psalm, into this moving, pathetical exclamation, "that men would therefore praise the Lord for His goodness, and declare the wonders that He doeth for the children of men!" His expressing Himself in so fervent a manner, implies both the importance and neglect of the duty.

⁓ George Whitefield (1714–1770)

THE INTENTIONS
OF THE HEART

Wouldn't God have found this out, since He knows the secrets of the heart?

Psalm 44:21

God hath no regard to the multitude of words, but to the purity of the intent. His greatest content and glory at that time, is to see the Soul in silence, desirous, humble, quiet, and resigned. Proceed, persevere, pray, and hold thy peace; for where thou findest not a sentiment, thou'lt find a door whereby thou mayest enter into thine own nothingness; knowing thy self to be nothing, that thou can'st do nothing, nay, and that thou hast not so much as a good thought.

How many have begun this happy practice of Prayer, and Internal Recollection, and have left it off, pretending that they feel no pleasure, that they lose time, that their thoughts trouble them, and that that Prayer is not for them, whil'st they find not any sentiment of God, nor any ability to reason or discourse; whereas they might have believed, been silent, and had patience. All this is no more, but with ingratitude to hunt after sensible pleasures, suffering themselves to be transported with self-love, seeking themselves, and not God, because they cannot suffer a little pain and dryness, without reflecting on the infinite loss they sustain, whereas by the least act of reverence towards God, amidst dryness and sterility, they receive an eternal reward.

~ Miguel de Molinos (1628–1696)

WHO HAS SEEN HIM?

But the tax collector, standing far off, would not even raise his eyes to heaven but kept striking his chest and saying, "God, turn Your wrath from me—a sinner!"

Luke 18:13

I have had a clear view of Jesus. I have seen Him, felt Him, and I have known Him in a far deeper way than simply by the outward physical appearance; I have felt the reality of His life begin to burn in my heart. I have seen in Christ the glory of a life that is totally submitted to the sovereignty of God. That glory has begun to take hold of me, and I have begun to see that this is the one life that God expects of any man He made in His own image.

I have seen the marks of the cross upon Him, and by His grace the marks of the cross have been put upon me and I am no longer my own; I am bought with a price, redeemed by His precious blood. Yes, I have seen Him—not in the outward physical sense only, but in the inward sense of a deep spiritual reality. I have had a clear view of Jesus and my life will never the be same again. We all...the weakest, the poorest, the most sinful, the most defiled. The spiritual aristocracy of the church of Jesus Christ...the sinner saved by grace. It is the soul who has come like the publican of old and said, "God be merciful to me a sinner," and it is the soul bowed before Calvary and seeing (as Paul saw) the glory of God in the face of Jesus Christ.

～ Alan Redpath (1907–1989)

DEVOTION

Devote yourselves to prayer; stay alert in it with thanksgiving.

Colossians 4:2

Some think that when Devotion and sensible Pleasure are given them, they are Favours of God, that thence forward they have him, and that the whole life is to be spent in breathing after that delight; but it is a cheat, because it is no more, but a consolation of nature, and a pure reflexion, wherewith the Soul beholds what it does, and hinders the doing, or possibility of doing any thing, the acquisition of the true light, and the making of one step in the way of perfection.

The Soul is a pure Spirit and is not felt; and so the internal acts, and of the will, as being the acts of the Soul and spiritual, are not sensible: Hence the Soul knows not if it liveth, nor, for most part, is sensible if it acteth. From this thou mayest infer, that that Devotion and sensible Pleasure, is not God, not Spirit, but the product of Nature; that therefore thou oughtest to set light by, and despise it, but firmly to persevere in Prayer, leaving thy self to the conduct of God, who will be to thee light in aridity and darkness.

~ Miguel de Molinos (1628–1696)

PRIVILEGE AND EXPERIENCE

"Son," he said to him, "you are always with me, and everything I have is yours."

Luke 15:31

"Thou are ever with me"; I am always near thee; thou canst dwell every hour of thy life in My presence, and all I have is for thee. I am a father, with a loving father's heart. I will withhold no good thing from thee. In these promises, we have the rich privilege of God's heritage. We have, in the first place, unbroken fellowship with Him. A father never sends his child away with the thought that he does not care about his child knowing that he loves him.

The father longs to have his child believe that he has the light of his father's countenance upon him all the day—that, if he sends the child away to school, or anywhere that necessity compels, it is with a sense of sacrifice of parental feelings. If it be so with an earthly father, what think you of God? Does He not want every child of His to know that he is constantly living in the light of His countenance? This is the meaning of that word, "Son, thou art ever with me."…Let that thought into your hearts—that the child of God is called to this blessed privilege, to live every moment of his life in fellowship with God. He is called to enjoy the full light of His countenance.

~ Andrew Murray (1828–1917)

DAILY FELLOWSHIP WITH GOD

Draw near to God, and He will draw near to you. Cleanse your hands, sinners, and purify your hearts, double-minded people!

James 4:8

The first and chief need of our Christian life is, Fellowship with God. The Divine life within us comes from God, and is entirely dependent upon Him. As I need every moment afresh the air to breathe, as the s sun every moment afresh sends down its light, so it is only in direct living communication with God that my soul can be strong. The manna of one day was corrupt when the next day came. I must every day have fresh grace from heaven, and I obtain it only in direct waiting upon God Himself.

Begin each day by tarrying before God, and letting Him touch you. Take time to meet God. To this end, let your first act in your devotion be a setting yourself still before God. In prayer, or worship, everything depends upon God taking the chief place. I must bow quietly before Him in humble faith and adoration, speaking thus within my heart: "God is. God is near. God is love, longing to communicate Himself to me. God the Almighty One, Who worketh all in all, is even now waiting to work in me, and make Himself known." Take time, till you know God is very near. When you have given God His place of honour, glory, and power, take your place of deepest lowliness, and seek to be filled with the Spirit of humility.

～ Andrew Murray (1828–1917)

INTERCESSION

In the same way the Spirit also joins to help in our weakness, because we do not know what to pray for as we should, but the Spirit Himself intercedes for us with unspoken groanings.

Romans 8:26

Thus the Spirit who cries "Abba Father" in the hearts of the blessed, knowing with solicitude that their sighing in this tabernacle can but weigh down the already fallen or transgressors, "more than intercedes with God in sighs unspeakable," for the great love and sympathy He feels for men taking our sighs upon himself; and, by virtue of the wisdom that resides in Him, beholding our Soul humbled "unto dust" and shut within the body "of humiliation," He employs no common sighs when He more than intercedes with God but unspeakable ones akin to the unutterable words which a man may not speak.

Not content to intercede with God, this Spirit intensifies His intercession, "more than intercedes," for those who more than conquer, as I believe such as Paul was, who says "Nay in all these we more than conquer." He simply "intercedes," I think, not for those who more than conquer, nor again for those who are conquered, but for those who conquer. Akin to the saying "what we ought to pray we know not how to as we ought, but the Spirit more than intercedes with God in sighs unspeakable," is the passage "I will pray with the Spirit, and I will pray with the understanding also: I will sing with the spirit; and I will sing with the understanding also."

～ Origen (185–254)

TEMPTATION
(PART 1)

I am not praying that You take them out of the world but that You protect them from the evil one.

John 17:15

As we have no strength to resist a temptation when it doth come, when we are entered into it, but shall fall under it, without a supply of sufficiency of grace from God; so to reckon that we have no power or wisdom to keep ourselves from entering into temptation, but must be kept by the power and wisdom of God, is a preserving principle. We are in all things "kept by the power of God" (1 Peter 1:5). This our Saviour instructs us in, not only by directing us to pray that we be not led into temptation, but also by His own praying for us, that we may be kept from it: "I pray not that thou shouldest take them out of the world, but that thou shouldest keep them from the evil"—that is, the temptations of the world unto evil, unto sin—which is all this is evil in the world; or from the evil one, who in the world makes use of the world unto temptation.

Christ prays His Father to keep us, and instructs us to pray that we be so kept. It is not, then, a thing in our own power. The ways of our entering into temptation are so many, various, and imperceptible, the means of it so efficacious and powerful—our weakness our unwatchfulness, so unspeakable—that we cannot in the least keep or preserve ourselves from it. We fail both in wisdom and power for this work.

～ John Owen (1616–1683)

TEMPTATION
(PART 2)

Let the heart, then commune with itself and say, "I am poor and weak; Satan is subtle, cunning, powerful, watching constantly for advantages against my soul; the world earnest, pressing, and full of specious pleas, innumerable pretences, and ways of deceit; my own corruption violent and tumultuating, enticing, entangling, conceiving sin, and warring in me, against me; occasions and advantages of temptation innumerable in all things I have done or suffer, in all businesses and persons with whom I converse; the first beginnings of temptation insensible and plausible, so that, left unto myself, I shall not know I am ensnared, until my bonds be made strong, and sin hath got ground in my heart: therefore on God alone will I rely for preservation, and continually will I look up to him on that account."

This will make the soul be always committing itself to the care of God, resting itself on Him, and to do nothing, undertake nothing, etc, without asking counsel of Him. So that a double advantage will arise from the observation of this direction, both of singular use for the soul's preservation from the evil feared …

～ John Owen (1616–1683)

THE WAY

But it is from Him that you are in Christ Jesus, who became God-given wisdom for us—our righteousness, sanctification, and redemption.

1 Corinthians 1:30

We know God only by Jesus Christ. Without this mediator, all communion with God is taken away; through Jesus Christ we know God…in proof of Jesus Christ we have the prophecies, which are solid and palpable proofs. And these prophecies, being accomplished and proved true by the event, mark the certainty of these truths and, therefore, the divinity of Christ. In Him, then, and through Him, we know God.

Apart from Him, and without the Scripture, without original sin, without a necessary mediator promised and come, we cannot absolutely prove God, nor teach right doctrine and right morality. But through Jesus Christ, and in Jesus Christ, we prove God, and teach morality and doctrine. Jesus Christ is, then, the true God of men. But we know at the same time our wretchedness; for this God is none other than the Saviour of our wretchedness. So we can only know God well by knowing our iniquities.

Therefore those who have known God, without knowing their wretchedness, have not glorified Him, but have glorified themselves. Not only do we know God by Jesus Christ alone, but we know ourselves only by Jesus Christ. We know life and death only through Jesus Christ. Apart from Jesus Christ, we do not know what is our life, nor our death, nor God, nor ourselves.

～ Blaise Pascal (1623–1662)

FOLLY

But look: joy and gladness, butchering of cattle, slaughtering of sheep, eating of meat, and drinking of wine—"Let us eat and drink, for tomorrow we die!"

Isaiah 22:13

Then there are those who think that life is this: "Eat and drink, for tomorrow we shall die." They view death as a deep sleep and a forgetting—"sleep and death, twin brothers"[as the saying goes]. And men think them religious! But there are others who reckon this present life of very little value. They are guided by this alone—to know the true God and His Word, to know the unity of the Father with the Son, the fellowship of the Father with the Son, what the Spirit is, what unity exists between these three, the Spirit, the Son, and the Father, and what is their distinction in unity.

These it is who know that the life for which we look is far better than can be told, if we arrive at it pure from all wrongdoing. These it is whose charity extends to the point of loving not only their friends, for, the Scripture says, "If you love those who love you, and lend to those who lend to you, what credit is it to you?" Since we are such and live this way to escape condemnation, can anyone doubt that we are religious? These points, however, are trifles from a great store, a few taken from many, lest we should trouble you further. For those who test honey and whey judge by a taste if the whole is good.

~ Cyril C. Richardson (1909–1976)

MARVELOUS GRACE

Indeed, we have all received grace after grace from His fullness.

John 1:16

I wish all professors to fall in love with grace. All our songs should be of His free grace. We are but too lazy and careless in seeking of it; it is all our riches we have here, and glory in the bud. I wish that I could set out free grace. I was the law's man, and under the law, and under a curse; but grace brought me from under that hard lord, and I rejoice that I am grace's freeholder.

I pay tribute to none for heaven, seeing my land and heritage holdeth of Christ, my new King. Infinite wisdom has devised this excellent way of free-holding for sinners. It is a better way to heaven than the old way that was in Adam's days. It has this fair advantage, that no man's emptiness and want layeth an inhibition upon Christ, or hindereth His salvation; and that is far best for me. But our new Landlord putteth the names of devours, and Adam's forlorn heirs, and beggars, and the crooked and blind, in the free charters. Heaven and angels may wonder that we have got such a gate of sin and hell. Such a back-entry out of hell as Christ made, and brought out the captives by, is more than my poor shallow thoughts can comprehend.

～ Samuel Rutherford (1600–1661)

FIRMLY ESTABLISHED

Therefore, as you have received Christ Jesus the Lord, walk in Him, rooted and built up in Him and established in the faith, just as you were taught, overflowing with gratitude.

Colossians 2: 6–7

Be not deceived with strange doctrines, "nor give heed to fables and endless genealogies," and things in which the Jews make their boast. "Old things are passed away: behold, all things have become new." For if we still live according to the Jewish law, and the circumcision of the flesh, we deny that we have received grace. For the divinest prophets lived according to Jesus Christ. On this account also they were persecuted, being inspired by grace to fully convince the unbelieving that there is one God, the Almighty, who has manifested Himself by Jesus Christ His Son, who is His Word, not spoken, but essential. For He is not the voice of an articulate utterance, but a substance begotten by divine power, who has in all things pleased Him that sent Him.

~ Philip Schaff (1819–1893)

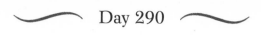

BROTHERLY LOVE

Above all, put on love—the perfect bond of unity.

Colossians 3:14

Let us therefore, with all haste, put an end to this [state of things]; and let us fall down before the Lord, and beseech Him with tears, that He would mercifully be reconciled to us, and restore us to our former seemly and holy practice of brotherly love. For [such conduct] is the gate of righteousness, which is set open for the attainment of life, as it is written, "Open to me the gates of righteousness; I will go in by them, and will praise the Lord: this is the gate of the Lord: the righteous shall enter in by it."

Although, therefore, many gates have been set open, yet this gate of righteousness is that gate in Christ by which blessed are all they that have entered in and have directed their way in holiness and righteousness, doing all things without disorder. Let a man be faithful: let him be powerful in the utterance of knowledge; let him be wise in judging of words; let him be pure in all his deeds; yet the more he seems to be superior to others [in these respects], the more humble-minded ought he to be, and to seek the common good of all, and not merely his own advantage.

∼ Philip Schaff (1819–1893)

EVERLASTING RIGHTEOUSNESS

Seventy weeks are decreed about your people and your holy city—to bring the rebellion to an end, to put a stop to sin, to wipe away iniquity, to bring in everlasting righteousness, to seal up vision and prophecy, and to anoint the most holy place.

Daniel 9:24

In the fullness of time descends the eternal Logos, "In the fullness of time God sent forth his Son made of a woman, made under the law, to redeem them that are under the law from the curse of it, being made a curse for us." The Lord Jesus Christ being clothed in human nature, fulfilled all righteousness; He submitted to every institution of God, and was pleased to obey the whole moral law; and afterwards, O can we think of it, O can you hear of it, without a heart leaping with joy, at last the Lord Jesus bled and died!

And when He was just expiring, just as He was about to bow down His head, and give up the ghost, what do ye think He said? He said, "It is finished!" As much as to say, "Now the arduous work, the difficult task I had undertaken, blessed be God, is now completely over; all the demands of the law are finished; now God's justice is satisfied; now a new and living way is opened by my blood to the holiest of all for poor sinners."…."Christ's obedience and death," all that Christ has done, and all that Christ has suffered for an elect world, for all that will believe on Him… Blessed be God for the epithet which in the text is put to this righteousness…but the angel calls it an everlasting righteousness: God give you to take the comfort of it!

~ George Whitefield (1714–1770)

READY?

Complete your outdoor work, and prepare your field; afterward, build your house.

Proverbs 24:27

We cannot shut our eyes to the fact that there is a fearful amount of laxity, unsubduedness, and self-indulgence going hand in hand with the evangelical profession of the day…so far as the intellect goes, into the truth of the sinner's title, who, if we are to judge from their style, deportment, and habits, are not "ready" in their moral condition—in the real state of their hearts. We are at times, we must confess, sadly cast down when we see our young friends decking their persons in the vain fashions of a vain and sinful world; feeding upon the vile literature that issues in such frightful profusion from the press; and actually singing vain songs and engaging in light and frivolous conversation.

It is impossible to reconcile such with "Be ye also ready." Those who have life in Christ, who are indwelt by the Holy Ghost, will be ready. But the mere professor—the one who has the truth in the head and on the lip, but not in the heart; who has the lamp of profession, but not the Spirit of life in Christ—will be shut out into outer darkness—in the everlasting misery of gloom and hell. Let us, as we take a solemn leave of you, put this question home to your very inmost soul, "Art thou ready?"

∼ C. H. Mackintosh (1820–1896)

DON'T BE DECEIVED

But if we walk in the light as He Himself is in the light, we have
fellowship with one another, and the blood of Jesus His Son cleanses us
from all sin.

1 John 1:7

Our Lord has said…unless we be born again from above, there is
no possible entrance into the kingdom of God…that which is born
of the devil can do nothing else but add sin to sin. To what end
do we pray, that "this day we may fall into no sin," if no such day
can be had? But if sinning can be made to cease in us for one day,
what can do this for us, but that which can do the same tomorrow?
What benefit in praying, that "God's will may be done on earth,
as it is in heaven," if the earth as long as it lasts must have as many
sinners, as it has men upon it?

How vainly does the church pray for the baptized person,
"that he may have power and strength to have victory, and to triumph against the devil, the world, and the flesh," if this victorious
triumph can never be obtained; if notwithstanding this baptism
and prayer, he must continue committing sin, and so be a servant
of sin, as long as he lives?…If at that same time we are to believe
that Christians, as long as they live, must in some degree or other
follow, and be led by the lusts of the flesh, the lust of the eyes, and
the pride of life?

～ William Law (1686–1761)

GIVE ALL UP TO CHRIST

You must follow the Lord your God and fear Him. You must keep His
commands and listen to His voice; you must worship Him and remain
faithful to Him.

Deuteronomy 13:4

Deal with God, and come to Him and say, "Lord of all, I belong to
Thee, I am absolutely at Thy disposal." Yield up yourselves. There
may be many who cannot go as Missionaries, but oh, come, give
up yourselves to God all the same to be consecrated to the work of
His Kingdom. Let us bow down before Him. Let us give Him all
our powers—our head to think for His Kingdom, our heart to go
out in love for men, and however feeble you may be, come and say:
"Lord, here I am, to live and die for Thy Kingdom."

Some talk and pray about the filling of the Holy Spirit. Let
them pray more and believe more. But remember the Holy Spirit
came to fit men to be messengers of the Kingdom, and you cannot expect to be filled with the Spirit unless you want to live for
Christ's Kingdom. You cannot expect all the love and peace and joy
of heaven to come into your life and be your treasures, unless you
give them up absolutely to the Kingdom of God, and possess and
use them only for Him. It is the soul utterly given up to God that
will receive in its emptying the fullness of the Holy Spirit.

～ Andrew Murray (1828–1917)

THE TRUE SHEPHERD

"I am the good shepherd. The good shepherd lays down his life for the sheep. The hired man, since he is not the shepherd and doesn't own the sheep, leaves them and runs away when he sees a wolf coming. The wolf then snatches and scatters them. This happens because he is a hired man and doesn't care about the sheep. I am the good shepherd. I know My own sheep, and they know Me, as the Father knows Me, and I know the Father. I lay down My life for the sheep."

John 10:11–15

"I am the good shepherd: the good shepherd giveth his life for the sheep." It is exceedingly interesting to know the many names by which Christ calls Himself in the Bible. These are above a hundred, I think a hundred and seven. He calls himself a rose, "I am the rose of Sharon," and a lily, "I am the lily of the valley."

The reason why He has so many names is that one name would not describe Him; He has so many offices that one name would not explain them; nay, all of them put together do not, for Paul said, "Unto me who am less than the least of all saints is this grace given, that I might preach among the Gentiles the unsearchable riches of Christ." Of all the names given, that of a shepherd is the sweetest. We understand things best by figures; so, at the beginning of this chapter, He contrasted Himself with a stranger, and in these words He contrasts Himself with a hireling, whose own the sheep are not.

~ Robert Murray McCheyne (1813–1843)

THE WORLD ISSUES
OF TODAY

"In fact, God knows that when you eat it your eyes will be opened and you will be like God, knowing good and evil."

Genesis 3:5

The gilded bait held out to Eve in the temptation was…was God's very purpose for the sinless pair before they fell. It seems that the word "likeness" in Genesis 1:26 signifies to "become like," indicating that the wonderful potentialities breathed into Adam constituting the image of God, were meant to be developed in a process which would "end in man being like his Creator" in dominion and rule over all things.

How tragic, then, that God Who alone could rightly develop and guide the use of these powers, should be shut outside the wonderful being He had created, and more terrible still that the very potentialities inherent in Him should now lie open to the hand of His enemy… Suffice it to say that the scheme was to lead men to "discoveries" of "natural Phenomena" under the name of "Psychic Science"…How they counterfeit in the soul realm the wondrous life of God in the spirit, cannot but strike those who know anything of the latter, and it is in this present development, and increase of the use of the powers of the soul, that peril lies for the children of God who are really "spiritual," and ignorant of these latent powers in the human frame.

⌒ Jessie Penn Lewis (1861–1927)

DIE, THEN!

And that is why I suffer these things. But I am not ashamed, because I know the One I have believed in and am persuaded that He is able to guard what has been entrusted to me until that day.

2 Timothy 1:12

I call to mind a bashful young farmer in the West, who had grown up far from the atmosphere of the church and to whom the habits of religious meetings were unfamiliar, saying to me when I urged upon him to come to the prayer meeting that night in a neighbouring farmhouse, and openly confess with the mouth his need of Christ, "I never could stand up and talk in that way before people, even though I wanted to; it would kill me to do it." "Well," I replied, "die then: I know how hard it is for you, but Christ commands the impossible. He told Peter to come to Him walking on the water, and as long as Peter kept his eye on the Lord, he also walked the waves. He commands you to confess Him before men and I shall expect you to do it tonight, even though you die in doing it."

To the meeting this timid man came. When he rose to speak he laboured as if he were Atlas lifting the world on his shoulders. The effort crushed the cowardice out of him; for before he sat down he sang the song of the new life. By faith he attempted the impossible: he seized the ideal he knew. Christ met him in the act, and he came into a saved state.

~ L. E. Maxwell (1895–1984)

BE PREPARED

LORD, reveal to me the end of my life and the number of my days. Let me know how short-lived I am.

Psalm 39:4

Nature hath given us one harvest every year, but death hath two; and the spring and the autumn send throngs of men and women to charnel-houses; and the summer long men are recovering from their evils of the spring, till the dog-days come, and the Sirian star makes the summer deadly; and the fruits of autumn are laid up for all the year's provision, and the man that gathers them eats and surfeits, and dies and needs them not, and himself is laid up for eternity; and he that escapes till winter only stays for another opportunity, which the distempers of that quarter minister to him with great variety.

Thus death reigns in all the portions of our time. The autumn with its fruit provides disorders for us, and the winter's cold turns them into sharp diseases, and the spring brings flowers to strew our hearse, and the summer gives green turf and brambles to bind upon our graves. Calentures and surfeit, cold and agues, are the four quarters of the year, and all minister to death; and you can no whither, but you tread upon a dead man's bones.

⁓ Jeremy Taylor (1613–1667)

GOD ORDERS BLESSINGS

But thank God that, although you used to be slaves of sin, you obeyed from the heart that pattern of teaching you were transferred to.

Romans 6:17

God does not order the wrong thing, but He uses it for our blessing; just as He used the cruelty of Joseph's wicked brethren, and the false accusations of Pharaoh's wife. In short, this way of seeing our Father in everything makes life one long thanksgiving, and gives a rest of heart, and more than that, a gayety of spirit, that is unspeakable. Someone says, "God's will on earth is always joy, always tranquillity." And since He must have His own way concerning His children, into what wonderful green pastures of inward rest, and beside what blessedly still waters of inward refreshment, is the soul led that learns this secret.

If the will of God is our will, and if He always has His way, then we always have our way also, and we reign in a perpetual kingdom. He who sides with God cannot fail to win in every encounter; and whether the result shall be joy or sorrow, failure or success, death or life, we may, under all circumstances, join in the apostle's shout of victory, "Thanks be unto God, which always causeth us to triumph in Christ!"

~ Hannah Whitall Smith (1832–1911)

HIS JOY OUR JOY

Now I am coming to You, and I speak these things in the world so that they may have My joy completed in them.

John 17:13

What was the joy that Jesus had? It is an insult to use the word happiness in connection with Jesus Christ. The joy of Jesus was the absolute self-surrender and self-sacrifice of Himself to His Father, the joy of doing that which the Father sent Him to do. Jesus prayed that our joy might go on fulfilling itself until it was the same joy as His. Have I allowed Jesus Christ to introduce His joy to me?

The full flood of my life is not in bodily health, not in external happenings, not in seeing God's work succeed, but in the perfect understanding of God, and in the communion with Him that Jesus Himself had. Be rightly related to God, find your joy there, and out of you will flow rivers of living water. Be a centre for Jesus Christ to pour living water through. The life that is rightly related to God is as natural as breathing wherever it goes. The lives that have been of most blessing to you are those who were unconscious of it.

⌒ Oswald Chambers (1874–1917)

INFLUENCED OF GOD'S SPIRIT

...ask that you may be filled with the knowledge of His will in all wisdom and spiritual understanding.

Colossians 1:9 KJV

Although it is with relation to the Spirit of God and his influences, that persons and things are called spiritual; yet not all those persons who are subject to any kind of influence of the Spirit of God, are ordinarily called spiritual in the New Testament. They who have only the common influences of God's Spirit, are not so called, in the places cited above, but only those who have the special, gracious, and saving influences of God's Spirit; as is evident, because it has been already proved, that by spiritual men is meant godly men, in opposition to natural, carnal, and unsanctified men. And it is most plain, that the apostle, by "spiritually minded," Romans 8:6, means graciously minded. And though the extraordinary gifts of the Spirit, which natural men might have, are sometimes called spiritual, because they are from the Spirit; yet natural men, whatever gifts of the Spirit they had, were not, in the usual language of the New Testament, called spiritual persons.

For it was not by men's having the gifts of the Spirit, but by their having the virtues of the Spirit, that they were called spiritual; as is apparent by Gal. 6:1: "Brethren, if any man be overtaken in a fault, ye which are spiritual, restore such a one in the spirit of meekness." Meekness is one of those virtues which the apostle had just spoken of, in the verses next preceding, showing what are the fruits of the Spirit. Those qualifications are said to be spiritual in the language of the New Testament, which are truly gracious and holy, and peculiar to the saints.

⁓ Jonathan Edwards (1703–1758)

SONG OF PRAISE TO GOD

How glorious is our heavenly King,
Who reigns above the sky!
How shall a child presume to sing
His dreadful majesty?
How great His power is none can tell,
Nor think how large His grace;
Not men below, nor saints that dwell
On high before His face.
Not angels, that stand round the Lord,
Can search His secret will;
But they perform His heavenly word,
And sing His praises still.
Then let me join this holy train,
And my first offerings bring:
Th' eternal God will not disdain
To hear an infant sing.
My heart resolves, my tongue obeys;
And angels will rejoice
To hear their mighty Maker's praise
Sound from a feeble voice.

~ Issac Watts (1674–1748)

EQUIPPED FOR EVERY GOOD WORK

A tinkling cymbal is an instrument of music, with which a skillful player can make such melodious and heart-inflaming music…and yet behold the cymbal hath not life…but because of the art of him that plays therewith…such music hath been made upon it. Just thus I saw it was and will be with them who have gifts, but want saving grace, they are in the hand of Christ, as the cymbal in the hand of David…so Christ can use these gifted men, as with them to affect the souls of His people in His church; yet when He hath done all, hang them by as lifeless, though sounding cymbals.

This consideration…were, for the most part, as a maul on the head of pride, and desire of vain glory; what, thought I, shall I be proud because I am a sounding brass? Is it so much to be a fiddle? Hath not the least creature that hath life, more of God in it than these?…a little grace, a little love, a little of the true fear of God, is better than all these gifts…that it is possible for a soul that can scarce give a man an answer, but with great confusion as to method, I say it is possible for them to have a thousand times more grace, and so to be more in the love and favour of the Lord than some who, by virtue of the gift of knowledge, can deliver themselves like angels.

～ John Bunyan (1628–1688)

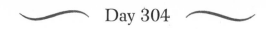

ALL MUST MEET GOD!

The fool says in his heart, "God does not exist." They are corrupt; they do vile deeds. There is no one who does good.

Psalm 14:1

Every one must meet God! The supreme question of life, then, is this: Are you ready to meet God? None of us can tell how soon it may be that we shall meet God. Are you ready? If not, I implore you to get ready before leaving this hall tonight. How can we meet God with joy and not with dismay? There is only one ground upon which man may meet God with joy and not with despair. That ground is the atoning blood of Jesus Christ.

God is infinitely holy, and the best of us is but a sinner. The only ground upon which a sinner can meet the holy God is on the is on the ground of the shed blood, the blood of Christ. Any of us, no matter how outcast or vile, can go boldly to the Holy of Holies on the ground of the shed blood, and the best man or woman that ever walked this earth can meet God on no other ground than the shed blood. There is only one adequate preparation for the sinner to meet God, that is the acceptance of Jesus Christ as our personal Saviour, who bore all our sins on the Cross of Calvary, and as our risen Saviour who is able to set us free from the power of sin.

~ R. A. Torrey (1856–1928)

TEACH THE CHILDREN

Teach a youth about the way he should go; even when he is old he will not depart from it.

Proverbs 22:6

"Thou shalt teach these words diligently unto thy children." And parents are commanded in the New Testament, to "bring up their children in the nurture and admonition of the Lord." The holy Psalmist acquaints us, that one great end why God did such great wonders for his people, was, "to the intent that when they grew up, they should show their children, or servants, the same."

And in Deut. 6 at the 20th and following verses, God strictly commands His people to instruct their children in the true nature of the ceremonial worship, when they should inquire about it, as He supposed they would do, in time to come. And if servants and children were to be instructed in the nature of Jewish rites, much more ought they now to be initiated and grounded in the doctrines and first principles of the gospel of Christ: not only, because it is a revelation, which has brought life and immortality to a fuller and clearer light, but also, because many seducers are gone abroad into the world, who do their utmost endeavor to destroy not only the superstructure, but likewise to sap the very foundation of our most holy religion.

～ George Whitefield (1714–1770)

CALLING THE PHYSICAL "SPIRITUAL"

He began to speak blasphemies against God: to blaspheme His name and His dwelling—those who dwell in heaven.

Revelation 13:6

It is said of the "Beast" in Revelation 13:5 that inspired by the Dragon he would be allowed to speak "blasphemies"...So rapidly are all the characteristics foreshown as accompanying the manifestation of the AntiChrist, coming to pass at the present hour, that it is difficult to keep pace with the need of unveiling them for the protection of those whose names are written in the "Book of Life of the Lamb slain from the foundation of the world" ...How wonderful to see that the Cross of Christ becomes to everything the "touchstone!"

If "supernatural power" can draw into activity psychic forces latent in the believer, then it is not safe to accept any manifestation of "power" as of God, except it comes by way of the Cross, and leads the believer into the path of the Cross. "Power" that results in the building up of "self" with compulsory forces at work upon others, simply means that the psychic powers have been developed, instead of being kept latent and unused by the exercise of the Cross. This alone makes way for the outflow of the Holy Spirit, who works upon the consciences of men, not by forcing and compelling power, but in conviction of the conscience by the light and truth of the Word of God.

⁓ Jessie Penn Lewis (1861–1927)

A SONG OF THE SOUL AND THE BRIDEGROOM OF CHRIST

For if you live according to the flesh, you are going to die. But if by the Spirit you put to death the deeds of the body, you will live.

Romans 8:13

"I will fear no wild beats; and pass over the mighty and the frontiers." The soul says also that it will cross the frontiers: these are the natural resistance and rebellion of the flesh against the spirit, for, as St. Paul says, the "flesh lusts against the spirit," and sets itself as a frontier against the soul on its spiritual road. This frontier the soul must cross, surmounting difficulties, and trampling underfoot all sensual appetites and all natural affections with great courage and resolution of spirit: for while they remain in the soul, the spirit will be by them hindered from advancing to the true life and spiritual delight.

This is set clearly before us by St. Paul, saying: "If by the spirit you mortify the deeds of the flesh, you shall live." This, then, is the process which the soul in this stanza says it becomes it to observe on the way to seek the Beloved: which briefly is a firm resolution not to stoop to gather flowers by the way; courage not to fear the wild beasts, and strength to pass by the mighty and the frontiers; intent solely on going over the mountains and the strands of the virtues, in the way just explained.

— St. John of the Cross (1542–1591)

GOD IS ALWAYS READY

I will take you to be My wife forever. I will take you to be My wife in righteousness, justice, love, and compassion.

Hosea 2:19

No one ought to think that it is difficult to come to Him, though it sounds difficult and is really difficult at the beginning, and in separating oneself from and dying to all things. But when a man has once entered upon it, no life is lighter or happier or more desirable; for God is very zealous to be at all times with man, and teaches him that He will bring him to Himself if man will but follow.

Man never desires anything so earnestly as God desires to bring a man to Himself, that he may know Him. God is always ready, but we are very unready; God is near to us, but we are far from Him; God is within, but we are without; God is at home, but we are strangers. The prophet saith: God guideth the redeemed through a narrow way into the broad road, so that they come into the wide and broad place; that is to say, into true freedom of the spirit, when one has become a spirit with God. May God help us to follow this course, that He may bring us to Himself.

⏤ William Ralph Inge (1860–1954)

OUR GUIDE

It remained that way continuously: the cloud would cover it, appearing like fire at night.

Numbers 9:16

This double aspect of all possible revelation of God, which was symbolized in comparatively gross external form in the pillar that led Israel on its march, and lay stretched out and quiescent, a guarding covering above the Tabernacle when the weary march was still, recurs all through the history of Old Testament revelation by type, and prophecy, and ceremony, in which the encompassing cloud was comparatively dense, and the light which pierced it relatively faint.

It reappears in both elements, but combined in new proportions, so as that "the veil—that is to say, His flesh" is thinned to transparency and all aglow with the indwelling luster of manifest Deity, so a light, set in some fair alabaster vase, shines through its translucent walls, bringing out every delicate tint and meandering vein of color, while itself diffused and softened by the enwrapping medium which it beautifies by passing through its pure walls. Both are made visible and attractive to dull eyes by the conjunction. He that hath seen Christ hath seen the Father, and he that hath seen the Father in Christ hath seen the man Christ as none see Him who are blind to the incarnate Deity which illuminates the manhood in which it dwells.

~ Alexander Maclaren (1826–1910)

SIN

Therefore do not let sin reign in your mortal body, so that you obey its desires.

Romans 6:12

Deadly sin is a death of the soul. To die is to lose life. But God is the life of the soul; since then deadly sin separates us from God, it is a death of the soul. Deadly sin is also an unrest of the heart. Everything can rest only in its proper place. But the natural place of the soul is God…deadly sin separates us from God; therefore it is an unrest of the heart. Deadly sin is also a sickness of the faculties, when a man can never stand up alone for the weight of his sins, nor ever resist falling into sin.

Therefore deadly sin is a sickness of the faculties. Deadly sin is also a blindness of the sense, in that it suffers not a man to know the shortness of the pleasures of lust, nor the length of the punishment in hell, nor the eternity of joys in heaven. Deadly sin is also a death of all graces; for as soon as a deadly sin takes place, a man becomes bare of all graces. Every creature must of necessity abide in God; if we fall out of the hands of His mercy, we fall into the hands of His justice. We must ever abide in Him. What madness then is it to wish not to be with Him, without whom thou canst not be!

— William Ralph Inge (1860–1954)

HOLY SPIRIT WORK

So he answered me, "This is the word of the LORD to Zerubbabel: 'Not by strength or by might, but by My Spirit,' says the LORD of Hosts."

Zechariah 4:6

The redeemed are not sanctified without Christ, who is made to them sanctification; hence the work of the Spirit must embrace the Incarnation of the Word and the work of the Messiah. But the work of Messiah involves preparatory working in the Patriarchs and Prophets of Israel, and later activity in the Apostles....Likewise this revelation involves the conditions of man's nature and the historical development of the race; hence the Holy Spirit is concerned in the formation of the human mind and the unfolding of the spirit of humanity...man's condition depends on that of the earth...and no less on the actions of spirits, be they angels or demons from other spheres...the Spirit's work must touch the entire host of heaven and earth.

To avoid a mechanical idea of His work as tho it began and ended at random...it must not be determined nor limited till it extends to all the influences that affect the sanctification of the Church. The Holy Spirit is God, therefore sovereign; hence He cannot depend on these influences, but completely controls them. For this He must be able to operate them; so His work must be honored in all the host of heaven, in man and in his history, in the preparation of Scripture, in the Incarnation of the Word, in the salvation of the elect.

⌒ Abraham Kuyper (1837–1920)

OBEDIENCE BRINGS BLESSING

Be careful to obey all these things I command you, so that you and your children after you may prosper forever, because you will be doing what is good and right in the sight of the LORD your God.

Deuteronomy 12:28

Though salvation is not by the works of the law, yet the blessings which are promised to obedience are not denied to the faithful servants of God. The curses our Lord took away when He was made a curse for us, but no clause of blessing has been abrogated.

We are to note and listen to the revealed will of the Lord, giving our attention not to portions of it but to "all these words." There must be no picking and choosing but an impartial respect to all that God has commanded. This is the road of blessedness for the Father and for His children. The Lord's blessing is upon His chosen to the third and fourth generation. If they walk uprightly before Him, He will make all men know that they are a seed which the Lord has blessed.

~ C. H. Spurgeon (1834–1892)

CONSEQUENCES OF THE FALL

You who are trying to be justified by the law are alienated from Christ;
you have fallen from grace.

Galatians 5:4

From the time when the first man gave a ready ear to the words of the enemy, mankind Have been deaf, so that none of us can hear or understand the loving utterances of the eternal Word. Something has happened to the ears of man, which has stopped up his ears, so that he cannot hear the loving Word; and he has also been so blinded, that he has become stupid, and does not know himself. If he wished to speak of his own inner life, he could not do it; he knows not where he is, nor what is his state. How can it be that the noble reason, the inner eye, is so blinded that it cannot see the true light?

This great shame has come about, because a thick coarse skin and a thick fur has been drawn over him, even the love and the opinion of the creatures, whether it be the man himself or something that belongs to him; hence man has become blind and deaf, in whatever position he may be, worldly or spiritual. Yes, that is his guilt, that many a thick skin is drawn over him, as thick as an ox's forehead, and it has so covered up his inner man, that neither God nor himself can get inside; it has grown into him.

~ William Ralph Inge (1860–1954)

THE MERCIES OF GOD

But God, who is rich in mercy, because of His great love that He had for us.

Ephesians 2:4

For to think on the mercy of our Lord, that He hath showed to me and to thee, and to all sinful captives that sometimes were in bondage to the devil, through the greatness and multitude of our sins; how He patiently suffered us to live in our sin, and in our heinous contempts of Him, and work no revenge on us for the same, as He most justly might have done, and might most worthily have cast us down headlong into Hell, if His love had not hindered Him; but out of love He spared us, and sent His grace into our souls, taking us out of the state of heinous sins, and by His grace hath turned our will entirely unto Him, and made us thereby, for the having of Him, and for His love, to forsake all manner of sin. The remembrance of His mercy and goodness…may justly cause and bring into a soul a great truth and confidence in our Lord, and a full hope of salvation, and greatly inflameth the desire of love to aspire to the joys of Heaven.

⌣ Walter Hilton (1340–1396)

THE WAY OF FAITH

You will keep the mind that is dependent on You in perfect peace, for it is trusting in You.

Isaiah 26:3

If you...are bent on becoming an utterly believing believer, one who pins all his confidence upon the veracity of God's naked Word, then hesitate not to take the simple and crucifying, the humbling and purifying way of faith—the only way in which prophets and apostles and martyrs have trod. Ask God to "put a thorn in every enjoyment, a worm in every gourd," that would either prevent your being wholly Christ's or would in any measure retard your growth in faith. Submit yourself to the divine will and let God cut every idolatrous prop away, whether of feeling or emotion or manifestation. Why demand to see your own faith, or *feel* His presence? Those who have done exploits in the Church of Christ have often experienced the greatest inner desolations.

～ L. E. Maxwell (1895–1984)

THE HUMANITY OF CHRIST

By these He has given us very great and precious promises, so that through them you may share in the divine nature, escaping the corruption that is in the world because of evil desires.

2 Peter 1:4

Think on the humanity of our Lord, as of His birth, of His Passion or of any other of His works, and feed thy thought with spiritual imagination thereof, for to move thine affection more to the love of Him…when it cometh freely of God's gift, with devotion and fervour of spirit, else a man will not likely find taste or devotion in it.

And if he have it not with such facility and sending of God, I think it not expedient that a man should much force himself in it, as if he would get it by violence; for so doing he might hurt his head and body too, and yet be never the nearer…it is good for a man to have in his mind and thought sometimes our Saviour's humanity…and if devotion come withal, and relish or gust found in it, then to hold it and follow it for a time, but leave off soon, and hang not long thereon.

And if devotion come not by thinking of the Passion, strive not, nor press too much for to have and come by such devotion or feeling in it, but take what will easily come; and if it come not easily betake thee to some other matter, wherein thou thinkest or hopest to find more devotion or gust.

∽ Walter Hilton (1340–1396)

GOD'S PERFECT PLAN FOR HIS CHILDREN

"For My thoughts are not your thoughts, and your ways are not My ways." This is the LORD's declaration.

Isaiah 55:8

When He works, His ways and His thoughts are declared by the prophet to be as far above our ways and our thoughts as the heavens are above the earth He makes no effort when He would execute what He has decreed; for to Him all things are equally easy; He speaks and causes the heavens and the earth to be created out of nothing, with as little difficulty as He causes water to descend or a stone to fall to the ground.

His power is co-extensive with his will; when He wills, the thing is already accomplished. When the Scriptures represent Him as speaking in the creation of the world, it is not to be understood as signifying that it was necessary that the word of command should issue from Him, in order that the universe He was about to create should hear and obey His will; that word was simple and interior, neither more nor less than the thought which He conceived of what He was about to do and the will to do it.

〜 Jeanne Marie Bouvier de la Mothe Guyon (1647–1711)

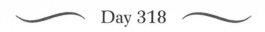
UNCONDITIONAL LOVE

We love because He first loved us.

1 John 4:19

It is God's love towards us that gives us everything…When He is able by His love to produce that love in us, He reigns within; He constitutes there our life, our peace, our happiness, and we then already begin to taste that blissful existence which He enjoys. His love towards us is stamped with His own character of infinity: it is not like ours, bounded and constrained; when He loves, all the measures of His love are infinite. He comes down from Heaven to earth to seek the creature of clay whom He loves; He becomes creature and clay with him; He gives Him his flesh to eat.

These are the prodigies of Divine love in which the Infinite outstrips all the affection we can manifest. He loves like a God, with a love utterly incomprehensible. It is the height of folly to seek to measure infinite love by human wisdom. Far from losing any element of its greatness in these excesses, He impresses upon His love the stamp of His own grandeur, while He manifests a delight in us bounded only by the infinite. O! how great and lovely is He in His mysteries! But we want eyes to see them, and have no desire to behold God in everything.

～ Jeanne Marie Bouvier de la Mothe Guyon (1647–1711)

GOD AND GRACE BE THY LEADER

I will instruct you and show you the way to go; with My eye on you, I will give counsel.

Psalm 32:8

Let fast who fast will, and be only who will, and let hold silence who so will, but hold thee by God that doth beguile no man; for silence and speaking, onliness and company, fasting and eating, all may beguile thee. And if thou hear of any man that speaketh, or of any that is still, of any that eateth or of any that fasteth, or of any that is in company or else by himself, think thou, and say, if thee list, that they conne do as they should do, but if the contrary shew in apert.

But look that thou do not as they do (I mean for that they do so) on ape's manner; for neither thou canst, nor peradventure thou art not disposed as they are. And, therefore, leave to work after other men's dispositions and work after thine own, if thou mayst know what it is. And unto the time that thou mayst know what it is, work after those men's counsel that know their own disposition, but not after their disposition; for such men should give counsel in such cases, and else none. And this sufficeth for an answer to all thy letter, as me thinketh; the grace of God be ever more with thee, in the name of Jesus.

～ Edmund Garratt Gardner (1869–1935)

LETTER TO SUFFERING SAINTS...FROM PRISON

Otherwise, wouldn't they have stopped being offered, since the worshipers, once purified, would no longer have any consciousness of sins?

Hebrews 10:2

Dear, suffering lambs, for the name and command of Jesus; be valiant for His truth, and faithful, and ye will feel the presence of Christ with you. Look at Him who suffered for you, who hath bought you, and will feed you; who saith, "Be of good comfort, I have overcome the world"; who destroys the devil and his works, and bruises the serpent's head. I say, look to Christ, your sanctuary, in whom ye have rest and peace. To you it is given not only to believe, but to suffer for His name's sake. They that will live godly in Christ Jesus, shall suffer persecution by the ungodly professors of Christ Jesus, who live out of Him. Therefore be valiant for God's truth upon the earth, and look above that spirit that makes you suffer up to Christ, who was before it was, and will be when it is gone.

Christ the Seed reigns; and His power is over all, who bruises the serpent's head, and destroys the devil and his works, and was before he was. So all of you live and walk in Christ Jesus; that nothing may be between you and God, but Christ, in whom ye have salvation, life, rest and peace with God.

~ George Fox (1624–1691)

THE GREATEST GIFT

This is My beloved Son. I take delight in Him. Listen to Him!

Matthew 17:5

When the Lord God and His Son Jesus Christ sent me forth into the world to preach His everlasting gospel and kingdom, I was glad that I was commanded to turn people to that inward Light, Spirit, and Grace, by which all might know their salvation and their way to God; even that Divine Spirit which would lead them into all truth, and which I infallibly knew would never deceive any.

But with and by this divine power and Spirit of God, and the Light of Jesus, I was to bring people off from all their own ways, to Christ, the new and living way; and from their churches, which men had made and gathered, to the Church in God, the general assembly written in heaven, of which Christ is the head. And I was to bring them off from the world's teachers, made by men, to learn of Christ, who is the Way, the Truth, and the Life, of whom the Father said, "This is my beloved Son, hear ye him"; and off from all the world's worships, to know the Spirit of Truth in the inward parts, and to be led thereby; that in it they might worship the Father of spirits, who seeks such to worship Him.

～ George Fox (1624–1691)

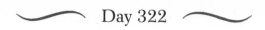

TO LIVE IS CHRIST

For me, living is Christ and dying is gain.

Philippians 1:21

The true discovery of a character is the discovery of its ideals. Paul spares us any speculation in his case. "To me to live," he says, "is Christ." This is the motto of his life, the ruling passion of it, which at once explains the nature of his success and accounts for it. He lives for Christ. "To me to live is Christ."… There is no fear about death being gain if we have lived for Christ. So, let it be: "To me to live is Christ." There is but one alternative—Paul's alternative, the discovery of Christ. We have all in some sense, indeed, already made that discovery.

We may be as near it now as Paul when he left Jerusalem. There was no notice given that he was to change masters. The new Master simply crossed his path one day, and the great change was come. How often has He crossed our path? We know what to do the next time: we know how our life can be made worthy and great—how only; we know how death can become gain—how only. Many, indeed, tell us death must be gain. Many long for life to be done that they may rest, as they say, in the quiet grave. Let no cheap sentimentalism deceive us. Death can only be gain when to have lived was Christ.

～ Henry Drummond (1851–1897)

DO YOU LOVE ME?

A second time He asked him, "Simon, son of John, do you love Me?" "Yes, Lord," he said to Him, "You know that I love You." "Shepherd My sheep," He told him.

John 21:16

Jesus did not say to make converts to your way of thinking, but He said to look after His sheep, to see that they get nourished in the knowledge of Him…Today we have substituted doctrinal belief for personal belief, and that is why so many people are devoted to causes and so few are devoted to Jesus Christ. People do not really want to be devoted to Jesus, but only to the cause He started. Jesus Christ is deeply offensive to the educated minds of today, to those who only want Him to be their Friend, and who are unwilling to accept Him in any other way.

Our Lord's primary obedience was to the will of His Father, not to the needs of people—the saving of people was the natural outcome of His obedience to the Father. If I am devoted solely to the cause of humanity, I will soon be exhausted and come to the point where my love will waver and stumble. But if I love Jesus Christ personally and passionately, I can serve humanity, even though people may treat me like a "doormat." The secret of a disciple's life is devotion to Jesus Christ…

～ Oswald Chambers (1874–1917)

MEN OF PRAYER

Rejoice in hope; be patient in affliction; be persistent in prayer.

Romans 12:12

Here is great need in this day for Christian business men to inform their mundane affairs with the spirit of prayer. There is a great army of successful merchants of almost every kind who are members of Christ's Church and it is high time these men attended to this matter. This is but another version of the phrase, "putting God into business," the realization and restraint of His presence and of His fear in all the secularities of life. We need the atmosphere of the prayer-closet to pervade our public sales-rooms and counting-houses.

The sanctity of prayer is needed to impregnate business. We need the spirit of Sunday carried over to Monday and continued until Saturday. But this cannot be done by prayerless men, but by men of prayer. We need business men to go about their concerns with the same reverence and responsibility with which they enter the closet. Men are badly needed who are devoid of greed, but who, with all their hearts carry God with them into the secular affairs of life…Praying men are God's agents on earth, the representative of government of heaven, set to a specific task on the earth.

∼ Edward M. Bounds (1835–1913)

BE ON THE ALERT!

Only be on your guard and diligently watch yourselves, so that you don't forget the things your eyes have seen and so that they don't slip from your mind as long as you live. Teach them to your children and your grandchildren.

Deuteronomy 4:9

All great amusements are dangerous to the Christian life; but among all those which the world has invented there is none more to be feared than the theatre. It is a representation of the passions so natural and so delicate that it excites them and gives birth to them in our hearts, and, above all, to that of love, principally when it is represented as very chaste and virtuous…it appears to innocent souls, the more they are likely to be touched by it.

Its violence pleases our self-love, which immediately forms a desire to produce the same effects which are seen so well represented; and, at the same time, we make ourselves a conscience founded on the propriety of the feelings which we see there, by which the fear of pure souls is removed, since they imagine that it cannot hurt their purity to love with a love which seems to them so reasonable.

So we depart from the theatre with our heart so filled with all the beauty and tenderness of love, the soul and the mind so persuaded of its innocence, that we are quite ready to receive its first impressions, or rather to seek an opportunity of awakening them in the heart of another, in order that we may receive the same pleasures and the same sacrifices which we have seen so well represented in the theatre.

~ Blaise Pascal (1623–1662)

GLORY AND PRAISE TO GOD

Not to us, Yahweh, not to us, but to Your name give glory because of Your faithful love, because of Your truth.

Psalm 115:1

Wherefore to dignity and wisdom we must add virtue, the proper fruit of them both. Virtue seeks and finds Him who is the Author and Giver of all good, and who must be in all things glorified; otherwise, one who knows what is right yet fails to perform it, will be beaten with many stripes (Luke 12:47). Why? you may ask. Because he has failed to put his knowledge to good effect, but rather has imagined mischief upon his bed (Ps. 36:4); like a wicked servant, he has turned aside to seize the glory which, his own knowledge assured him, belonged only to his good Lord and Master.

It is plain, therefore, that dignity without wisdom is useless and that wisdom without virtue is accursed. But when one possesses virtue, then wisdom and dignity are not dangerous but blessed. Such a man calls on God and lauds Him, confessing from a full heart, "Not unto us, O Lord, not unto us, but unto Thy name give glory" (Ps. 115:1). Which is to say, "O Lord, we claim no knowledge, no distinction for ourselves; all is Thine, since from Thee all things do come."

~ Bernard of Clairvaux (1090–1153)

A LETTER TO CHRISTIANS

Dear friends we must consecrate not only ourselves—body and soul—but all we have. Some of you may have children; perhaps you have an only child, and you dread the very idea of letting it go. Take care, take care; God deserves your confidence, your love, and your surrender. I plead with you; take your children and say to Jesus: "Anything Lord, that pleases Thee." Educate your children for Jesus. God help you to do it. He may not accept all of them, but He will accept of the will, and there will be a rich blessing in your soul for it. Then there is money.

When I hear appeals for money from every Society; when I hear calculations as to what the Christians of England are spending on pleasure, and the small amount given for Missions, I say there is something terrible in it. God's children with so much wealth and comfort, and giving away so small a portion! God be praised for every exception! But there are many who give but very little, who never so give that it costs them something, and they feel it. Oh, friends! Our giving must be in proportion to God's giving. He gives you all. Let us take it up in our Consecration prayer: "Lord, take it all, every penny I possess. It is all Thine." Let us often say "It is all His." You may not know how much you ought to give. Give up all, put everything in His hands, and He will teach you if you will wait.

~ Andrew Murray (1828–1917)

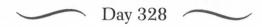

CONCERN FOR OUR TIME

There is an occasion for everything, and a time for every activity under heaven.

Ecclesiastes 3:1

God hath given to man a short time here upon earth, and yet upon this short time eternity depends: but so, that for every hour of our life (after we are persons capable of laws, and know good from evil) we must give account to the great Judge of men and angels. And this is it which our blessed Saviour told us, that we must account for every idle word; not meaning that every word which is not designed to edification, or is less prudent, shall be reckoned for a sin; but that the time which we spend in our idle talking and unprofitable discoursings; that time which might and ought to have been employed to spiritual and useful purposes—that is to be accounted for.

For we must remember that we have a great work to do, many enemies to conquer, many evils to prevent, much danger to run through, many difficulties to be mastered, many necessities to serve, and much good to do; many children to provide for, or many friends to support, or many poor to relieve, or many diseases to cure; besides the needs of nature and of relation, our private and our public cares, and duties of the world, which necessity and the providence of God have adopted into the family of religion.

~ Jeremy Taylor (1613–1667)

DON'T LET TEMPTATIONS OVERPOWER YOU

Then the Lord knows how to rescue the godly from trials and to keep the unrighteous under punishment until the day of judgment.

2 Peter 2:9

If it should ever happen that through some of these temptations and your own weakness, you waver and perhaps fall into sin, and thus lose the way for a time, return as soon as possible to the right path by using such remedies as the Church ordains. Do not think of your past sins, for that will harm you and favour your enemies; but make haste to go on your way as if nothing happened. Think only of Jesus, and of your desire to gain His love, and nothing will harm you.

Finally, when your enemies see that you are so determined that neither sickness, fancies, poverty, life, death, nor sins discourage you, but that you will continue to seek the love of Jesus and nothing else, by continuing your prayer and other spiritual works, they will grow enraged and will not spare you the most cruel abuse. They will make their most dangerous assault by bringing before you all your good deeds and virtues, showing that all men praise, love, and honour you for your sanctity. This they will do to make you vain and proud. But if you offer your life to Jesus you will consider all this flattery and falsehood as deadly poison to your soul, and will cast it from you.

～ Henry Suso (1296–1366)

A NEW BEGINNING

"For God loved the world in this way: He gave His One and Only Son, so that everyone who believes in Him will not perish but have eternal life."

John 3:16

How glorious, then, is the blessing which every one receives that believes in the Lord Jesus. Not only does there come a change in his disposition and manner of life; he also receives from God out of heaven an entirely new life. He is born anew, born of God: he has passed from death into life. This new life is nothing less than Eternal Life. This does not mean, as many suppose, that our life shall now no more die, but shall endure into eternity.

No: eternity life is nothing else than the very life of God, the life that He has had in Himself from eternity, and that has been visibly revealed in Christ. This life is now the portion of every child of God. This life is a life of inconceivable power. Whenever God gives life to a young plant or animal, that life has in itself the power of growth, whereby the plant or animal as of itself becomes large. Life is power. In the new life, that is, in your heart, there is the power of eternity. More certain than the healthful growth of any tree or animal is the growth and increase of the child of God, who in reality surrenders himself to the working of the new life.

～ Andrew Murray (1827–1917)

THE HANDS OF THE FATHER

And Jesus called out with a loud voice, "Father, into Your hands I entrust My spirit." Saying this, He breathed His last.

Luke 23:46

Neither St. Matthew nor St. Mark tells us of any words uttered by our Lord after the Eloi. They both, along with St. Luke, tell us of a cry with a loud voice, and the giving up of the ghost; between which cry and the giving up, St. Luke records the words, "Father, into thy hands I commend my spirit." St. Luke says nothing of the Eloi prayer of desolation. St. John records neither the Eloi, nor the Father into thy hands, nor the loud cry.

He tells us only that after Jesus had received the vinegar, He said, "It is finished," and bowed His head, and gave up the ghost... we shall never be able, I say, to rest in the bosom of the Father, till the fatherhood is fully revealed to us in the love of the brothers. For He cannot be our father save as He is their father; and if we do not see Him and feel Him as their father, we cannot know Him as ours. Never shall we know Him aright until we rejoice and exult for our race that He is the Father. He that loveth not his brother whom he hath seen, how can he love God whom he hath not seen? To rest, I say, at last, even in those hands into which the Lord commended his spirit, we must have learned already to love our neighbour as ourselves.

～ George MacDonald (1824–1905)

TRUTH IS GOD'S WAY

So Jesus said to the Jews who had believed Him, "If you continue in My word, you really are My disciples."

John 8:31

The truth can neither be communicated nor be received without being as it were before the eyes of God, nor without God's help, nor without God being involved as the middle term, since he is the truth. It can therefore only be communicated by and received by "the single individual," which, for that matter, every single human being who lives could be: this is the determination of the truth in contrast to the abstract, the fantastical, impersonal, "the crowd"— "the public," which excludes God as the middle term (for the personal God cannot be the middle term in an impersonal relation), and also thereby the truth, for God is the truth and its middle term… It is clear that to love the neighbor is self-denial, that to love the crowd or to act as if one loved it, to make it the court of last resort for "the truth," that is the way to truly gain power, the way to all sorts of temporal and worldly advantage—yet it is untruth; for the crowd is untruth.

— Søren Kierkegaard (1813–1855)

AN ABUNDANCE OF LOVE

You are from God, little children, and you have conquered them, because the One who is in you is greater than the one who is in the world.

1 John 4:4

Some souls, by virtue of the love that God gives them, are so cleansed that all creatures and everything they hear, or see, or feel by any of the senses, turns them to comfort and gladness; and the sensuality receives new savor and sweetness in all creatures. And just as previously the sensual appetites were carnal, vain, and corrupt, because of the pain of original sin, so now they are made spiritual and clean, without bitterness and biting of conscience.

And this is the goodness of our Lord, that since the soul is punished in the sensuality, and the flesh shares the pain, that afterward the soul be comforted in the sensuality, and the flesh join in joy and comfort with the soul, not carnal, but spiritual, as it was a fellow in tribulation and pain. This is the freedom and the lordship, the dignity, and the worth that a man has over all creatures, which dignity he may so recover by grace here, that every creature appear to him as it is. And that occurs when by grace he sees, he hears, he feels only God in all creatures. In this way a soul is made spiritual in the sensuality by abundance of love, that is, in the nature of the soul.

~ Walter Hilton (1340–1396)

JESUS CHRIST HAS WON...

We are to "STAND," not struggle. "Having done all things, stand." The shield of FAITH is able to quench all the fiery darts of the evil one (Ephesians 6).

"Faith does nothing; faith lets God do it all"—the victory for us. "I live," says Paul, "yet not I, Christ LIVES IN ME." "Ye are of God," says John, "and have overcome them." How? Why? "Because greater is HE that is IN YOU, than he that is in the world" (1 John 4:4).

...The secret of Victory is the Indwelling-Christ. Victory is in trusting, not in trying. "This is the Victory that overcometh the world"—and SIN—"even our faith" (1 John 5:4).

...Yet all growth takes place without effort. "No man by taking thought can add one cubit to his stature," said our Lord. And this is true of our spiritual stature.

~ Unknown

ESTABLISHED IN
FAITH AND UNITY

So if you have been raised with the Messiah, seek what is above, where the Messiah is, seated at the right hand of God.

Colossians 3:1

Study, therefore, to be established in the doctrines of the Lord and the apostles, that so all things, whatsoever ye do, may prosper both in the flesh and spirit; in faith and love; in the Son, and in the Father, and in the Spirit; in the beginning and in the end; with your most admirable bishop, and the well-compacted spiritual crown of your presbytery, and the deacons who are according to God.

Be ye subject to the bishop, and to one another, as Jesus Christ to the Father, according to the flesh, and the apostles to Christ, and to the Father, and to the Spirit; that so there may be a union both fleshly and spiritual. Study, therefore, to be established in the doctrines of the Lord and the apostles, that so all things, whatsoever ye do, may prosper, both in the flesh and spirit, in faith and love, with your most admirable bishop, and the well-compacted, spiritual crown of your presbytery, and the deacons who are according to God. Be ye subject to the bishop, and to one another, as Christ to the Father, that there may be a unity according to God among you.

~ Philip Schaff (1819–1893)

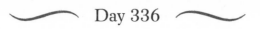

IMPORTANCE OF GOD'S LAW

Teach me to do Your will, for You are my God. May Your gracious Spirit lead me on level ground.

Psalm 143:10

The Law is a mirror to show a person what he is like, a sinner who is guilty of death, and worthy of everlasting punishment. What is this bruising and beating by the hand of the Law to accomplish? This, that we may find the way to grace. The Law is an usher to lead the way to grace. God is the God of the humble, the miserable, the afflicted. It is His nature to exalt the humble, to comfort the sorrowing, to heal the broken-hearted, to justify the sinners, and to save the condemned.

The fatuous idea that a person can be holy by himself denies God the pleasure of saving sinners. God must therefore first take the sledge-hammer of the Law in His fists and smash the beast of self-righteousness and its brood of self-confidence, self-wisdom, self-righteousness, and self-help. When the conscience has been thoroughly frightened by the Law it welcomes the Gospel of grace with its message of a Savior who came into the world, not to break the bruised reed, nor to quench the smoking flax, but to preach glad tidings to the poor, to heal the broken-hearted, and to grant forgiveness of sins to all the captives.

～ Martin Luther (1483–1546)

FAITHFUL FOLLOWERS

The LORD answered me: Write down this vision; clearly inscribe it on tablets so one may easily read it.

Habakkuk 2:2

Our supreme duty is that which we owe to God, and the next appertains to the soul. And yet these two are such loving correlates, that though every one of the is a duty of supreme consequence, and such as by no means we may presume to neglect or omit, yet cannot we possibly perform any one of them without the other. So that whosoever will serve God doth at the same time provide for his own soul; and he that is careful for his own soul doth at the same time serve God.

So that the state of these two sovereign duties in man, is by a certain compendious dependency and co-intention rendered very easy, while the faithful performance of the one is a perfect consummation of both: for by the unspeakable tenderness and mercy of God, the good we do to our own souls is the most acceptable service and sacrifice that we can offer unto Him.

～ Eucherius of Lyons (380–449)

THE BLESSING SECURED

And don't get drunk with wine, which leads to reckless actions, but be filled by the Spirit.

Ephesians 5:18

What folly it would be for a man who had lost a lung and a half, and had hardly a quarter of a lung to do the work of two, to expect to be a strong man and to do hard work, and to live in any climate! And what folly for a man to expect to live—God has told him he cannot live—a full Christian life, unless he is full of the Holy Ghost! And what folly for a man who has only got a little drop of the river of the water of life to expect to live and to have power with God and man!

Jesus wants us to come and to receive the fulfilment of the promise, "He that believeth in me, streams of water shall flow out from him." Oh, begin to say, "If I am to live a right life, if I am in every part of my daily life and conduct to glorify my God, I must have the Holy Spirit—I must be filled with the Spirit." Are you going to say that? Talking for months and months won't help. Do submit to God, and as an act of submission say, "Lord, I confess it, I ought to be filled, I must be filled; help me!" And God will help you.

— Andrew Murray (1828–1917)

VICTORY OVER THE WORLD THROUGH FAITH

For whatsoever is born of God overcometh the world: and this is the victory that overcometh the world, even our faith.

1 John 5:4 KJV

A man certainly does not overcome the world unless he gets above being engrossed and absorbed with its concerns. The man who gains the victory over the world must overcome not one form only of its pursuits, but every form—must overcome the world itself and all that it has to present as an allurement to the human heart. Overcoming the world implies overcoming the fear of the world… and a state of worldly anxiety. The victory under consideration implies that we cease to be enslaved and in bondage to the world in any of its forms. There is a worldly spirit and there is also a heavenly spirit; and one or the other exists in the heart of every man and controls his whole being. Those who are under the control of the world of course have not overcome the world.

No man overcomes the world till his heart is imbued with the spirit of heaven. "To me," said Paul, "it is a small thing to be judged of man's judgment." So of every real Christian; his care is to secure the approbation of God; this is his chief concern, to commend himself to God and to his own conscience. No man has overcome the world unless he has attained this state of mind. Almost no feature of Christian character is more striking or more decisive than this—indifference to the opinions of the world. Men who are not thus dead to the world have not escaped its bondage. The victorious Christian is in a state where he is no longer in bondage to man. He is bound only to serve God.

~ C. G. Finney (1792–1875)

SUFFERING

I will rejoice and be glad in Your faithful love because You have seen my affliction. You have known the troubles of my life.

Psalm 31:7

Men who love God are so far from complaining of their sufferings, that their complaint and their suffering is rather because the suffering which God's will has assigned them is so small. All their blessedness is to suffer by God's will, and not to have suffered something, for this is the loss of suffering. This is why I said, Blessed are they who are willing to suffer for righteousness, not, Blessed are they who have suffered.

All that a man bears for God's sake, God makes light and sweet for him. If all was right with you, your sufferings would no longer be suffering, but love and comfort. If God could have given to men anything more noble than suffering, He would have redeemed mankind with it: otherwise, you must say that my Father was my enemy, if he knew of anything nobler than suffering. True suffering is a mother of all the virtues.

～ William Ralph Inge (1860–1954)

PURITY OF HEART

And let the peace of the Messiah, to which you were also called in one body, control your hearts. Be thankful.

Colossians 3:15

Let us then draw near to Him with holiness of spirit, lifting up pure and undefiled hands unto Him, loving our gracious and merciful Father, who has made us partakers in the blessings of His elect. For thus it is written, "When the Most High divided the nations, when He scattered the sons of Adam, He fixed the bounds of the nations according to the number of the angels of God. His people Jacob became the portion of the Lord, and Israel the lot of His inheritance." And in another place [the Scripture] saith, "Behold, the Lord taketh unto himself a nation out of the midst of the nations, as a man takes the first-fruits of his threshing-floor; and from that nation shall come forth the Most Holy."

— Philip Schaff (1819–1893)

TIME

"I will rebuke the devourer for you, so that it will not ruin the produce of your land and your vine in your field will not fail to produce fruit," *says the* LORD *of Hosts.*

Malachi 3:11

It seems that most believers have difficulty in realizing and facing up to the inexorable fact that God does not hurry in His development of our Christian life. He is working from and for eternity! So many feel they are not making progress unless they are swiftly and constantly forging ahead. Now it is true that the new convert often begins and continues for some time at a fast rate. But this will not continue if there is to be healthy growth and ultimate maturity. God Himself will modify the pace. This is important to see, since in most instances when seeming declension begins to set in, it is not, as so many think, a matter of backsliding.

John Darby makes it plain that "it is God's way to set people aside after their first start, that self-confidence may die down. Thus Moses was forty years. On his first start he had to run away. Paul was three years also, after his first testimony. Not that God did not approve the first earnest testimony. We must get to know ourselves and that we have no strength. Thus we must learn, and then leaning on the Lord we can with more maturity, and more experientially, deal with souls."

~ Miles Stanford (1914–1999)

ABIDING COMFORTER

To provide for those who mourn in Zion; to give them a crown of beauty instead of ashes, festive oil instead of mourning, and splendid clothes instead of despair and they will be called righteous trees, planted by the LORD to glorify Him.

Isaiah 61:3

If I am walking along the street with a very disfiguring hole in the back of my dress…it is certainly a very great comfort to me to have a kind friend who will tell me of it. And similarly it is indeed a comfort to know that there is always abiding with me a divine, all seeing Comforter, who will reprove me for all my faults, and will not let me go on in a fatal unconsciousness of them…it is far more to a man's interest that he should see his own faults than that anyone else should see them, and a moment's thought will convince us that this is true, and will make us thankful for the Comforter who reveals them to us.

I remember vividly the comfort it used to be to me, when I was young, to have a sister who always…kept me in order…I was always made comfortable, and not uncomfortable, by her presence. But when it chanced that I went anywhere alone, then I would indeed feel uncomfortable…The declaration is that He "comforts all our waste places"; and He does this by revealing them to us, and at the same time showing us how He can make our "wildernesses like Eden," and our "deserts like the garden of the Lord."

~ Hannah Whitall Smith (1832–1911)

CHRIST THE HEAD OF THE CHURCH AND SOURCE OF ITS AUTHORITY

There are different ministries, but the same Lord.

1 Corinthians 12:5

He rules the Church, not by force, but by His Word and Spirit. All human officers in the Church are clothed with the authority of Christ and must submit to the control of His Word...The power of the Church is spiritual, because it is given by the Holy Spirit, is a manifestation of the power of the Spirit, pertains exclusively to believers, and can be exercised only in a spiritual way It is also a purely ministerial power, which is derived from Christ and is exercised in His name.

God is a God of order, who desire that all things in the Church be done decently and in order. For that reason He made provision for the proper regulation of the affairs of the Church, and gave the Church power to carry the laws of Christ into effect. Colossians 1:18, "And He is the head of the body, the Church: who is the beginning, the firstborn from the dead; that in all things He might have the preeminence."

～ Louis Berkoff (1809–1833)

SACRAMENTS

Or are you unaware that all of us who were baptized into Christ Jesus were baptized into His death? Therefore we were buried with Him by baptism into death, in order that, just as Christ was raised from the dead by the glory of the Father, so we too may walk in a new way of life.

Romans 6:3–4

The Word of God is complete as a means of grace, but the sacraments are not complete without the Word. This must be maintained over against the Roman Catholics, who teach that the sacraments contain all that is necessary unto salvation. The Word and the sacraments differ in the following particulars: (a) the Word is absolutely necessary, while the sacraments are not; (b) the Word serves to beget and to strengthen faith, while the sacraments can only strengthen it; and (c) the Word is for all the world, but the sacraments only for believers and their seed…

A sacrament is a holy ordinance instituted by Christ, in which by sensible signs the grace of God in Christ is represented, sealed, and applied to believers, and they, in turn, express their faith and obedience to God.

~ Louis Berkoff (1809–1833)

THE SOUL WINNER'S REWARD

The fruit of the righteous is a tree of life, but violence takes lives.

Proverbs 11:30

It is far more pleasant to remember that there is a reward for bringing men to mercy, and that it is of a higher order than the premium for bringing men to justice; it is, moreover, much more within our reach, and that is a practical point worthy of our notice. We cannot all hunt down criminals, but we may all rescue the perishing. God be thanked that assassins and burglars are comparatively few, but sinners who need to be sought and saved swarm around us in every place.

Here is scope for you all; and none need think himself shut out from the rewards which love bestows on all who do her service. At the mention of the word REWARD, some will prick up their ears, and mutter "legality." Yet the reward we speak of is not of debt, but of grace; and it is enjoyed, not with the proud conceit of merit, but with the grateful delight of humility…When we endeavor to lead men to God, we pursue a business far more profitable than the pearl fisher's diving or the diamond hunter's searching. No pursuit of mortal men is to be compared with that of soul winning.

~ Charles H. Spurgeon (1834–1892)

WALK IN THE SPIRIT

For you were once darkness, but now you are light in the Lord. Walk as children of light.

Ephesians 5:18

You will never be an overcomer until you are Spirit filled. The Bible says: "Walk in the Spirit and ye shall not fulfill the lust of the flesh" (Gal. 5:16). It is only as you are filled with the Holy Spirit that you are able to overcome your besetting sin. The Holy Spirit makes you a victorious Christian. Without His fullness you will be defeated, you will be a slave to sin. God wants to set you free. He wants to make you an overcomer.

You cannot overcome yourself. Only the Holy Spirit within you can overcome. The Christian life is the outliving of the indwelling Christ. Only as He indwells in the fullness and power of the Holy Spirit will your outward life be the kind of a life it should be. Therefore, in order to have power over sin you must be filled with the Spirit…If you are going to be an effective witness you must be filled with the Spirit. Otherwise you will witness in the energy of the flesh and accomplish nothing. If you want your testimony to count for God, you must testify in the power of the Holy Ghost.

~ Oswald J. Smith (1889–1986)

FALSE HOPE

For false messiahs and false prophets will rise up and will perform signs and wonders to lead astray, if possible, the elect.

Mark 13:22

Utopias of historical progress cannot seduce those who believe in Christ. Utopias are the straws to which those cling who have no real hope; utopias are as unattractive as they are incredible, for those who know what real hope is. Utopias are not a consequence of true hope but a poor substitute for it and therefore a hindrance and not a help.

The hope that is in Jesus Christ is different from all utopias of universal progress. It is based on the revelation of the crucified one. It is, therefore, not an uncertain speculation about the future but a certainty based upon what God has already revealed. One cannot believe in Jesus Christ without knowing for certain that God's victory over all powers of destruction, including death, is the end towards which the time process moves as its own end.

～ Emil Brunner (1889–1966)

STANDARD OF RIGHTEOUSNESS

They will fear the name of Yahweh in the west and His glory in the east;
for He will come like a rushing stream driven by the wind of the LORD.

Isaiah 59:19

Most men dislike a teaching which lays upon them strict moral requirements that check their natural desires. Yet they like to be considered as Christians, and listen willingly to the hypocrites who preach that our righteousness is only that God holds us to be righteous, even if we are bad people, and that our righteousness is without us and not in us, for, according to such teaching, they can be counted as holy people.

Woe to those who preach that men of sinful walk can not be considered pious; most are furious when they hear this, as we see and experience, and would like all such preachers to be driven away or even killed; but where that cannot be done, they strengthen their hypocrite preachers with praise, comfort, presents and protection, so that they may go on happily and give no place to the truth, however clear it may be.

~ Andreas Osiander (1498–1552)

ALWAYS GIVE THANKS

Speaking to one another in psalms, hymns, and spiritual songs, singing and making music from your heart to the Lord, giving thanks always for everything to God the Father in the name of our Lord Jesus Christ.

Ephesians 5:19–20

We can always find something to be thankful for, and there may be reasons why we ought to be thankful for even those dispensations which appear dark and frowning. A man owes a debt of obligation to him for anything which will recall him from his wanderings, and which will prepare him for heaven. Are there any dealings of God towards men which do not contemplate such an end? Is a man ever made to drink the cup of affliction when no drop of mercy is intermingled? Is he ever visited with calamity which does not in some way contemplate his own temporal or eternal good?

Could we see all, we should see that we are never placed in circumstances in which there is not much for which we should thank God. And when, in His dealings, a cloud seems to cover His face, let us remember the good things without number which we have received, and especially remember that we are in the world of redeeming love, and we shall find enough for which to be thankful.

~ Albert Barnes (1872–1951)

THE WAY TO DIVINE KNOWLEDGE

His divine power has given us everything required for life and godliness through the knowledge of Him who called us by His own glory and goodness.

2 Peter 1:3

If Reason seems to have any Power against Religion, it is only where Religion is become a dead Form, has lost its true State, and is dwindled into Opinion; and when this is the Case, that Religion stands only as a well-grounded Opinion, then indeed it is always liable to be shaken; either by having its own Credibility lessened, or that of a contrary Opinion increased.

But when Religion is that which it should be, not a Notion or Opinion, but a *real Life growing up in God*, then Reason has just as much power to stop its Course, as the barking Dog to stop the Course of the Moon. For true and genuine Religion is *Nature*, is *Life*, and the *Working* of Life; and therefore, where-ever it is, Reason has no more Power over it, than over the Roots that grow secretly in the Earth, or the Life that is working in the highest Heavens. If therefore you are afraid of Reason hurting your Religion, it is a Sign, that your Religion is not yet as it should be, is not *a self-evident Growth of Nature and Life within you*, but has much of mere Opinion in it.

～ William Law (1686–1761)

BE STRONG IN THE GRACE THAT IS IN CHRIST JESUS

That has come to you. It is bearing fruit and growing all over the world, just as it has among you since the day you heard it and recognized God's grace in the truth.

Colossians 1:6

This grace of God is your strength, as it is your joy; and it is only by abiding in it that you can really live the life of the redeemed. Be strong, then, in this grace; draw your joy out of it; and beware how you turn to anything else for refreshment, or comfort, or holiness. Though a believing man, you are still a sinner; a sinner to the last; and, as such, nothing can suit you but the free love of God. Be strong in it. Remember that you are saved by believing, not by doubting. Be not then a doubter, but a believer.

Draw continually on Christ and His fullness for this grace. If at any time you are beguiled away from it, return to it without delay; and betake yourself to it again just as you did at the first. To recover lost peace, go back to where you got it at first; begin your spiritual life all over again: get at once to the resting-place. Where sin has abounded, let grace much more abound. Do not go back to your feelings, or experiences, or evidences, in order to extract from them renewal of your lost peace. Go straight back to the free love of God. You found peace in it at first; you will find peace in it to the last. This was the beginning of your confidence; let it be both last and first.

～ F. Horatius Bonar (1808–1889)

ACCOUNTABLE TO GOD

Because these are days of vengeance to fulfill all the things that are written.

Luke 21:22

Pilate sat in the court of the castle of Antony to condemn Jesus to death; and from that very point was made the last and successful assault on the temple and city. They intimidated Pilate by pretending great loyalty to Caesar, whom they claimed as their only king; and under his imperial sway their nation was broken into fragments by the very hosts of Caesar. They rejected the true Messiah with His mighty works as well as words; and lent themselves as silly dupes to the control of Messianic pretenders and false prophets.

When Pilate declared Christ innocent and sought to release Him, they assumed all responsibility, saying, "His blood be on us and on our children," and that very generation gave their blood for His. Never was there any imprecation more prophetic. An individual may have his retribution beyond this life, for he lives beyond this life. A nation, however, is a temporal state, and its sins must be avenged, if at all, in this world. "Institutions are mortal: men immortal: the historical temporal judgment is of institutions and of organisms: the final judgment is of individuals, each one giving account of himself unto God."

— Arthur T. Pierson (1867–1911)

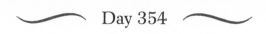
COURAGE

For I am persuaded that not even death or life, angels or rulers, things present or things to come, hostile powers, height or depth, or any other created thing will have the power to separate us from the love of God that is in Christ Jesus our Lord!

Romans 8:38–39

I will go anywhere, as long as it be forward.
If you have men who will only come
    if they know there is a good road, I don't want them.
I want men who will come if there is no road at all.
I will place no value on anything I have or may
    possess except in relation to the kingdom of Christ.
I determined never to stop until I had come
    to the end and achieved my purpose.
Fear God and work hard.

~ David Livingstone (1813–1873)

Day 355

THE INNER LIFE

I know your works. Because you have limited strength, have kept My word, and have not denied My name, look, I have placed before you an open door that no one is able to close.

Revelation 3:18

What men stand most in need of, is the knowledge of God. They know, to be sure, by dint of reading, that history gives an account of a certain series of miracles and marked providences; they have reflected seriously on the corruption and instability of worldly things; they are even, perhaps, convinced that the reformation of their lives on certain principles of morality is desirable in order to their salvation; but the whole of the edifice is destitute of foundation; this pious and Christian exterior possesses no soul.

The living principle which animates every true believer, God, the all and in all, the author and the sovereign of all, is wanting. He is, in all things, infinite—in wisdom power and love—and what wonder, if everything that comes from his hand should partake of the same infinite character and set at nought the efforts of human reason…His power is co-extensive with His will; when He wills, the thing is already accomplished.

〜 Francois Fénélons (1651–1715)

DYING TO SELF

Then Jesus said to His disciples, "If anyone wants to come with Me, he must deny himself, take up his cross, and follow Me."

Matthew 16:24

We have a clear Example in Lucifer, and also in Adam the first Man, of what self doeth, when it getteth the Light of Nature to be its own, and when it can walk with the Understanding in its own Dominion.

We see also in Men learned in Arts and Sciences, that when they get the Light of this outward World or Nature into the Possession of their Reason, nothing cometh of it but Pride of themselves. And yet all the World so vehemently desireth and seeketh after this Light as the best Treasure; and indeed it is the best Treasure this World affordeth, if it be rightly used. But while self, viz. Reason, is captivated and fast bound in a close and strong Prison, that is to say, in the Anger of God, and in Earthliness, it is very dangerous for a Man to make use of the Light of Knowledge in self, as if it were in the Possession of self.

~ Jacob Boehme (1575–1624)

THE SIGNS OF THE TIMES

"And in the morning, 'Today will be stormy because the sky is red and threatening.' You know how to read the appearance of the sky, but you can't read the signs of the times."

Matthew 16:3

One of the Signs given of the near Approach of the Kingdom of Power and Glory, is, the Divisions and Contentions that will arise through the Malice and Subtlety of the Enemy among the true *Sion*-Waiters, the Children of the Kingdom themselves; so that the *Father* of the Family will be drawn to come himself and quiet them, and set all in due Order.

This Sign we have verifyed already; and by the strong Drivings of the Holy Spirit upon many at this time, we conceive the good Hopes and Assurance that *God* is indeed drawing near to do it; wherefore we would bestir our selves, and excite all engaged in the same blessed Hope with us to such a frame of Spirit, as may be fit to receive the God of Unity and Love. For tho' the wrack the Enemy may make, may hasten the Deliverance, yet God cannot be expected to manifest Himself in the Power of His Kingdom, but in such as Conquer and hold out the Hour of Temptation; standing steadfast in the true Child-like Simplicity…

~ Jane Lead (1624–1704)

REGENERATION

Then the eyes of both of them were opened, and they knew they were naked; so they sewed fig leaves together and made loincloths for themselves.

Genesis 3:7

Man was created by God after His own Image, and in His own Likeness, a living Mirror of the Divine Nature; where Father, Son, and Holy Ghost, each brought forth their own Nature in a creaturely Manner. As the Son, who is begotten of the Father, is the Brightness of the Father's Glory, and the Holy Ghost proceedeth from the Father and the Son, as an amiable, moving Life of both; so it was in this created Image of the Holy Trinity. In it, the Father's Nature generated the Nature of the Son, and the Holy Ghost proceeded from them both, as an amiable, moving Life of both.

This was the Likeness or Image of God, in which the first Man was created, a true Offspring of God, in whom the Divine Birth sprung up as in the Deity, where Father, Son, and Holy Ghost saw themselves in a creaturely Manner. In the Divine Nature the Father cannot possibly be separated from the Son, nor the Holy Ghost from both, or either of them. But such Separation could come to pass in the Trinity, become creaturely, or in the created living Image of the Trinity.

⁓ William Law (1686–1761)

METHOD OF PRAYER

When Abram was 99 years old, the LORD appeared to him, saying, "I am God Almighty. Live in My presence and be blameless."

Genesis 17:1

All are capable of prayer, and it is a dreadful misfortune that almost all the world have conceived the idea that they are not called to prayer. We are all called to prayer, as we are all called to salvation. Prayer is nothing but the *application of the heart to God,* and the internal exercise of love. St. Paul has enjoined us to "pray without ceasing;" (1 Thess. v. 17,) and our Lord bids us watch and pray, (Mark 13:33, 37): all therefore may, and all ought to practise prayer.

I grant that meditation is attainable but by few, for few are capable of it; and therefore, my beloved brethren who are athirst for salvation, meditative prayer is not the prayer which God requires of you, nor which we would recommend... Nothing is so easily obtained as the possession and enjoyment of God. He is more present to us than we are to ourselves. He is more desirous of giving Himself to us than we are to possess Him; we only need to know how to seek Him, and the way is easier and more natural to us than breathing.

～ Jeanne Marie Bouvier de la Mothe Guyon (1647–1711)

INWARD HUMILITY

*The fear of the L*ORD *is what wisdom teaches, and humility comes before honor.*

Proverbs 15:33

O what a great Happiness is it for a Soul to be subdued and subject! what great Riches is it to be Poor! what a mighty honour to be despised! what a height is it to be beaten down! what a comfort is it to be afflicted! what a credit of knowledge is it to be reputed Ignorant! and finally, what a Happiness of Happinesses is it to be Crucified with Christ! This is that lot which the Apostle gloried in, *Nos autem gloriari oportet in cruce Domini nostri Jesu Christi*) (Gal. 6:14.)

Let others boast in their Riches, Dignities, Delights and Honours; but to us there is no higher honour, than to be denied, despised and crucified with Christ. But what a grief is this, that scarce is there one Soul which despises spiritual pleasures and is willing to be denied for Christ, imbracing his Cross with love, *Multi sunt vocati; pauci vero electi*, (Matt. 22.) says the Holy Ghost: many are they who are call'd to perfection, but few are they that arrive at it: because they are few who embrace the Cross with patience, constancy, peace, and resignation.

— Miguel de Molinos (1628–1696)

TRUE ILLUMINATION

But you are a chosen race, a royal priesthood, a holy nation, a people
for His possession, so that you may proclaim the praises of the One who
called you out of darkness into His marvelous light.

1 Peter 2:9

For thou must grow from above and from beneath to be the Image of God again. Just as a young plant is agitated by the wind, and must stand its ground in heat and cold, drawing strength and virtue to it from above and from beneath by that agitation, and must endure many a tempest, and undergo much danger before it can come to be a tree, and bring forth fruit. For through that agitation the virtue of the sun moveth in the plant, whereby its wild properties come to be penetrated and tinctured with the solar virtue, and grow thereby. And this is the time wherein thou must play the part of a valiant soldier in the Spirit of Christ, and co-operate thyself therewith.

For now the Eternal Father by His fiery power begetteth His Son in thee, who changeth the fire of the Father, namely, the first principle, or wrathful property of the soul, into the flame of love, so that out of fire and light (*viz.* wrath and love) there cometh to be one essence, being, or substance, which is the true temple of God. And now thou shalt bud forth out of the vine Christ, in the vineyard of God, and bring forth fruit in thy life, and by assisting and instructing others, show forth thy love in abundance, as a good tree.

～ Jacob Boehme (1575–1624)

ACTIONS!

I will pay attention to the way of integrity. When will You come to me?
I will live with a heart of integrity in my house.

Psalm 101:2

It is indeed a most lamentable consequence of the practice of regarding religion as a compilation of statutes, and not as an internal
principle, that it soon comes to be considered as being conversant
about external actions rather than about habits of mind. This sentiment sometimes has even the hardiness to insinuate and maintain
itself under the guise of extraordinary concern for practical religion; but it soon discovers the falsehood of this pretension, and
betrays its real nature.

The expedient, indeed, of attaining to superiority in practice
by not wasting any of the attention on the internal principles from
which alone practice can flow, is about as reasonable, and will answer about as well, as the economy of an architect who should account it mere prodigality to expend any of his materials in laying
foundation, from an idea that they might be more usefully applied
to the raising of the superstructure. We know what would be the
fate of such an edifice.

~ William Wilberforce (1759–1833)

WORDS OF WISDOM

There are many trades in which a man can hardly work—or simply cannot work—without sinning.

All that which our blessed Saviour wrought in his mortal body, he did it for our example and instruction, to the end that, following his steps, according to our poor ability, we might without offense pass over this present life.

Purity of heart and simplicity are of great force with Almighty God, who is in purity most singular, and of nature most simple.

Many things seem good and yet are not, because they be not done with a good mind and intention; and therefore our Saviour saith in the Gospel, "If thy eye has naught, all thy body shall be dark." For when the intention is wicked, all the work that follows is naught, although it seemed to be never so good.

〜 St. Gregory the Great (540–604)

CHRISTIAN FREEDOM

You will know the truth, and the truth will set you free.

John 8:32

Christian freedom, in my opinion, consists of three parts. The first: that the consciences of believers, in seeking assurance of their justification before God, should rise above and advance beyond the law, forgetting all law righteousness…

The second part, dependent upon the first, is that consciences observe the law, not as if constrained by the necessity of the law, but that freed from the law's yoke they willingly obey God's will…

The third part of Christian freedom lies in this: regarding outward things that are of themselves "indifferent," we are not bound before God by any religious obligation preventing us from sometimes using them and other times not using them, indifferently…

Accordingly, it is perversely interpreted both by those who allege it as an excuse for their desires that they may abuse God's good gifts to their own lust and by those who think that freedom does not exist unless it is used before men, and consequently, in using it have no regard for weaker brethren…

Nothing is plainer than this rule: that we should use our freedom if it results in the edification of our neighbor, but if it does not help our neighbor, then we should forego it.

~ John Calvin (1509–1564)

STANDING
ON HIS PROMISES

As we continue to face the daily issues that test our faith, as Christians, the challenge of the Apostle Paul rings as true today as ever. He exhorted the Christians in Corinth that in light of the resurrection of the Lord Jesus they are to stand firm, let nothing move them and always give themselves fully to the work of the Lord because they know their labor in the Lord is not in vain or empty. If there was ever a time in the history of the church for steadfastness, the need is today.

We must be people of the Word of God, standing firm on its teachings, not being moved away from it by accusations of intolerance or political correctness. We need to be like people of old spending great amounts of time memorizing and meditating on the Scriptures, rather than captivated with reality television, situation comedies, and the endless number of sports extravaganzas. For our labor to not be empty or in vain, we need to do it by the Book. God's Word is clear and His expectations for us are understandable.

The question is whether we will have the hunger for the Word created by the Holy Spirit or will we be satisfied to munch on the morsels of worldly and fleshly appetites. Will we cry out to God and ask Him to create an insatiable hunger to know Him and His Word? It is only by the sustaining work of the Holy Spirit using His Word that we can stand firm, not be moved, and give ourselves fully to the work of the Lord. May it be so in each of our lives.

⌒ Public Domain

CONTRIBUTORS

Thomas à Kempis (1380–1471) Born in Kempen in the duchy of Cleves. Educated by a religious order called the Brethren of the Common Life, and in due course joined the order, was ordained a priest, became sub-prior of his house (in the low Countries). Composed and compiled *The Imitation of Christ.*

St. Thomas Aquinas (1225–1274) Born in Aquino, Italy and represents the pinnacle of the philosophical and theological school that flourished between 1100 and 1500 and attempted to reconcile faith with reason and the works of Aristotle with the scriptures. Received Th.M in Paris, France.

St. Augustine (345–440) A theologian of the early Christian church. Author of *The Confessions* and *The City of God.* St. Augustine, FL is named for him.

T. Austin-Sparks (1888–1971) London, England. Educated in both England and Scotland. At the age of 25 he was ordained as a pastor.

Henry W. Baker (1821–1877) Born at Belmont House, Vauxhall, Surrey, England. He attended Trinity College at Cambridge, was ordained in 1844, and became assistant curate at Great Hockesley, near Colchester, Essex. In 1851, he became Vicar of Monkland Priory Church in Herefordshire, England. He was editor-in-chief of the Anglican *Hymns Ancient and Modern*, and contributed hymns, tunes, and translations.

Raymond V. Banner (1937–) Graduated from Grace Bible Institute, Bob Jones University, and Dallas Seminary and lives in Mount Ayr, Iowa.

Louis Berkoff (1809–1833) Fundamentalist. Writer of Systematic Theology offered today in many seminaries.

Jacob Boehme (1575–1624) "chosen servant of God," was born in Alt Seidenburg, Germany. Ordained minister.

F. Horatius Bonar (1808–1889) Born in Edinburgh. Member of the Free Church of Scotland. Ordained minister and pastured Chalmers Memorial Church in Edinburgh. Best known for his songs and poems.

Edward M. Bounds (1835–1913) Lawyer, Faithful Pastor, Army Chaplain, Devotional Writer, Beloved Husband-Father, Powerful Preacher and a Man of Fervent Prayer.

Thomas Boston (1677–1732) Born in Duns, Berwickshire; read arts and divinity at Edinburgh; Ordained minister. An English Puritan.

Matthew Bridges (1800–1894) Hymn writer. The Friars, Maldon, Essex, England. Though raised as an Anglican, Bridges converted to Roman Catholicism in 1848. He lived in Quebec, Canada, for some years, but eventually returned to England.

John Bunyan (1628–1688) The most popular religious writer in the English language. He enjoyed peace and a cheerful confidence in the mercy of God.

Emil Brunner (1889–1966) Teacher Unsurpassed. Referred to as "divine-human encounter," or "man in revolt," or "the divine imperative."

Jeremiah Burroughs (1599–1646) Graduate of Emmanuel College, Cambridge, and the "teacher" of an English congregation in Rotterdam. After his return from exile in 1641 he became "Gospel preacher" to "two of the greatest congregations in England, viz: Stepney and Cripplegate" (London). Belonged to the front rank of English puritan preachers and played a prominent part in the Westminster Assembly of divines.

John Calvin (1509–1564) French reformer and theologian. One of the most important figures of the Reformation. Studied the ideas of Luther and moved into the Protestant camp by 1533. On November 1 of that year, he delivered a speech in which he attacked the established church and called for reforms.

B. H. Carroll (1843–1914) Born in Carrollton, MS. Pastor, teacher, denominational leader, author. He led in the founding of Southwestern Baptist Theological Seminary, and served as president of the seminary in Fort Worth; Loved reading; Authored, Interpretation of the English Bible-commentaries.

George Washington Carver (1860–1943) Educator, Agricultural/Food Scientist, Farmer. Born a slave. Managed to obtain a high school education. Admitted as the first black student of Simpson College, Indianola, Iowa. Attended Iowa Agricultural College (now Iowa State University) where, while working as the school janitor, he received a degree in agricultural science. Had a post at Tuskegee.

Oswald Chambers (1874–1917) Scottish Baptist minister converted under Spurgeon's ministry. He stressed availability to God.

Gilbert K. Chesterton (1874-1936) One of the finest writers of the 20th century. His book, *The Everlasting Man*, led a atheist C. S. Lewis to become a Christian.

Charles Coffin (1676–1749) Wrote *The Advent of Our King* and over 100 hymns. Principal of the college at Beauvais. 1718-Rector of the University of Paris. In 1727, he published some of his Latin poems, and in 1736, the bulk of his hymns appeared in the *Paris Breviary* and *Hymni Sacri Auctore Carolo Coffin*.

Lettie Cowman (1870–1960) Wesleyan missionary to Japan who, with her husband Charles E. Cowman, co-founded the Oriental Missionary Society in 1901.

Fanny J. Crosby (1820–1915) Hymn writer whose sacred songs are sung wherever the English language is spoken.

James G. Deck (1807–1884) Educated for the army, and became an officer in the Indian service. Retired from the army and joined the Plymouth Brethren.

A. C. Dixon (1854–1925) Wake Forest College and Southern Baptist Theological Seminary. In 1906, he accepted the pulpit of the Chicago Avenue Church (Moody Memorial Church) and he spent the war years ministering at Spurgeon's Tabernacle in London.

Philip Doddridge (1702–1751) Non-conformist divine and hymn-writer.

Henry Drummond (1851–1897) Born in Scotland, a gifted evangelist who assisted Dwight L. Moody during his revival campaigns. Theological writer, revivalist, explorer, geologist, ordained minister, and a professor of theology.

George Duffield (1818–1888) Hymnologist. Graduated from Yale University and Union Theological Seminary. Ordained Presbyterian minister.

Johannes Eckhart (1260–1327) German Dominican philosopher.

Jonathan Edwards (1703–1758) One of the greatest preachers and churchmen in American history, was born in East Windsor. Entering Yale at the age of thirteen, Edwards graduated at the head of his class. Credited with bringing about the first Great Awakening of American history, beginning in 1734.

G. H. Lang (1874–1958) A Plymouth Brethren writer; a man of uncommon spirituality. His life was devoted to the study of God's Word.

William Law (1686–1781) English spiritual writer. Fellow of Emmanuel College, Cambridge. Writer and Priest.

Jane Lead (1624–1704) *17th Century Prophetess of God.*

St. Eucherius of Lyons (380–449) Bishop of Lyons and ascetic author. Theologian.

Francois Fénélons (1651–1715) *French.* Christian Counsel from a 300-year-old writing.

C. G. Finney (1792–1875) A master at presenting the intricacies of a Systematic Theology. A Voice from the Philadelphian Church Age.

John Flavel (1630–1691) Born at Bromsgrove in Worcestershire. Puritan theologian. English Presbyterian.

George Fox (1624–1691) Born in Fenny Drayton, Leicestershire. Founder of the Society of Friends (Quakers) University College, Oxford. Ordained minister. Leonard Ravenhill referred to Fox as The Unshakable Shaker.

Theodorus J. Frelinghuysen (1691–1748) Born in West Friesland: After receiving a thorough classical education he began the study of theology, was ordained to the ministry in the Reformed Dutch Church.

Robert Grant (1779–1838) Wrote "Oh, Worship the King." Received a BA and a MA from Magdalene College, Cambridge and became a lawyer in 1807. A member of Parliament for Inverness, a Privy Councilor in, Judge Advocate General, and was knighted in 1834. He then returned to India to be Governor of Bombay. His work appeared in the *Christian Observer* (1806-1815), Elliott's *Psalms and Hymns* (1835), and *Sacred Poems*, published posthumously by his brother in 1839, and reprinted in 1844 and 1868.

St. Gregory the Great (540–604) Doctor of the Church; born in Rome. One of the most notable figures in Ecclesiastical History. Gave explanation of the religious situation of the evolution of the form of <u>medieval</u> <u>Christianity</u> from the Middle Ages.

William Gurnall (1617–1679) Emanuel College, Pastor of the Church of Christ, Lavenham, Suffolk.

Jeanne Marie Bouvier de la Mothe Guyon (1647–1711) Born at Montargis. Madame Guyon was arrested again in 1695 for teaching heresy and spent 6 years in prison.

Matthew Henry (1662–1714) Welsh-born, English nonconformist minister and Bible commentator. He is remembered for his practical and devotional multi-volume Exposition of the Old and New Testaments which is still published.

Petrus Herbert (1533–1571) An ordained a priest of the Brethren's Unity in 1562, became a member of the Select Council in 1567, and was Consenior of the Unity. He was sent as a deputy to confer with John Calvin, and in 1562 to arrange with Duke Christoph of Württemberg for the education at Tübingen of young men from the Bohemian Brethren. He was also one of the deputies sent to Vienna in 1564 to present the revised form of the Brethren's Confession of Faith to the Emperor Maximilian II, and in 1566 to present their new German hymn book. Herbert was one of the principal compilers of the enlarged edition of the 1566 hymn book published as Kirchengeseng, and contributed some 90 hymns to it (in the 1639 edition, 104 hymns are marked as his).

Dick Hillis (1913–2005) An American Protestant Christian missionary to China, author and founder of "Formosa Crusades", later "Orient Crusades", now "One Challenge International".

Walter Hilton (1340–1396) English mystic. An innovator. Hilton urged holiness.

William Ralph Inge (1860–1954) Anglican Platonist author. Ordained Deacon. Educated at Eton College and King's College, Cambridge. Professor of divinity at Jesus College, Cambridge. In 1911, he was chosen to be the Dean of St. Paul's Cathedral in London. He was a columnist for 25 years for the *Evening Standard* and a trustee of London's National Portrait Gallery.

Samuel Johnson (1709–1784) Next only to William Shakespeare is perhaps the most quoted of English writers. Born in Lichfield, Staffordshire. He was deaf in the left ear, almost blind in the left eye, and dim of vision in the right eye. He responded to his disabilities by a fierce determination to be independent and to accept help and pity from no one.

St. John of the Cross (1542–1591) Mystical doctor and founder of the Discalced Carmelites. John Keble (1792–1866) Anglican tractarian leader. Ordained Priest in 1816, tutor at Oxford.

Søren Kierkegaard (1813–1855) Danish existentialist philosopher. Born in Copenhagen. Profound and prolific writer in the Danish "golden age." Educated at a prestigious boys' school (*Borgedydskolen*), then attended Copenhagen University where he studied philosophy and theology.

Abraham Kuyper (1837–1920) Pastor, theologian, scholar, journalist, educator and statesman. Founded the Antirevolutionary Party, the first Dutch political party and the first Christian Democratic party in the world. Established the Free University, a Christian university established on Reformed principles. Elected to the Second Chamber of the Dutch Parliament and served as Prime Minister.

William Law (1686–1781) English spiritual writer. Fellow of Emmanuel College, Cambridge. Writer and Priest.

Brother Lawrence (1610–1691) Born Nicholas Herman in Herimenil, Lorraine, a Duchy of France. Saved at age 18. Author of *The Practice of the Presence of God*.

C. S. Lewis (1898–1963) Anglican professor at both Oxford and Cambridge. He held to the orthoxdox Christian faith and remains perhaps the greatest recent apologists.

Abraham Lincoln (1809–1865) Hodgenville, Kentucky, little formal schooling. Self-educated, elected to the Illinois House of Representatives. Admitted to the bar in 1836. Became Vice-Presidential candidate for the (new) Republic Party in 1856 and was elected 16th President of the United States. Lincoln's slave emancipation principles led to the Civil War between the North and the South in 1861.

David Livingstone (1813–1873) African Explorer. A curious combination of missionary, doctor, explorer, scientist, and anti-slavery activist. Received a gold medal from the London Royal Geographical for being the first to cross the entire African Continent from west to east.

Martin Luther (1483–1546) Born in Eisleben. He attended school in Mansfeld, Magdeburg, Eisenach and Erfurt to become a lawyer. However, he decided to enter the Augustinian monastery in Erfurt. This decision culminated in the development of the Reformation of the Church.

George MacDonald (1824–1905) Scottish novelist and poet. Educated at university in Aberdeen, and Highbury College. A Congregational minister. Famous writer of youth and adult books.

Charles Henry Mackintosh (1820–1896) Businessman in Limerick, in 1844 he opened a school at Westport, undertaking the educational work with enthusiasm. He was active in the Irish Revival of 1859–1869.

Alexander Maclaren (1826–1919) Expository minister. Next to Spurgeon's, this Scottish preacher's sermons have been the most widely read of their time.

L. E. Maxwell (1895-1984) Founded Prairie Bible Institute in Three Hills, Alberta, Canada, in 1922. He was a professor, principal, and president and a prolific author.

Robert Murray McCheyne (1813–1843) His seven-year ministry attracted great crowds.

F. B. Meyer (1847–1929) Baptist Ambassador for Keswick holiness spirituality. One of the most prominent English Baptist ministers.

Miguel de Molinos (1628–1696) Born in Muniesa, Spain. Spanish quietist. Ordained minister. In 1675, he published his Spiritual Guide a small handbook teaching that Christian perfection is achieved by a mixture of contemplation.

Dwight L. Moody (1837–1899) Dispensational evangelist who was highly successful in Europe and America. Founder of the Moody Bible Institute.

George Muller (1805–1898) Prussian-born English evangelist and philanthropist. A man of faith and prayer, he established orphanages in Bristol and founded the Scriptural Knowledge Institution for Home and Abroad. Was a divinity student at the University of Halle which qualified him to preach in the Lutheran state church.

Andrew Murray (1828–1917) Born in a Dutch Reformed parsonage in Graaff Reinet, South Africa. It was here that his father, the Rev. Andrew Murray, Sr., was ministering to the Dutch settlers. Such men as David Livingstone and Robert Moffat frequently passed through their home on their way to the coast.

Watchman Nee (1903–1972) Born in Swatow, Fukien province, China in 1903. He was converted at the age of 17. Missionary to China learned to live as a Chinese in order to minister to them. Arrested and imprisoned, for his faith, by the Communists in and died in prison in 1972.

Origen (185–254) Ordained priest. Considered the greatest theologian and biblical scholar of the early Eastern church. His father Leonides had given him an excellent literary education. His father died in the persecution of 202, and he himself narrowly escaped the same fate. At the age of 18, Origen was appointed to succeed Clement of Alexandria as head of the catechetical school of Alexandria, where he had been a student.

Andreas Osiander (1498–1552) German reformer, was born at Gunzenhausen, near Nuremberg. Educated at Leipzig, Altenburg arid Ingolstadt. Ordained minister, he was appointed Hebrew tutor in the Augustinian convent at Nuremberg and appointed preacher in the St Lorenz Kirche, and about the same time he publicly joined the Lutheran party, which ultimately led to the adoption of the Reformation by the city.

John Owen (1616–1683) Theologian. Was born of Puritan parents at Stadham in Oxfordshire. Admitted at age 12 to Queen's College, Oxford, where he took his B.A. and M.A.

Blaise Pascal (1623–1662) French theologian, mathematician, and philosopher.

Edward Perronet (1726–1792) Moravian minister. He was one of the editors of the Brethren's German hymn book, published in 1566, to which he contributed many hymns.

Folliott S. Pierpont (1835–1917) Born at Spa Villa, Bath, England, and was educated at Queen's College.

Arthur T. Pierson (1837–1911) Philadelphian Church Era. Preached over 13,000 sermons, wrote over fifty books and Bible lectures. Consulting editor for the Scofield Reference Bible, and was the author of the classic biography, *George Muller of Bristol.*

Aurelius C. Prudentius (348–413) Born into the upper class. After working as a lawyer, he served a judge. At age 57, he retired and began to write sacred poetry.

Alan Redpath (1907–1989) Newcastle-upon-Tyne, United Kingdom. Accountant with Imperial Chemical Industries. In 1936, joined National Young Life Campaign until 1940 when he became pastor of Duke Street Baptist Church, Richmond, London, until 1953, when he came pastor of Moody Memorial Church in Chicago.

Cyril C. Richardson (1909–1976) Union Theological Seminary Professor.

Samuel Rutherford (1600–1661) Scottish Presbyterian divine. Attended the University of Edinburgh and was Professor of Philosophy in that University. One of the Scots commissioned, appointed in 1643 to the Westminster Assembly.

John of Ruysbroeck (1293–1381) Flemish mystic with a religious education including considerable training in theology and philosophy.

Philip Schaff (1819–1893) German-American theologian and church historian.

Christian L. Scheidt (1709–1761) Hymn writer.

Cyriacus Schneegass (1546–1597) Born in Buffleben, Germany. Graduated with an M.A. from the University of Jena. Pastor of the St. Blasius church at Friedrichroda. Also adjunct to the Superintendent of Weimar, and signed the Formula of Concord in 1579.

Joseph Scriven (1819–1886) Born at Ballymoney Lodge, Banbridge. His Baptismal entry is recorded in Seapatrick Parish Church, Banbridge. B.A. degree at Trinity College, Dublin. Cadet at the Military College, Addiscombe.

Hannah Whitall Smith (1832–1911) Arminian evangelical; wife of popular evangelist Robert Pearsall Smith. Taught the joy of Christ throughout a difficult life.

Oswald J. Smith (1889–1986) a Canadian pastor and evangelist.

Charles Haddon Spurgeon (1834–1892) Born in Kelvedon, Essex. Became a Baptist pastor at the New Park Street Chapel and later the Metropolitan Tabernacle in London at age 20. In 1887, Spurgeon left the Baptist Union because no action was taken against people in the church charged with fundamental errors.

James Stalker (1848–1927) Scottish preacher. More widely known in America than any other Scottish preacher of his day. Spent twenty of his later years as a professor.

Miles Joseph Stanford (1914–1999) Writer of Christian materials. Outspoken proponent on the subjects of Dispensationalism and the Growth Truths of Romans 6-8.

James S. Stewart (1822–1894) Baptist minister. County Judge of Rowan County.

Henry Suso (1296–1366) German mystic. Theology student of Meister Eckhart in Cologne. Noted preacher in Switzerland and the area of the Upper Rhine.

Louis T. Talbot (1890–1976) Dispensational evangelical who founded Talbot Theological Seminary. Leading defenders of the gap theory, also helped popularize famous timeline charts.

Jeremy Taylor (1613–1667) Cambridge, England. Anglican bishop. Educated at Caius College in Cambridge and a fellow of All Souls College in Oxford; rector of Uppingham, Rutlandshire. He ran a school in Wales and served as chaplain to the Earl of Carberry at Golden Grove, Carmathenshire. Preached in Lisburn and Portmore. Bishop of Down and Connor in January and a member of the Irish Privy Council; entrusted with the diocese of Dromore; and was Vice Chancellor of the University of Dublin.

R. A. Torrey (1856–1928) Is to Bible exposition what C. S. Lewis is to Christian philosophy. Successor to D. L. Moody's ministry upon Moody's death.

A. W. Tozer (1897–1963) Arminian fundamentalist pastor in the Christian and Missionary Alliance, which grew out of the late-19th-century Holiness movement.

Thomas Traherne (1636–1674) Born in Hereford, England. English metaphysical poet and writer. Educated at the University of Oxford and ordained as an Anglican clergyman.

Charles G. Trumbull (1872–1941) He was the editor of The Sunday School Times, a respected Christian journal with a weekly circulation of more than 100,000 in the United States and abroad in the early 1900s. He was one of the foremost promoters of the Keswick holiness movement, and in 1913 he helped found America's Keswick Conference Center in southern New Jersey. He was an editor and played a key role in the formation of the Victorious Life Testimony, a series of conventions held on the deeper life. He wrote several books, including *What is the Gospel*, and *Taking Men Alive*.

Henry Wace (1836–1924) Dean of Canterbury.

B. B. Warfield (1851–1921) Born in "Grasmere" near Lexington, Kentucky. Surrendered to the ministry at age 21, entering Princeton Seminary for his training. Succeeded A. A. Hodge as a professor of Theology at Princeton, a post he occupied for over 33 years.

Anna Laetitia Waring (1823–1910) Born in Neith, Glamorganshire, Wales. Her most widely known hymns are: "Father, I know that all my life," "Go not far from me, O my Strength," and "My heart is resting, O my God."

Isaac Watts (1674–1748) Augustan; Southampton grammar school under John Pinhorne Academy at Stoke Newington: 1690; D.D., University of Edinburgh.

Charles Wesley (1707–1788) Westminster school: Christ Church, B.A. from Oxford, Christ Church, Oxford (M.A.) Ordained minister. Cofounder of Methodism and arguably the greatest hymn writer ever.

John Wesley (1703–1791) Anglican clergyman, evangelist, and cofounder of Methodism. Graduated from Oxford University and became a priest in the Church of England. Participated in a religious study group in Oxford organized by his brother Charles its members being dubbed the "Methodists" for their emphasis on methodical study and devotion.

Geroge Whitefield (1714–1770) Post Reformation. Born in Gloucester. Entered Pembroke College, Oxford at age 18. Member of a religious group known as the Holy Club or the Oxford Methodists that included John and Charles Wesley. Minister of Savannah, Georgia. Back in England he was appointed Chaplain.

William Wilberforce (1759–1833) Hailed as a "Renewer of Society," was the conscience of Parliament. Educated at St John's College, Cambridge. Elected to the House of Commons from Hull and Yorkshire. Became an Evangelical Christian.

Woodrow Wilson (1856–1924) 28th President, United States of America. Nobel Prize for Peace: 1919.

Christopher Wordsworth (1807–1885) English bishop and man of letters, Master of Trinity; born in London, and was educated at Winchester and Trinity, Cambridge. He became senior classic, and was elected a fellow and tutor of Trinity, shortly afterwards he took holy orders.